MARXIAN POLITICAL ECONOMY
An outline

MARXIAN POLITICAL ECONOMY

An outline

JAMES F. BECKER

Professor of Economics
New York University

CAMBRIDGE UNIVERSITY PRESS

CAMBRIDGE

LONDON   NEW YORK   MELBOURNE

Published by the Syndics of the Cambridge University Press
The Pitt Building, Trumpington Street, Cambridge CB2 1RP
Bentley House, 200 Euston Road, London NW1 2DB
32 East 57th Street, New York, NY 10022, USA
296 Beaconsfield Parade, Middle Park, Melbourne 3206, Australia

© Cambridge University Press 1977

First published 1977

Printed in the United States of America

Library of Congress Cataloging in Publication Data
Becker, James F. 1921-
Marxian political economy.
1. Marxian economics. I. Title.
HB97.5.B329 1976   335.4   76-9172
ISBN 0 521 21349 5

Contents

PART TWO: THE LABOR THEORY OF VALUE

PART THREE: RELATIONSHIPS BETWEEN PRICES AND VALUES

Contents

Acknowledgments

It is conventional to acknowledge one's indebtedness to individuals whose influence has been appreciable. My creditors are numerous, so much so that I would not know where to begin or where to end an enumeration. Certainly my students have been indispensable; three generations have listened to and criticized my views as they assumed gradually their present form. Similarly, my colleagues at New York University have been helpful, especially with their tolerance and forbearance, qualities not at all common in academia and in any event remarkable on the scale of my experience. Among my Marxist friends, comment over the years has taken a heavy toll of my misconceptions. Friends and relatives have helped, often more than they realize, sometimes by saying nothing and sometimes by being their faithful and critical selves. For particular aid I owe much to Doug Dowd, Russ Nixon, Ed Nell, Arthur Felberbaum, and Ed Tonna. My gratitude to all of you is very great.

Above all, whether one knows it or not, admits it or not, one owes a debt to circumstances more powerful than one's own devotion to foibles. For some decades the tide of protest literature has been rising, and this is part of that stream. Having myself come to maturity in a troubled epoch—of depression, World War II and its noxious aftermath, the cold war, of the new imperialism—a mounting anger at first afflicted both mind and spirit. Unaware at first that this feeling had any connection with matters of social class, my early endeavors to understand the chaos, to find law if not order within it, were pounded and beaten by events until I was forced to admit that the theories of the standard repertoire could only be brought into agreement with the main facts by twisting them beyond all

ix

point of contact with their assumptions and authentic formulations. For a time, confidence born of youth and a dexterous imagination preserved my faith in these theories, and these might have served indefinitely were it not for those world events of revolution and war, especially the Chinese revolution and the war in Southeast Asia, which forced the issue whether to abandon science or to find one up to the tasks that such events portended. No doubt many a Marxist has been made by the Pentagon; but if Saul has his thousands, David has his tens of thousands, and the Pentagon and the like fade into insignificance in comparison with the surging movement of the oppressed to whose ranks, I gradually discovered, I myself belong. It is not the oppressors—who never learn—but the oppressed who, in discovering their oppression, discover themselves.

Events have contributed to this all-important awareness on my part, but this by no means negates the constructive influence referred to of students, colleagues, friends, and relatives. It means merely that, among them, those most oppressed have contributed the most to this work. To them I am most indebted. I wish now to thank them—those who are still living—from the bottom of my heart. For the rest of this work, circumstances suffice to explain it.

November 1976

J. F. B.

Introduction

Scientific inquiry and the materialist standpoint

Despite the striking worldwide revival of theoretical Marxism – a revival whose signs include a heightened flow of books and monographs, some increase in the number of courses of academic instruction in colleges and universities (not unopposed), a growing volume of discourse in the media, and so on – a study such as this requires some explanation. Its subject is the rather formidable one of Marxian economics and its applications to political economy, a field only partly lit and from which mists of incantation now and again arise.

While Marx spent the great bulk of his energies as a mature scientist in precisely this realm of inquiry, much of the current revival has centered, curiously enough, on political (Frankfurt school,) social psychological (psychologists and alienation theorists), sociological ("new class" theorists), or other theories. My intention, however, is to follow Marx's own lead, to reconstruct his economic theories, and to use them to analyze the advanced capitalism. The goal is to explain the present phase of development in those countries and regions where the mode first put in its modern appearance and within which it is now entering its dotage. Eventually, we shall come to an assessment of the present state of class structure and relations and to an assessment, indeed, of the very hypothesis of class struggle itself. Is such a struggle at the center of the process of social change in the advanced context? We shall see. First, however, the economic theory; then the matter of present travail.

Thus this study begins with an explication of the theoretical apparatus itself, the apparatus used by Marx in his own work, and which is absolutely indispensable to a meaningful interpretation of

the advanced capitalism. The initial discussion will include also occasional reference to dialectical materialism, the philosophy of
science whose principles control the formulation and application of
the economics. Our intent is to reconfirm both the principles and
the theories by working with them systematically in order to show
what it is they reveal. Yet our mainstay in these endeavors is the
economics, the theory of the general and of the special roles played
by the organization of productive activity in the evolution of a social
formation, and in particular the one we know as capitalism.

In concentrating upon the economics, we are following the main
path cut by Marx, but we have every intention of avoiding a
dogmatic procedure justified by authoritative reference to the
master; an authentic rather than authoritarian presentation is what
is desired. Implicit within Marxian methods and theories is the
premise that it is the tools, rather than the person who uses them,
that embody whatever of scientific and political utility the science
may provide. This is the reason that much attention must always be
paid to matters of theoretical detail, matters that require some
work on the part of the reader - work, hopefully, with rewards proportioned to it. Let us examine a bit more closely this suggestion
that the powers of general foresight are disclaimed by Marxism.

There is no question in my mind that Marxian theory does convey
enormous insight into the functioning of the mode of production
and all that attends it. However, neither Marx nor Engels conceived
of social science as a quest for laws of motion that, once known,
would expose to view the entire course of future development.
Among natural scientists, La Place is perhaps best known for his
avowal of this extravagant ambition, this deterministic view of the
possibilities of science. Given the state of planetary relations at one
point in time, the whole future movement of the celestial system
could, he supposed, be predicted. While many of Marx's critics,
and even some of his friends, perhaps themselves overburdened with
aspiration, often impute to Marx a similar conception of scientific
possibilities, they are quite mistaken in so doing. They will be
equally mistaken in imputing to this writer a similar misconception.
Marxism rejects altogether the mechanistic and deterministic
philosophy of science and the hopeless and frenzied quests to which
it sometimes leads. Engels here explains an alternative view:

According to the materialist conception of history, the *ultimately* determining element in history is the production and reproduction of social life. More than this

neither Marx nor I have ever asserted . . . . The economic situation is the basis, but the various elements of the superstructure – political forms of the class struggle and its results, to wit: constitutions established by the victorious class after a successful battle, etc., juridical forms, and even the reflexes of all these actual struggles in the brains of the participants, political, juristic, philosophical theories, religious views and their further development into systems of dogmas – also exercise their influence upon the course of the historical struggles and in many cases preponderate in determining their *form. There is an interaction of all these elements in which, amid all the endless hosts of accidents (that is, of things and events whose interconnection is so remote or so impossible of proof that we can regard it as non-existent, as negligible) the economic movement finally asserts itself as necessary.* Otherwise the application of the theory to any period of history would be easier than the solution of a simple equation of the first degree.[1]

This unrealistic dream of the first-degree equation even today disturbs the rest of the troubled economist; but, despite the assistance of the computer and other mechanical aids lending color and seeming substance to the vision, the ideal is as futile now as ever it was. Why is this so?

It is not because the Marxian economics is dialectical, but because social evolution is itself dialectical, that the deterministic methodology is futile. To put it briefly, the laws that influence the process of historical development must always be viewed as tendencies, albeit sometimes very powerful ones. They exert their influence "under certain conditions and after long periods," as Marx said of the tendency of the general rate of profit to fall.[2] When they do exert their influence, moreover, they generally give rise to countertendencies that may themselves influence the course of development. If the rate of profit tends to fall, for example, it will induce various reactions on the part of businessmen, politicians and legislators, workers, and so on, and the net effect of these reactions may even be to forestall, at least for a time, the decline in the rate of profit itself. The essential point is that the Marxian premise is one of dialectical interrelations and interactions within the social universe, and not the premise of a unilateral and mechanical law. This does not mean that there are no scientific laws; it does not mean that the rate of profit does not finally fall. It means only that the investigator seeking an unconditional law of development has set for himself an impossible task no matter what the degree of his equations. As Engels expressed it, "To us so-called 'economic laws' are not eternal laws of nature but historical laws which arise and disappear. . . ."[3]

The implications of the dialectical philosophy are numerous. Among them is the implication that a continuing inquiry into, say, the course of capitalist development and, further, into the very theoretical apparatus by means of which inquiry is conducted is a scientific responsibility. Inquiry along these lines is imperative in order to keep pace with a universe in flux. Particularly at the leading edge of the advance, signs of underlying change are numerous and persistent and in need of study. Hence our aim is not merely to describe the principles of the science and of the economics but to put them to work and, by so doing, to demonstrate both the effectiveness of the tools and the nature of the changes taking place.

Interpretation and misinterpretation: first principles

Marx's theories, including his economic theories, have often been described before, and this study makes free use of secondary sources. However, it happens that for the first time Marx's writings on economics have become available in the English language virtually in their entirety, especially now that the *Grundrisse* is available.[4] The serious student of economics therefore has direct access to Marx and can, if he chooses, bypass secondary sources in his endeavor to learn an authentic system. This holds for the present study, too, except that our intent is not to substitute for the original material as much as to facilitate and make easier a subsequent approach to it.

Marx himself was well aware of the difficulties of comprehending his analytics and often refused, beyond some point, to make concessions on behalf of the interested reader. He felt, for example, that the presentation in *Capital* of the law of value and its operation could only become clear given a willingness of the reader to work on the subject: ". . . even if there were no chapter on 'value' in my book, the analysis of the real relations which I give would contain the proof and demonstration of the real value relations."[5] A certain scholarly labor is necessary for comprehension, then, and Marx was often irritated with misinterpretations of his theories offered by "vulgar" economists. These misinterpretations, he declared, "show what these priests of the bourgeoisie have come down to, when workers and even manufacturers and merchants understand my book and find their way about in it, while these 'learned scribes' (!) complain that I make excessive demands on their understanding."[6]

Time has not done too much, unfortunately, to remedy the complaints of the "learned scribes." Misinterpretations and distortions of the economics still abound, some of them provided by economists who should know better, and some by Marxists, many of whom still regard *Capital* as one of those nineteenth-century books that modern improvements have rendered superfluous. Nor did Marx exaggerate the problem of intellectual laziness and intransigence. Thus it would not be realistic to assume that such determined opposition could be overcome by yet one more presentation of reasoned argument. On the other hand, there are good reasons for making the effort to do so. It may be that, to some extent, the recent revival of interest in "old" theories evidences a greater goodwill toward Marx even if, at the same time, a new and more passionate hostility also flourishes. Furthermore, a century of work within standard economics has contributed certain tools and even concepts that should enable the student of Marx to enter more easily into a real understanding of his doctrines. An example is the input–output economics of Wassily Leontief.[7] It is easier now to see that Marx's economics is an input–output economics, one in which, I would say, the Leontief system appears as a rather special case. Or, again, because the subject of economic growth has come into vogue in standard economics, a vogue now to be superseded by the fact of stagnation, perhaps students of the subject may better be prepared for a general organic account of social interrelations.

Actually, a considerable part of the conventional economics is what it is because of the proddings of its critics, especially its Marxian critics, and this reaction has, in turn, prepared the way for a new extension of communications among social scientists. But more important by far in bringing conventional economics into contact with social realities – however tenuous that contact – is the force of ineluctable circumstance: of economic collapse, depression, inflation, depression and inflation, domestic and international conflict in which economic causation is of decisive importance, and so on. Events are the wind before which economics must bend or break, and what bending there has been is a hopeful omen for the possibility of further reformation. The scientific mind cannot remain closed to contemporary social needs, and this forces the study of those theories most capable of identifying and ministering to them. Insofar as the scientific need corresponds to social needs, the Marxian science will prosper. The science is far from impossible to understand, however difficult it may be to present it simply and effectively. It has that remarkable quality of making our world more understandable, the quality of historical and contemporary applicability that makes it invaluable to students of society.

We are speaking, of course, of the authentic economics, not of its neo-Marxian simulants. Among the many interpretations extant are some curious misinterpretations of the economics by friends, by enemies, and by that rather mysterious and omnipresent body of friendly enemies. Among the latter, Joan Robinson offers a fairly typical view. "It was inevitable, and in a certain sense right," she declares, "that Marxism should have developed into a faith rather than a science."[8] In Robinson's generation this view of Marxism as secular religion was widespread and to some extent justified. In the thirties, the forties, and even into the fifties of this century the religious Marxist was all too common from one standpoint and not common enough from another. There was far too great an emphasis upon ideological and political to the neglect of analytical, scientific work. Yet there was nothing inevitable or right about this. Referring to that same generation of Communist intellectuals, more familiar with ideology than with science, Louis Althusser writes, "We had been trained to treat science, a status claimed by every page of Marx, as merely the first-comer among ideologies."[9] Friends as well as friendly enemies can be quite cognizant of the degeneration of the tradition. To a lesser extent friends and enemies would agree as to the basic causes of the degeneracy, perhaps.[10] But while this is a problem that should not lightly be glossed over, certain causes of the decline are rather obvious. Exhausted by the ardors of revolution and civil war, by the simple struggle for physical survival, by great depressions, by the rise of nazism and fascism; called upon again and again to provide immediate, workable solutions to overwhelming social problems; harassed and hounded by authorities, "changing our countries more often than our shoes," as Brecht put it; subject to discrimination and to the ridicule of philistine "intellectuals," those who might have been the new scientists of Marxism were perforce concerned with other things.

In the light of these familiar and appalling conditions it would seem absurd to trace the decline of Marxian science to doctrinal failures of Marx himself. Yet many have looked here for the basic error (and we cite Robinson only for convenience):

. . . there are certain deficiencies in the Marxian apparatus which have often been noticed. The lack of a measure of physical output, to supplement *value* (a unit of labor time) cripples the analysis of real income; the definition of a key concept the organic composition of capital – is ambiguous; the treatment of the relation between the level of real wages and the money wage bargain is unsatisfactory. And so forth.[11]

This is not the point at which to show the vacuity of these charges; we shall come to each of them in due course. Our purpose, rather, is to note the differing responses of intellectuals of recent generations to the deterioration of the science.

Compare Robinson's reaction, for instance, with that of Althusser. "We had to retreat," Althusser says, "and, in semi-disarray, *return to first principles*."[12] Here is the difference between the Marxist and the friendly enemy. The latter criticizes, often *ex cathedra*, and shies away from the reconstructive return. He may, instead, flee to some new master, erecting under other, more honorable auspices some "new" theoretical system to restore the disillusioned spirit[13] – and disillusion has been a potent force in the flight from Marxism. Or the critic may fly to a higher level of abstraction, to a critique of criticism, or to a critique of critics, to the frontiers of philosophy, to the arms of psychoanalytics – there are always retreats available. The friend returns to first principles in order to determine whether or not they are in fact deficient. Where they are or where elaboration or extension is required, then there is work to be done. Thus we observe quite different reactions to the circumstances. We find both those revisionists who seek either to abandon or to modify radically the premises of Marx's theories and, typically, without their prior examination, and, also, those antirevisionists, such as Althusser and his followers, who rise to the theoretical challenge and undertake, where possible, real work of doctrinal reconstruction. It should now be clear why the present study is so much concerned with first principles, especially those of the economics, Marx's own favorite subject in which he has always been the unexcelled master – and will long continue to be, it is safe to say.

Certainly no return to first principles is easy; it is not even easy to say when one is in fact returning to first principles. Even among those who have abandoned the Marxian science, many believe they are returning to it and declare their intention of doing so. There is, in other words, a question after all of what principles are, or should be, first. For some, the return has been to philosophy or to psychoanalytics;[14] for others, a new social psychology or a new sociology is the mirage in view; there is a new politics and, it appears, a new economics, a "radical" economics quite divorced from Marxian "errors." For a growing number, however, the return is to Marx's own starting point as a social scientist: to the old labor theory of value and to the economics that derives from that theory. From this starting point much was once achieved, and the scientific issue among friends and friendly enemies is whether from this point a new beginning can be made. The premise from which the present study proceeds is that the abandonment of this starting point is the fundamental error from which scientific difficulties have long since multiplied in geometric proportion. The alleged defects of the labor theory of value turn out to be, on close examination, quite unsubstantial. Further, as one extends the theoretical structure from labor value premises to contemporary history, the theory, instead of breaking down, becomes a steadily more powerful instrument for probing into the secrets of the present order, into its structure of political as well as economic power. Marxists who have fled the labor theory have simply succumbed to bourgeois legends of the unsoundness of the theory.

Time will tell, no doubt, whether or not the economics will endure and come eventually to dominate the standard economics. But certainly there can be no authentic presentation of that economics that does not begin from its beginnings and proceed from thence to the examination of contemporary history. There is only one way to begin in order really to test the theory, and we propose to do precisely that – within the limits of an outline, of course. Beginning with the first principles of the labor theory, principles on which rest all of the other branches of Marxian science – its sociology, politics, philosophy, social psychology, and all else – we proceed gradually to extend our points of contact between the theory and contemporary society, looking always for what the theory *cannot*, at the same time watching for what it *must*, explain. What we offer is an exercise in theoretical history. In this type of writing one must begin from premises that have historical roots in social life, and this is the point from which the labor theory of value begins. From thence the theory must develop in such a fashion as to embrace all that needs to be explained. From the premises one proceeds to the explanation of social history and to the politically important work of elaborating a program for effecting a transition to socialism.

The very act of reconstructing and reapplying to the advanced capitalism the economic principles of Marxism would seem to suggest that the ordinary economics is not up to this work. Let this not stand as mere implication. The standard economics is not up to it. To the extent to which we succeed here in our undertaking, the study stands, therefore, as a reproach to conventional economics. The reproach will be spelled out in particular as well as in general ways. The subtitle of *Capital* is *A Critique of Political Economy*, and the present volume could well be subtitled *A Critique of Economics*, that is, the school or standard economics that is the mainstay of Western academia.

The growing exasperation with the standard economics, not only among young students but among older students, too, is by now a familiar fact of academic life. And it must be admitted by any candid viewer, that conventional textbooks in the subject[15] offer strange and yawning gaps in their discourse. While much attention is paid to theoretical mechanics, including their mathematical and statistical expression, the science chooses to ignore the role of economic circumstance in relation to the larger issues of the day: war, its causes and cures (if any); civil unrest; social inequality and inequity; political, racial, religious, and sexual repressions; revolution and counterrevolution; and other issues. Those who might look to the economist to descend to the question of economic causality in these matters look in vain. Instead, one is often told that this spiritual and scientific desiccation is the very sign of science. As economic and social crises deepen, the assurance is less and less convincing. Economics ends, then, not with a bang, but with a whimper.

Contrary to what most economists themselves believe, much of the irrelevance of the school economics to the problems of our time is built into the economics itself.[16] At certain critical junctures we shall try to show how this has come about. But the reader who stands in wonderment at our repeated criticisms of mainstream deficiencies must realize the importance of the issue. To the extent to which the Marxian explanation is valid – for the bourgeoi economist, to be sure, this is thinking the unthinkable – the or thodox explanation cannot be. These are *not* similar theoretical systems except at the level of formal structure (and even then parallels are limited). While it is true that there are theoretical overlappings between standard and Marxian economics, for example, in their conceptions of effective demand, such junctures may best be interpreted as confirming the Marxian system rather than refuting it, at least to the extent that the Marxian explanation proves generally satisfactory. Further, the superiority of the Marxian economics will be seen in its capacity to provide guidance for us in engineering a further developmental advance beyond the confines of the capitalist mode of production. We are not speaking now of the devising of utopias called communism or socialism or postindustrial society. We are speaking of practical goals, goals that can be worked for and implemented in systematic fashion, whose realization is calculated to meliorate much of the distress in which we find ourselves in the present phase of economic and social development. The Marxian political economy is superior to the standard system because it is capable of defining operationally useful goals that are within our powers of realization. In contrast, not only is standard economics oblivious even now to the true nature of the present crisis, preoccupying itself with rationalizing the status quo or even the status quo ante, it stands helpless before the dragon, waving ineffectual policies while awaiting the arrival of Saint George.

A sketch of the outline

The present work follows the main sequence from theory to policy just outlined. As an outline, it lays no claim to comprehensiveness but seeks to realize limited objectives: to introduce to the student of economics what is politically and in our view scientifically the most spectacular of the theoretical systems of social science; to bring to the reader the rudimentary knowledge needed for his own direct exploration of Marx's work; to reveal some of the critical defects of standard economics, both by direct criticism of it and by description of a superior alternative; to provide an interpretation of Marx's work that helps one to understand its permanent relevance to social studies; to reveal some of the principal instrumentalities necessary to comprehending the functioning of the advanced capitalism, to perceiving the laws of motion governing the contemporary order; to explain the need to effect a transition to socialism and to suggest some essentials of a program appropriate to this transition. Yet the work remains an outline, a compendium of elementary principles rather than a definitive system in its own right, a sketch of problems and of methods of solving them rather than a portrait. This much said, even an outline offers difficulties, and it is desirable, therefore, to sketch the outline. The work proceeds from what is more or less familiar to what is unfamiliar and from first to second approximations to the advanced capitalism.

The first two parts, Part One, on the reproduction schemes, and Part Two, on the labor theory of value, describe elementary concepts, principles, and methods that are more or less familiar.[17] The famous schema of reproduction on a constant, expanding, or declining scale serve not merely to express basic features of capitalist reproduction but also help with the definition of concepts and theoretical variables and with establishing premises for later work. They serve as vehicles for acquainting the reader with the vocabulary of the economics together with its rules of discourse. The applicability of the theory to analysis of the historical process is indicated, and social history begins to enter the argument as a means of clarifying and correcting the theoretical apparatus under construction. The first part includes a restatement of the theory of capital accumulation as described in *Capital I*, "The General Law of Capitalist Accumulation."[18]

In Part Two we proceed further into the theoretical foundations of the system, emphasizing its total dependence upon the labor theory of value and bringing to the fore those aspects of the labor theory that are scientifically critical. The effort is directed to laying bare premises and postulates in order that the whole may be better understood. Marx himself, we know, undertook the most meticulous inquiries into these theoretical underpinnings. Within the limits of available space, we do likewise. Logically, this portion of the text should precede the reproduction schemes of Part One. But as Althusser has pointed out, it is better to introduce the labor theory to the beginner after he has first had an opportunity to see the general direction in which it will ultimately carry him, after he has seen enough of the economics to be able to appreciate more fully the strategic as well as scientific importance of the theory.[19]

In Parts One and Two, in addition, we reintroduce into the economics what is an integral but not well-known and not well-publicized segment of it, the theory of unproductive labor and its consumptions (unproductive consumptions). Students who have not studied the whole of Marx's work, and of course the many who assume that *Capital I* contains all that is noteworthy in the economics, are commonly unfamiliar with the theory of unproductive labor. Even scholars often bypass Marx's extended and vastly important treatment of the subject – a subject most dear to Marx's classical forebears, by the way. With Chapter 3 we bring again to its rightful place in fundamentals a theory whose consideration can no longer be postponed. The reason for this restoration is not to do justice to its creator. Primarily, the current need for the theory traces to the course of capitalist development, a course that has brought capital to shoals on which it threatens to founder, and one to which its captains are bound, not by honor so much as by the dictates of forces over which they have little control and whose very existence falls to some extent outside the range of their comprehension. There is rather more hope, however, that serious students will be able to grasp the almost unbelievable perversity of the capitalist engine of accumulation, for there are growing numbers whose lack of ideological commitment allows them to contemplate with open mind the operation of laws of motion whose functioning is inconsistent with an indefinite continuance of the existing mode of production.

In Parts One and Two we portray the theoretical-historical structure descending from its premises in the labor theory of value, a structure that thus conforms to what many scientists have found to be an ideal form of scientific argument.[20] At the apex of the theory are the definitions and postulates from which lower-level theorems may be successively deduced, the latter explaining what is to be observed in social history. As far as the upper theorems are concerned, they, too, Marx always insisted, should be historically relevant, and we are prepared to repeat his insistence on the scientific need for and, finally, adequacy of, the labor theory of value. We shall see that his claims must be taken seriously from the scientific and historical standpoints. Despite the contrary opinion of the vulgar, who wish to dump the theory, the theory holds firm in all essentials. If one follows carefully the theses of these chapters (1, 2, 3), he should be able to read with an improved understanding the famous Chapter 1 of *Capital I*, a chapter of considerable difficulty and one notorious for the disagreements to which it has given rise.

Coming now to Part Three ("Relationships Between Prices and Values"), we broach a topic dear to the standard economics, the subject of price and price theory. Here our objective is twofold: to clarify relations between prices and values theoretically and to show in historical terms – counting "the present as history," as Paul Sweezy puts it – exactly how the laws of price-value relations assert themselves within the advanced capitalism and in the latter's associations with the rest of the world. Part Three describes the Marxian theory of price, a theory whose very existence has been concealed by ideological gas. It will be seen that the theory uses the famous laws of supply and demand, both micro and macro, in its analyses of the real world; but it also uses a great deal of fundamental material not dreamed of in the standard philosophy.

The Marxian theory of price, of which the so-called transformation problem is an important and misleading aspect, is above all a theory of relations between prices and values as these relations shift and change in the course of capitalist accumulation. Relations between prices and values generated within the capitalist economy come eventually into quite peculiar and eccentric constellations that, in turn, have an intimate and even decisive bearing on the development of economic crises. The standard theory of price, by contrast, is in all essentials an equilibrium theory showing (if that is the word) how prices determine an equilibrium tendency or, alternatively, how prices define a normal relation to each other, a relation whose possibility of realization is thought to be politically feasible and desirable in the interest of equilibrium. In standard economics, competitive pricing is taken to be a rational and self-equilibrating process, and the theory of competitive price, which is the subject of mechanistic theorizing ad nauseum in standard texts, is a *normative* theory masquerading as science. That the Marxian theory of price is nonnormative is best indicated by the explanation it provides of the role of the pricing system in the development of economic crises. Our discussion of price-value relations in Part Three, therefore, concludes with an analysis of the development of the present crisis of the advanced capitalism (Chapter 8). While this analysis was first undertaken in the winter of 1974, it continues to hold at the present time (winter 1976) as the crisis continues to develop within the constraints indicated in the analysis: the tendency to imbalance between monetary and exchange values in the aggregate; the tendency of particular prices to deviate systematically from particular values (unequal exchange); the tendency for the general rate of profit to fall, a tendency reflecting in the advanced capitalism a combination of forces pushing in the same direction. While our analysis relates primarily to the United States, the laws function in approximately similar fashion throughout the whole range of countries; the crisis is perfectly general.

With Part Four we come to the development of class structure and relations, the perennial issue of Marxian political economy of the nature and form of the class struggle in its latest phase. We consider here some of the alleged failures of class analysis, that is, the disappearance of the proletariat and the rise of the new middle classes to predominance. Chapters 9, 10, and 11 extend and broaden the traditional analysis in order to deal more fully with the current situation while at the same time reverting to Marx (Chapter 9 in particular) in order to obtain the clues needed for this work.

In this matter of class structure and relations the Marxian science has, reputedly, nothing new to offer. In one sense, this charge is not too wide of the target. Marx's comments on the sociopolitical development of capitalism probed much further into the future than his critics have ever admitted. One of the reasons that his analysis is not more widely known is, perhaps, that it was not easy to understand what he was saying on this subject, because the main developments to which he referred had not until recently put in a decisive and overwhelming appearance within the advanced capitalism. Marx's own fast-sliding remarks simply sailed past batters who were unaware that anything was being thrown at them. This is not the first occasion, and it will probably not be the last, that the master's views have antedated both the events and the scholar's understanding of them. Be this as it may, our analysis, resting upon the labor theory of value, tends to combine with historical evidences to confirm not merely the suggestions of *Capital* (and especially of *Capital III*) but even those of the earlier *Manifesto* as well. In view of the combination of theory and evidences presented in Part Four, much of the carping to which the theory has been subject appears to be motivated by other than objective considerations.

Finally, we take up rather briefly certain economic and political problems involved in the transition to socialism from the advanced capitalism. In our concluding chapter (Chapter 12), we seek to demonstrate the utility of the theory for devising and implementing specific means of solving both economic (e.g., full employment) and politico-social (e.g., class tensions) problems. A case is made for socialist control and management of social resources on the grounds that only by breaking capitalist relations of production can the most deep-rooted problems of our epoch be dealt with. We argue, further, that the understanding as well as the dissolution of these problems is contingent upon an appreciation of Marxian theory and that an understanding of them, at least, is not at all beyond the reach of people of average intelligence, education, and willingness to think. Not that these are sufficient conditions for understanding the theory and the problems to which it points; there are many whose allegiances are to other views and other values. On the other hand, while there are many within the working class whose formal educations are deficient, they will understand much instinctively, as it were, as a consequence of their own direct experience and analysis of it. The reader who comes at our world primarily from the theoretical side, through the medium of Marxian analysis, should not be surprised if certain of his conclusions bring him into essential agreement with those of ordinary working people.

This volume must certainly not be regarded as a work that moves from simplicity to ever greater complexity. To some extent the very reverse is the case; as Marx says: "Every beginning is difficult holds in all sciences." The further one proceeds with the analysis, the simpler and more understandable the world becomes, for, after all, the object of science is to enhance comprehension. The idea that scientific truth is so complex and intricate that only the rare individual can grasp it is, to be sure, an idea with which the standard disciplines, themselves in desperate straits, torture and plague the minds of their students. It is an idea whose main function is to cater to intellectual cultism within the academic establishment.

Thus at the conclusion of this volume it is hoped that the reader will understand exactly what we mean when we say that socialism is not at all an inevitable, but a necessary, outcome of the process of capitalist development. Socialism is, we shall see, a very real possibility and an effort to make a transition to it is imperative. Whether or not the effort will be successful will depend on the working out of specific terms and relations among social classes both at national and international levels. What specific kinds of relations and terms of interchange are required to effect a global transition to socialism is too large a subject for inclusion in this brief outline. We do wish to underscore, nevertheless, the importance of attempting to define those relations and those terms and of trying to implement them globally.

If at the conclusion of this work one is able to see more clearly the nature of our social predicament, and if one sees, therefore, the relevance of theoretical Marxism, then our immediate objective will have been achieved. It must be understood, however, that socialism is not inevitable, and that its realization out of the advanced capitalism, while of the utmost importance, requires work, struggle, and planning. Neither Marx nor any true Marxist can take the course of events for granted. Adam Smith's warning is to the point: "But though empires, like all the other works of men, have all hitherto proved mortal, yet every empire aims at immortality."[21] Some empires, no doubt, aim rather more at immolation than at immortality. In the interests of mankind their aim must be improved.

The Marxian political economy provides guidance for all who seek to establish a human dominion over the development of the productive forces. This is as true for people of the advanced capitalism as it has proved to be true for those in the economically undeveloped and exploited world. Unlike conventional economics, however, the Marxian economics gives no assurance of automatic salvation. It offers no unstudied hopes, provides no panaceas. But the need is universal for a methodology big enough to grapple with the real issues of social life and strong enough to throw them.

PART ONE
The reproduction schemes

1

Methodological glasses
for the longer view

An approach to historical processes

As everyone knows, the main theses of Marxian political economy are two in number. The first is that conflict among social classes is a prime mover of history. The second is that the exercise of the productive force of social labor is a predominant and ultimately decisive concern of man in society. We begin with a simple elaboration of these theses and with the simple relation that they bear to each other. There is but one preliminary observation to be made.

The basic postulate is that of an evolving universe moving under the impress of definite laws of development, although not in a deterministic fashion as is sometimes implied in rigid concepts of law. The laws controlling the reproduction of social life are not at all obvious; thus there is a general problem of methodical procedures to be faced. Special methods of inquiry are required, and it is at this juncture that the two theses referred to may be brought to the fore. Their function is heuristic in the first instance. They are hypotheses serving as guides for the investigator, helping him to extract from the historical context the specific laws controlling the reproduction of social life.[1] The guides to inquiry of which Marxism avails itself are numerous, of course; we single out only two that were preeminent in Marx's own study of historical development. In turning these to the question of general, hypothetical relations between social classes and the force of productive labor, the character of the two proposals becomes evident.

Man does not live by bread alone, it is true, but it is certain that he does not live at all without it. It is inescapable that the energies of social labor are always and everywhere socially necessary in that

19

bread must be forthcoming. This simple necessity stands as an unassailable premise and makes the labor theory of value imperative for inquiries anthropological, archeological, economic historical, and so on, for inquiries extending far beyond the confines of modern capitalism.[2] The labor theory points directly to a form of human activity that is socially indispensable. Hence, properly qualified, the theory relates to modern capitalism as well as to precapitalist economic formations.

In its broadest aspect the labor theory proposes that the social activity devoted to reproduction of the material means of life provides critical support for the sustenance of all other varieties of social activity. The energy expended by working people, in the broadest sense of that phrase, insofar as it produces and reproduces the economic essentials of life, provides the material means of supporting its own activity together with all other forms of social activity. Because the need for material sustenance is all pervasive, it is evident that all of social life depends upon the maintenance of the vitality of the labor engaged in processes of economic reproduction. Indeed, the only other social activity comparable to this as absolute necessity is that of biological reproduction.[3] These two activities have always been accorded a theoretical primacy in the Marxian tradition.

Our hypothesis may be made more specific. The labor power that reproduces life's economic underpinnings must itself be kept in working condition by maintenance of its own material foundations. In the production and reproduction of the material base the tools, equipment, raw materials, and, indeed, the technique of production itself, must themselves be reproduced. These are instruments of labor, means of production, and men have utilized such instruments systematically since millennia ago they finished with foraging. Further, there are the direct means of *subsistence* consumed by labor in its reproductive work: food, clothing, shelter, and so on.[4] These two sets of material means comprise the main categories of the means of reproduction necessarily utilized – and, incidentally, *used up* by labor – in the course of labor's socially necessary work.

All of this may appear quite obvious, but one should not underrate complexities. With reference to biological reproduction, for instance, it is well known that the secrets of biological processes are only slowly giving way to science and to their own rational organization. The same is true of economic reproduction. Many of its secrets are still to be extracted from historical data through the hard digging of inquiry. "Few men know what they would be at," Lord Byron once observed, and the comment is even now applicable to our understanding of economic reproduction. We do not suggest that the relevant laws are simple, much less self-evident. It is only certain that society must make provision, even if only semiconsciously, as through the media of tradition and custom, for securing and ensuring that economic reproduction regularly takes place.

To ensure the reproduction of material resources there must always be a regularized flow of productive labor power. This is the means through which the material means themselves may be reproduced. This is a simple premise of the labor theory. The necessity for maintaining this flow within variegated ecological circumstances will, we suppose, shape the institutional and class structure of social life, although, of course, the specific ways that it does so can be shown definitely only by the study of social history proper. The extent and character of modifications of social life that are imposed by economic necessity, the penalties that follow from failures of social mechanisms of adjustment — these are substantial objectives of historical study aimed at eliciting a more specific knowledge of the laws of motion of social life and their *modus operandi*. Hence the importance of study of the mode of production. Study alone will confirm – or fail to confirm – the premises from which scientific inquiry departs. Marxists believe that history confirms their assumptions. But whether or not this is true, the premise that the power of productive labor both sustains and requires sustenance is the touchstone from which the labor theory departs and to which it returns. But what of the class struggle? The two theses, of class conflict and of the primacy of processes of economic reproduction, are related to each other in simple fashion.

The productivity of social labor is, and since neolithic times has commonly been, sufficiently developed that labor yields a surplus product. Returning to our observation that labor itself must be sustained, that it must reproduce what it uses up of the means of production and the means of subsistence, the term "productivity" in this connection refers to what is produced in *excess* of this minimum reproduction requirement. On what does this productivity depend? It depends on what has been called variously the level of technique and technology, the level of development of the productive forces, the state of the industrial arts (Thorstein Veblen), or, simply and somewhat misleadingly, the level of development. Working with its means of production within a given technical and social milieu, labor has long had the power to do more than simply reproduce itself. Historically, our arrival at the point where we could do something more than the required economic minimum set the stage for the appearance of class society. Class society became possible in that some portion of the population then could, by the expedient of supporting itself from the surplus generated, engage in activities more or less far removed from those of the reproductive workers. This proposition is, again, a hypothesis. We do not say that the appearance of the surplus made unavoidable class society, except in the very loosest and retrospective sense of the phrase; we say, rather, that it made class society *possible*. This is something else again. The rise of productivity and the generation of surplus were a precondition for class society, a necessary but not sufficient condition for its emergence. Recall that the labor theory is meant to aid and encourage inquiry rather than to stifle it; we need to know more of the historical details of the origins of class society.

In this quest the labor theory can offer more pointed suggestions that may be helpful. While the productivity of social labor is a prerequisite for the appearance of social classes, their appearance will signify an opposition of their economic interests that traces to the economic reproductive substructure of society. There will be a class whose interest in economic reproduction will be self-interest, to be sure, but upon whose reproductive activity nevertheless the entire edifice of social activity is founded: the working class. There will be another class, or classes, whose direct interest is not reproductive but appropriative, since its livelihood is contingent upon possession and utilization of the surplus. The former, with its interest in productive consumption, is the "producing" class, and in the Marxian terminology the term "producers" refers always to its members. The latter consists of those who consume unproductively in the broad sense that their activity does not culminate directly in reproduction of the community's material means of production or of consumption either one.[5]

The famous opposition of class interests of which Marxists speak is the one just described, the opposition of the productive to the unproductive interest. This is the fundamental oppposition that underlies class tensions and which, when sharpened by circumstance, may threaten a breakdown in social relations. But even if tensions do not result in breakdown, in collapse and civil war, they may profoundly influence the social structure in political, ideological, or in other dimensions – all to be watched for in the study of particular cases. When, for instance, we come to the consideration of contemporary capitalism, such guides as these will be brought into play. It will then be time enough for the reader to appraise the usefulness of the methods and assumptions proposed.

Passing once more over the argument thus far, we repeat that there is what Hegel called a world history to be explained. There a historical process of which the present is but a segment, an interlude, but one that, of course, demands our careful attention. In order to approach world history scientifically, to explore properly the interconnected histories of peoples, nations, tribes, one must equip himself with aids to his queries. While the need for heuristic devices is agreed upon by all philosophers of science, those we propose relate directly to the thesis of class structure and conflict and to the labor theory. These devices, in turn, may be cast in various forms, any or all of which may be helpful in given instances. Take as an example a proposition utilized by Marx in his exploration of the development of modern capital.

Technique and the division of labor

In approaching a particular social order, whether of past or present, one may expect to find operative within it a certain division of labor, a more or less elaborate and articulate structure of occupations embracing the whole of productive and also of unproductive activity. This division of labor will reflect directly the necessary division of work specialties corresponding to the technical development of the productive forces. One would expect to find in hoe culture, say, not only a certain simplicity of technique, but a correspondingly limited and simple division of labor. Where technique is more advanced and the productive forces more developed, the divisions will be more numerous, the varieties of labor power greater and, perhaps, more sophisticated, specialization in all its dimensions more marked and otherwise developed. The higher the level of technique, the plateau on which the reproductive worker stands, the more extended the division of labor and the higher the level of labor productivity. These important propositions were, of course, known before Marx. The latter, however, took them, placed them more securely within a general framework of principles such as we discuss here and used them in the exploration of ancient as well as modern society. We see that there is nothing mysterious or obscure in the reference so frequently made to forces of production in the Marxian economics. The reference is to a congerie of workers, functioning within a given division of labor, utilizing technique (and technology) characteristic of their level of technical development, and engaged in reproducing the community's means of production and means of consumption. Though simple, these ideas are absolutely fundamental to sound historical and economic inquiry.

We repeat what we have already said in still more precise terms. The evolution of the productive forces to the point where a regular reproduction of surplus could take place doubtless took the human race a very long time to accomplish, perhaps thousands of millennia and an equal number of false starts before economic foundations and, hence, social reproduction as a whole were securely established. The forms of social organization emerging with these struggles reflected in one way or another, in one circumstance or another, the necessity of ensuring the reproductive activity underlying the whole social structure. The eventual appearance of a product in excess of the amounts and kinds needed simply to replace used-up means of production (tools, instruments, raw materials) and means of consumption, or what are termed wage goods within the capitalist mode of production (food, clothing, shelter, etc.), heralded a new phase of social development, a new phase of human history. A modification of older forms of primitive communism and the appearance of newer ones, and especially of those featuring more or less pronounced class formations, gradually took place. With a higher productivity it had become possible to support out of the social surplus additional divisions and social classes whose activities were no longer tied directly to the reproductive foundation.

None of this is intended to declare sharp and immutable dichotomies between productive and unproductive labor, between working and ruling class, as ubiquitous phenomena in all precapitalist modes of production. The intent of actual inquiry is to reveal the variety and complexity of activities in all of their interrelations. Here we state only principles. We simply say that men have always been concerned – if not consciously in full awareness of the laws to which they were subject, then in groping and tentative fashion – for preservation of the means of ensuring their material and, hence, social existence. Much less do we suggest a perennial preoccupation of economic man with making alternative choices among competing ends so as to maximize his satisfactions. This latter principle, sometimes confused with Marxism, is so simplistic that insight into social history proceeding upon that premise must be more by accident than design. Imputing hedonistic motives to men within modes of production far removed from capitalism is a highly suspect procedure, as the American economic anthropologists under Karl Polanyi have emphasized.[6] Polanyi, in fact, puts it well when he tells us that under primitive conditions economic life is embedded with a matrix of noneconomic activities of ritual and ceremony, custom and convention. On the other hand, the kind of economic necessity to which we have referred does make its mark on society, and the matrix of noneconomic institutions must always be carefully scrutinized for signs of its impress, for its recognition, so to speak, of basic needs. While the work of economic reproduction is and has always been carried out in intimate interrelation with what are *seemingly* noneconomic ritual, ceremony, and, furthermore, extended family interrelations of gens, tribe, and family, these intimate interrelations are the very substance of which history is composed and into whose character and function one must inquire.

Contrary to rumor, there is nothing whatsoever in the Marxian methodology to forestall the most detailed inquiry aimed at discovering precisely what *was* what or what *is* what. If we say, for instance, that the level of development of the productive forces makes possible historically a certain separation of mental from manual labor – to cast the proposition in but one of several possibly useful forms[7] – this may only help one to specify with the aid of available evidences the *exact* form and degree of this separation and the role played by it in historical development. If as early as Neolithic times productivity sufficed to support superstructures more or less divorced from, and often quite parasitic to, productive labor – as happened with the emergence of slavery – still the substance of history is embedded in the phrase "more or less" and is to be determined objectively. The contention is that the labor theory and class conflict hypotheses are *useful* and will indeed prove *necessary* for explaining the gradual emergence of varied class-structured orders out of earlier or more primitive social forms. This principle applies not only to the analysis of prehistoric, antique, and feudal modes of production but to the modern capitalistic and socialistic forms as well.

For all of the otherwise great differences among prehistoric, antique, and modern social-economic formations, they in one respect still resemble each other. They feature more or less distinct and clear-cut divisions between ruling and producing classes, between unproductive and productive labor. With respect to modern society, too, surplus product in the form of surplus value underlies and supports its class arrangements and alignments. Needless to say, this comment hardly exhausts the subject of the numerous and subtle connections between social surplus and class structure and conflict. Were this all there is to be said, our study could close before it begins. The intention is to mark the starting point of our analysis, and the surplus value hypothesis is both a useful and necessary starting point.

As for today, in appropriate form, as a theory of values being exchanged within the money-market-commodity context of modern capitalism, the labor theory of value has an extraordinary explanatory power. Carefully and systematically applied, the theory augments enormously one's understanding of the nature and functioning of contemporary capitalism. Modern society, like ancient society, still rests upon economic foundations that, when shaken, threaten to topple the superstructure and sometimes the substructure as well. But all of this still remains to be seen.

The theory of simple reproduction[8]

It may be lamentable – and both friends and enemies of Marxism have decried the fact – but the propositions so far referred to may be elaborated into a detailed and sophisticated theoretical structure for the explanation of social history. To this point the emphasis has been upon general methodological premises from which the study of contemporary society may proceed. The next task is to proceed from these foundations to the work of theory construction, reconstruction, and elaboration. One must proceed also to the actualities to be encompassed by this theoretical framework. These objectives entail new difficulties. "There is no royal road to knowledge!" is true enough. On the other hand, a beginning of

Marxian economics has already been made and what follows is merely a further specification of its ideas, extending what has already been read and understood. The theory of simple reproduction is such an extension.

A somewhat more careful spelling out of the theory will enable sharper distinctions to be drawn among important concepts, as between social reproduction taken in its entirety, including the functions of unproductive labor, for instance, and the reproduction of the fundamental substructure with its productive labor. As a whole, we have seen, social reproduction embraces both the continuing sustenance of unproductive and of productive activity; it means putting social activity on a permanent footing in both of its economic aspects. At the base, there is first of all the system of economic reproduction proper. The reproduction of productive activity consists of the system of reconstituting the tools, instruments, raw materials, foodstuffs, clothing, shelter, and other things, at a rate sufficient to replace these items as they wear out or are used up in the course of working them. The surplus beyond this output of necessaries, whatever it may be, consists of material means, perhaps physically similar in form to the foregoing for the most part, but destined to be used in support of activity that does *not* itself yield a product or service essential to the underlying process of economic reproduction. The consumption taking place in the second sphere does not contribute to economic reproduction. Instead, it typically consists of activities pointed toward the continuing appropriation of surplus being generated out of the productive base. This consumption draws upon, and must continue to draw upon, the surplus product regularly thrown up out of the energies of productive labor.

Although it is not necessary to be a student of economics to comprehend what is most important and peculiar to the system being described, that system is composed of certain required economic interrelations among those inputs, all of which are destined for productive use, and its outputs, some portion of which, in particular the excess portion, is destined for unproductive employment. All of the reproduction schemes of the Marxian economics are in fact input–output systems of this general kind, so that a small effort spent in grasping their main features will save perplexity subsequently. Figure 1.1 will be helpful.

In this graph the volume of inputs is measured on the horizontal

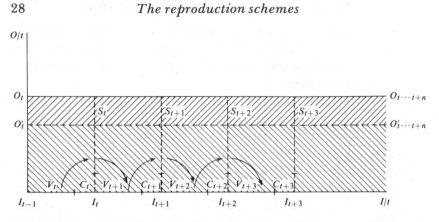

Figure 1.1. Simple Reproduction (fixed technique). Measuring input quantities on the horizontal and output on the vertical, the theory of simple reproduction proceeds as follows. If the (value) magnitude of the initial inputs is I_t, then at the close of the period of production t this value will have transmitted itself in its entirety to the value of the output of which it becomes a part. The reproduced value, O'_t, is not the whole of the value of the output, however. If the productivity of labor suffices, there will be a surplus, S_t. The value of the entire output, O_t, is then the reproduced value plus the surplus value. If *only* the reproduced values are put back into motion with each period, these same relations will hold for each period: $I_t = O_t = I_{t+1} \ldots I_{t+n}$. We assume also that the ratio of the surplus value to the input is the same for each period. Both input and output scales are then unchanging. The area shaded to the right represents the flow of surplus product through time, the area shaded to the left the flow of consumed and reproduced values. In applying the scheme of simple reproduction to primitive and archaic societies in an effort to understand their class and other internal relationships, exchange values will not manifest themselves directly in those relationships since community production is not involved. Instead one must "look and see" whether, for example, the extent of kinship responsibilities is governed by labor times required for production without assuming at the outset that such is necessarily the case. In precapitalist production, simple reproduction may better be thought of as involving necessary and surplus labor or product rather than the values of wage goods, means of production, surplus, etc. On the other hand, an anthropologist may be *forced* to a labor theory of value, where quantities exchanged are measured in units of labor time, in order to explain what he observes. Compare R. F. Salisbury, *From Stone Age to Steel,* Melbourne University Press, 1962.

axis (I/t) and of outputs is measured on the vertical axis (O/t). The distances measured horizontally and vertically will measure quantities of the material means of production and means of subsistence *used up* (measured on the horizontal axis) and *reproduced* (measured on the vertical axis) over a fixed period of time. The state of productive technique is fixed and unchanging along with the size of the total population and of the work force. These are primary features of what is termed "simple" reproduction. In a process of simple reproduction the given outputs of period t (totaling an amount measured by the distance $I_t - I_{t-1}$) are used up (consumed) in the course of that period. Suppose that by the close of that period of production, labor power has succeeded in *reproducing precisely* all items consumed in support of productive work.

This reproduced product necessary for economic reproduction is measured by the distance O'_t on the vertical axis. Now the working community stands ready to enter the next period of production, $t + 1$, with the same required volume of material means of reproduction as it entered period t.

Suppose in addition to the reproduced output, O'_t, a surplus product appears at the close of the period. This is the portion of the total output O_t that is to be used *unproductively* in the sense that its subsequent consumption does *not* result in the appearance of any new or excess product at some subsequent point in time. With each period surplus product appears, a result of the productivity of the living labor power functioning at the lower level of economic reproduction. We see, then, how it is possible for an entire social system, a system composed of productive activity, on the underside, and unproductive activity, on the upper side, to endure for an indefinite period of historical time – provided the material means required for the support of each kind of activity are always regularly forthcoming, as in the case of simple reproduction we are describing. For each and every period each portion of the total population, productive and unproductive alike, finds available *for the purpose of reproducing itself* the material means that it requires. The workers reproduce the means of production and the means of subsistence that they use up in their work. The leisure class (as Veblen referred to it) finds available and regularly *appropriates* a surplus product that sustains it in the activities in which it engages, whatever those activities may be.

While a reproductive scheme of this simple kind has a great deal of utility for inquiry into precapitalist modes of production, it is necessary to modify it somewhat in order to apply it to the analysis of capitalism as a mode of social reproduction. Assume, therefore, a market economy in which all inputs, including labor power, are bought and sold at market prices, the same applying to outputs of every kind – those destined for productive as well as unproductive use. The inputs being used up in reproductive activity by productive labor are, like labor power itself, bought and sold at prices established by supplies and demands for these means of production and these wage goods. As for the laborers, they are paid money wages with which they turn around and purchase the means of consumption (wage goods) that they require in order to maintain their own energy as working people, and so, too, as regards the output of social product. The output that is destined for productive use (O' in period t, for example) is sold in part to entrepreneurs (means of production) and to workers (means of consumption) who then use them productively as input in the following period.

The portion of the output that goes to unproductive consumption, S_t from period t, for example, is sold to its unproductive consumers during the period $t + 1$. These consumers use this product to support themselves in the life style to which they are accustomed and in the unproductive work in which they are engaged, such as the work involved in appropriating and consuming the surplus as it regularly rises up out of productive activity. For as long as the surplus appears and reappears, is appropriated and consumed by the unproductive class; for as long as the productive inputs are consumed and reproduced, then put back into motion once more as inputs of a subsequent period – for as long as the material means of life are produced and reproduced on the required scale, the social order may also reproduce the characteristic activities of its main classes of consumers.

It is desirable to run through once more the theory of simple reproduction in order to introduce the notion of value, the quantitative dimension of the inputs and outputs of capitalist reproduction. In ordinary parlance, value refers most often to the money value of a commodity, to its price, or to its price times its quantity (the expenditure to be made). In simple reproduction under capitalism the values of commodities are, similarly, exchange values or values in exchange, to use the older phrase. As noted, these values in exchange may be measured in monetary units; so many dollars worth of means of production, so many worth of means of consumption, and so on. But within the labor theory of value it is maintained that, in addition, these values in exchange are in principle measurable in units of labor time: so many man-hours worth of this item, a means of production, say; so many man-hours worth of that, a consumption good. In order to avoid for the time being, the complications of introducing all at once two different standards and measures of exchange value, suppose we simply assume that the prices of all commodities making up the socially necessary inputs and outputs of the reproductive system also measure (strictly speaking, are proportional to) the exchange values of these commodities measured in units of labor time (of socially necessary labor time, the labor time required on the average to produce and reproduce each item of necessary input). A brief

recapitulation of reproduction in terms of these exchange values
will help to make clear the Marxian conception of the essential
character of capitalist and other reproductive systems.

In the theory of simple reproduction, we abstract from changes
in technique of production, changes in population, and so on, in
order to concentrate better upon relations within and between the
main spheres of productive and of unproductive activity. At the
beginning of a period of reproduction – a period of time long
enough to put into motion the productive inputs of the period,
reproduce them, generate the accompanying surplus value, and sell
them to buyers so as to realize a profit (the object of entrepreneurial
activity) – a certain total value of inputs is available for productive
consumption. Call their total value 100 billions (of dollars, pounds,
marks, rubles, etc., worth of commodities). This total input
divides, let us say, into 80 billions of means of consumption for
labor (wage goods) and 20 billions of means of production
(including the capital goods of conventional economics). In the terminology of Marxian economics (taken up in more detail in
Chapter 2), there is an input of constant capital in the amount of 20
billions and of 80 billions of variable capital or wage goods (or the
labor power that those goods will support in productive work). At
the close of the period of reproduction, under capitalism as under
other modes of production, what has been used up has been
reproduced and comprises a part of the total value of the output.
This portion of the total output O'_t consists of the value of the
reproduced wage goods and reproduced means of production, and
these stand ready, along with living labor, to participate in productive activity in the period following, $t + 1$. The surplus product is
sold "at its value" of, say, 50 billions, and is consumed by the
capitalists in the course of their activity as entrepreneurs and as
consumers. The sale of the surplus product provides that portion of
the capitalist's total revenues that he designates as profit. It is evident in Figure 1.1 that if all output sells at its value, the profits to be
made cannot *exceed* the value of the surplus product of each
period.

Some general remarks on the theory of simple reproduction

But enough, for the moment, with this business of theoretical
mechanics, important as it may be. The theory merely spells out
more precisely what may be termed "conditions of simple reproduc-

tion"; it helps to specify the circumstances under which the production and reproduction of commodities, after all an intrinsic and characteristic feature of life in all society, can continue in such a way as to sustain indefinitely the main categories of activity characteristic of the social whole. When the productive inputs demanded by the state of technique are transformed through the agency of creative labor into an array of final products, identical with and proportional to the inputs consumed in process, the possibility of economic reproduction obtains. The reproduced values being equal in magnitude *and* in kind to those used up in their own creation, the community at the close of a period will find itself in possession of all the means of livelihood for the subsequent period – and thus for each and every period as long as the reproduction conditions are met.

We are dealing here with flows rather than with stocks of commodities, the point being that, given a certain population and a level of development of the productive forces, certain rates of flow of certain means of production and means of subsistence are necessary to sustain economic together with other social processes. While these flow magnitudes will be defined in the following chapter, it is important to understand at the outset that the very necessity of defining these flows arises from the prior need to understand reproductive processes per se.

Further, we have emphasized the flow of surplus value as a stream from which is regularly drawn the material means of supporting whatever unproductive activities may characterize the capitalist superstructure. Later on, a part of our inquiry will turn upon a precise identification of those activities and, also, upon the forces governing their magnitudes relative to the magnitude of productive resources caught up in the economic substructure and there processed by productive labor. Clearly, the method of abstraction being utilized permits a considerable elaboration of useful concepts and propositions, and it is this, together with the historical applicability of the model, that makes its study worthwhile.

In regard to surplus value itself, what needs to be kept in mind is that it *may be* functionally entirely extraneous to economic reproduction, a portion of the social product accruing to others than its producers. However, if the surplus is unproductively consumed, the exact nature of this consumption, including the specific social functions that it serves, is to be determined by historical as much as by abstract inquiry. This principle applies to the study of capitalism as it applies to the study of other modes of production and to interrelations between or among them. Suffice it to say, however, that the social roles of unproductive and of productive consumption, or, as they are referred to within the context of the labor theory of value, of unproductive and of productive labor, are assumed to be of the greatest significance in shaping the course of social development, including the development of modern capitalism, the final object of our examination.

While the importance of these concepts is underscored only in a general way at this time, a more careful definition of unproductive and of productive labor must be given later. For the moment the general conceptions suffice, and our discussion helps to bring front and center an assertion of Marx's whose importance may be too easily underrated:

> Whatever the form of the process of production in a society, it must be a continuous process, must continue to go periodically through the same phases. A society can no more cease to produce than it can cease to consume. When viewed, therefore, as a connected whole, and as flowing on with incessant renewal, every social process of production is, at the same time, a process of reproduction.[9]

This must be taken not as a mere theoretical abstraction, but as a proposition whose vital import is contained in the innocent word "must." No matter what the mode of production, we shall find this necessity impressed upon the institutions and customs, the morals and mores, of peoples solving the fundamental economic problem. Where these impressions do not obtain, and where the mechanism of economic and social reproduction becomes eccentric in relation to elemental necessities, the consequences *may* be disastrous: "No society can go on producing, in other words no society can reproduce, unless it constantly reconverts a part of its products into means of production, or elements of fresh products."[10]

Even as it stands here, more or less stripped of historical flesh, the skeletal structure of simple reproduction suggests dialectical possibilities for the student of history to contemplate. On the one side, unproductive consumption, and the labor that it supports, shows itself as a form of what might be termed "dead-end consumption," a consumption that, unlike productive consumption, fails to lead to a real replacement of economically vital energies or, what comes to the same thing, the material means of replacing or regenerating those energies of productive labor. On the other hand, it appears as a mass potentially productive of value, a potential that might, under certain conditions, be transformed into positive

activity, into some kind of increment of productive work. But insofar as simple reproduction itself is concerned, the using up of the
surplus may take place under historically varied circumstances
featuring a wide variety of particular uses of surplus product,[11] for
example, in precapitalist society when the surplus maintains the
elders, as in tribal society; or when it supports the military or leisure
class, as in Sparta or Egypt; or when it provides a foundation for all
of those religious, ceremonial, or other cultural activities whose
contributions to basic economic reproduction are at best indirect.
And yet, we should not be surprised to discover in historical study
times and places where, for instance, the surplus supports activities
which, like a gyroscope, tend to stabilize and regularize the
reproduction of economic necessaries. Nor should we be surprised
to find on occasion the consumption of surplus by those whose activities only corrode or undercut economic foundations.

At its most general level of applicability, the theory reminds us
that while the variety of social forms is as large as history reveals it
to be, social life always consists of interrelated but sometimes
disparate and even dichotomous processes. Within the theory the
economic foundations of social life appear to involve a recycling
process whose input–output interrelations are geared to ensuring
that what is used up is always reproduced through the activity of
social labor, so that the material means of life are always forthcoming. More than this, it reminds us that out of the productivity of
social labor a surplus arises whose consumption may have quite different implications. This is not to denigrate unproductive consumption in all its historical forms, nor to deny that it may play, or may
have played, a useful and even necessary role in the evolution of
human society. The supportive role played by unproductive consumption in relation to the underlying recycling can and must be
seen in all its manifestations, in the historical contexts in which they
show themselves. So, too, for the negative contributions of unproductive consumption to the economic base; they must also be
seen for what they are. These principles hold, of course, for the examination of all of the phases of modern capitalist development.

A note on modes of production

With preliminaries out of the way, we may again raise the question
of the kinds of social formations that history offers for our inspec-

tion and that may be analyzed with the instruments we are discussing. What *is* a mode of production, however?

The phrase designates a particular set or constellation of material forces and relations characterizing the organization of reproduction at a given level of development of the productive forces. The theory is intended to imply the existence of different modes, and it suggests a rough correspondence between the level of productive technique utilized in economic reproduction and the peculiar kinds of relations of production that oversee and govern its exercise, ensuring that reproduction takes place. At a given technical level of the productive forces (of labor power and the means of production with which it works) there are given relations of production (as defined by the general division of social labor) that envelop the technique and those who exercise it within an organizationally distinctive arrangement. As a rule, these are relations of unproductive to productive labor, and they tend to guarantee that, while certain responsibilities for social production are assigned to productive labor, rights of appropriation of a portion of the social product are reserved to the unproductive.

In rather more familiar terms, the modes that Marx and Engels distinguish are, in rough chronological order: primitive communism, slavery, the Asiatic mode, feudalism, capitalism, and, among those hopefully to come, socialism and communism. In addition, the theory implies that there are modal sequences involving "transitions" between or among certain of the modes. The determination of these sequences, both as historical fact and as possible successions, deserves the most careful study in order that the laws governing these successions may be understood. Their study will, presumably, shed some light on our present problems of transition to socialism, a transition badly needed but still uncertain of realization.[12]

Among those unacquainted with, or perhaps careless in interpretation of, Marx's writings, it has often been said that he projected a unilateral and fixed sequence among modes along the general path of social development, a sequence that all men would be required to follow en route to communism. In the mechanistic view the great engine of class struggle and conflict would eventually carry mankind from its inception in primitive communism through slavery, feudalism, capitalism, and socialism to communism. A careful study of Marx's writings reveals no simple escalator, however. Since the rediscovery of his now famous Asiatic mode of production the realization has dawned among many that he also intended his famous modes to be used heuristically, for research quite as much as for narrow polemicizing.[13] Mankind must not be thought of as proceeding through some preordained sequence to a promised land. Not only may some peoples find themselves unable to effect transitions to technically and socially, perhaps, more advanced states, but some modes may be bypassed in the process. Further, there may be variants of the primary modes yet to be identified through historical study, and either an elaboration or a simplification of the main categories may one day be accomplished theoretically. Finally has come the realization that transitions between modes may be marked by regressions as well as by forward movement.[14] The supposition of a linear movement toward socialism can never do justice to the complexity of history.

None of this means, need we add, that history is "full of sound and fury, signifying nothing." It is more than a tale told by fools or a story of heroes and hero worshipers, princes and paupers, of cataclysmic but meaningless accidents and events. We want the real story, the natural history of the development of mankind, the rough and dialectical course of social evolution, and it is the aim of Marxian science to tell that story with accuracy and in such a manner that its lessons may be applicable to the great work of continuing the process of social development in all possible dimensions. These goals require a serviceable theoretical system, one intrinsically capable of suggesting and explaining the variety and complexity that must inevitably be encountered, and of converting what is learned to a feasible practice for improving and changing the present state, whatever that state may be. Improvement, after all, is the one thing of which mankind always stands in need, as John Stuart Mill insisted. The determination to satisfy this social need is fundamental to Marxism. This human end underlies the probings of Marxian science in its continuing effort to explain the various epochs and phases of social history and the interconnections among them. It is the end that explains its political probings as well, governing its tactics and strategies of practice.

Still the immediate goal must obviously be more limited than a survey and explanation of world history. It is to identify and assess the operation of the main forces and counterforces contained within the current phase of capitalist development. Within this order, within this phase, we seek to analyze the changing interrelations among forces and relations of production. Within the mature capitalism, the surplus emerging from the efforts of productive labor still constitutes the material base of class society, but, as we shall see, that society assumes a distinctive aspect not only in its capitalistic form but in the latest phase of that formation. In this phase, superstructure and substructure are still blended together in a capitalistic amalgam in which the cash nexus and the market still predominate; but times *have* changed, for all that. Our analysis seeks to show just how they have changed – and what this means for socialism. In pursuing this elusive and difficult subject, we need more theoretical tools than we have yet examined. Although productive labor generates the all-important surplus, the manner in which it does so must be determined before the superstructure built upon it, and before relations between the superstructure and the substructure, can be further analyzed.

2

Simple and complex accumulation: the productive consumption of capital

The capitalist mode as an analytical problem

The central core of the Marxian political economy is a general theory of the development and functioning of the productive forces, a theory that serves as a lever for prying open the secrets of social structure, its class composition, its organizational forms. The theory must illumine, moreover, not just the particular social formation but also the general movement among social formations, including, of course, the rise of modern capitalism and its development under the pressure of definite forces or laws of motion, some of which may be operative within more than one social formation, some of which will be peculiar to particular formations, for instance, to capitalism itself.

Were we to come at our mode in strict chronological sequence, then, we would come to it by examining its emergence from its historical predecessor, in the case of capitalism, Western feudalism; and the transition from feudalism to capitalism is one of the subjects to which Marxian scholars have made signal contributions, not to mention Marx's own indispensable leads for inquiry into the phenomenon.[1] *Hic et nunc*, however, we can pay only passing attention to this fascinating subject and offer only a quick summary statement of the movement from feudalism to capitalism in order to help us to locate (so to speak) the main feature of capitalism that must always excite the historian's imagination, the remarkable industrial accumulation that, succeeding the transition, excelled in the pace and scope of its development anything previously experienced. Marx's sketch is a sufficient reminder of the main features of the "miracle":

The discovery of America, the rounding of the Cape, opened up fresh ground for the rising bourgeoisie . . . the increase in the means of exchange and in commodities generally, gave to commerce, to navigation, to industry, an impulse never before known, and thereby, to the revolutionary element in the tottering feudal society, a rapid development.

. . . The feudal system of industry, under which industrial production was monopolized by the closed guilds, now no longer sufficed for the growing wants of the new markets. The manufacturing system took its place. . . . Meantime, the market kept ever growing, the demand ever rising . . . steam and machinery revolutionized industrial production. The place of manufacture was taken by the giant Modern Industry, the place of the industrial middle class, by industrial millionaires, the leaders of industrial armies, the modern bourgeoisie. . . .

. . . We see, therefore, how the modern bourgeoisie is itself the product of a long course of development, of a series of revolutions in the modes of production and of exchange.[2]

All this is taken pretty much for granted now, at least in broad outline. From this enormous tableau we wish to extract only the figure of capitalist growth, especially in its industrial and subsequent phases. What is to be explained is the undoubted fact that within this mode production has undergone a remarkable and continuing expansion, an expansion carrying all the way to the present, although at progressively reduced rates, and featuring expansions in other than industrial dimensions also, as we shall see. The opening of *Capital I* singles out the same figure for analysis: "The wealth of those societies in which the capitalist mode of production prevails, presents itself as 'an immense accumulation of commodities,' its unit being a single commodity. Our investigation must therefore begin with the analysis of a commodity."[3] For the moment, however, it is not *the* commodity, but the magnitude of the *mass* of commodities, the enormous and extending (until relatively recently) scale of their production, that poses a first challenge to our theory of reproduction. How does the growth in the immense aggregate of commodities come about? In a more theoretical phraseology, how does simple reproduction become a process of simple accumulation?

As we proceed with these questions, we should keep in mind some preliminaries. In considering growth under capitalism, for instance, it must be remembered that there are *two* levels and *two* dimensions in which all flows of relevant input and output values must be examined. There are, first, flows of essentially monetary or pecuniary values, the money values of the commodities as given by their market prices and the quantities of them purchased (or sold). Second, these commodities may also be viewed – indeed, must be so viewed, for such they are – as embodiments of labor energy expended in the course of their production, as envelopes containing the labor power spent in producing them. This dualistic conception must be explored eventually in every detail. It does not suffice to stress only the labor flows required for production, labor to which no thinking student of social history can remain oblivious. For understanding the accumulation of capital both aspects of reality must constantly be born in mind because both are integral to the capitalist mode.

At the former monetary level it is as obvious as it is significant that the system is geared to profit and that this motive propels it with enormous force toward ultimate destinations, whatsoever they may be. On the other level, but also geared to the impulse of gain, the reproduction of material energies takes place and must take place (as in simple reproduction), even though this reproduction is *not* itself the primary object of activity. The goals of the system reside at the monetary level. Beneath the veil of money, as in simple reproduction, is the real process of reproduction that does and must take place. Under capitalism, too, human labor power and congealed labor, means of consumption and means of production, must be conjoined in continuing reproductive work. What is peculiar to capitalism is the cash nexus holding together in exchange relations *all* of the elements of the reproductive process. In contrast with precapitalist modes, the human and the inanimate means of social reproduction are all produced for monetary gain; and they are utilized in production for this purpose. Whether en route to the factory as machines or raw materials, or on their way to the worker's stomach as food, they are conveyed by the mechanisms of money capital, the monetary counterpart and carrier of all of society's material means of reproduction.

In exploring the substructure of real-value flows, it is essential to be precise concerning their technical and economic characteristics as reproductive elements. Here, too, the scientific interest requires that we distinguish two basic categories of material means and their pecuniary counterparts, their money capitals. The first of these, means of production, Marx designates constant capital; the second, the means of subsistence or consumption of the productive worker, he designates variable capital. (Their more exact definitions follow in a moment.) Under capitalism, as under any other mode, these material requisites are "there," their reproduction is a social imperative. Yet economic reproduction has become a byproduct of the profitable investment in, sale, and repurchase of commodities, the form that all flows assume within the money-market economy.

Thus, under capitalism, as under any other mode, the material substructure of reproductive activity supports everything, including itself. From the brain and sinews of social labor flow the real values of means of production and means of consumption which, like labor power itself, move through commodity markets to their reproductive destinations. From the productive forces that generate them they move through commodity markets to support all of the activities, productive and unproductive, economic and otherwise, to which the mode of production lends its sanctions. From thence they move in support of the entire structure of social activities, productive and unproductive alike. Under capitalism, too, no one works or plays without material means of support, and, peculiarly, it is the monetary conveyors of the commodities, the flows of money, credits, and all associated monetary paraphernalia, that determine the ultimate destinies of the real flows on which social life depends. Do these monetary flows determine the proper conjuncture of real-value relations that the continuation of social life requires? Do they extend and strengthen these relations, at least in certain phases of the development process? Or is there here an irreconcilable contradiction, retarding and weakening the substructure, placing fetters upon the productive forces?

The world of monetary or pecuniary quantities that receives the attention of profit-seeking entrepreneurs, of the economists seeking their explanations for what is going on (and, too often, their excuses for it), and, perforce, of labor seeking to reproduce itself – this world of monetary values is a veneer of considerable hardness and depth, concealing at times much of the universe of material and energetic interrelations, including class interrelations, that are the real substance of social life. In removing the veneer so as to expose what is beneath it, we shall employ a certain number of theoretical definitions and premises.

Definitions and postulates: surplus value once more

It is not at all an exaggeration, in fact, to say that the terms "variable" and "constant" capital reflect postulates concerning the functioning of this mode of production that are absolutely basic to its comprehension. Indeed, the entire complex of definitions and postulates surrounding these conceptions is of the utmost theoretical importance. Because question has so often been raised in regard to their scientific consistency, explicitness, and adequacy, let us lay them out as best we can.

The adjectives "variable" and "constant" designate the two basic types of inputs that, under capitalism, are conveyed by money capital or money expenditure into their respective roles as productive capitals. They were chosen to remind us of certain behavioral characteristics of each of these forms of social capital when functioning within processes of production. Thus constant capital Marx defines as, "that part of capital . . . which is represented by the means of production, by the raw material, auxiliary material, and instruments of labor, *does not in the process of production undergo any quantitative alteration of value.*" [4] There is more than simple definition here. There is a declaration of the role played by this capital in the production of value. That role may be described by the simple equation $C_i = C_o$, where C_i is the value in exchange of the instruments, raw materials, *used up* within the period, and C_o is that portion of the total value of the output that is the direct equivalent of and the consequence of the using up of the value, C_i. In sum, a given constant capital always transmits to the value of the output *its own precise value equivalent* — hence the name constant capital.

Similarly a hypothesis attaches to Marx's definition of variable capital. The latter is "that part of capital, represented by labor power, does in the process of production undergo an alteration of value. . . . *It both reproduces the equivalent of its own value and also produces an excess, a surplus value, which may itself vary, may be more or less according to circumstances.*" [5]

Like C, V reproduces its own value equivalent in the output: $V_i = V_o$. In addition, however, it adds to this reproduced value a further value increment, a quantity S, so that $V_i \leq V_o + S$ by the amount of S, whatever the latter's magnitude may be. This is the famous surplus value hypothesis attributing to variable capital a capacity to create a value over and above its reproduced equivalent. Working for a given interval of time at a certain level of technical development, living labor commonly adds an increment of value to the combined and reproduced values of C_i and V_i.

This capacity of generating a surplus, which the French physiocrats of the eighteenth century had attributed to land, appears to the labor value theorist to be wholly a property of living labor. The latter possesses this capacity of yielding a surplus when working in combination with material means, land and capital, or both. As we have seen, the total of the given input values is commonly less than the value of the output $(C_i + V_i \leqq C_o + V_o + S_o)$ by the amount of the surplus, "which may itself vary, may be more or less according to circumstances." The circumstances referred to are principally those relating to the level of technique at which the given labor power is operating. In order words, the relative magnitude of the surplus is determined by the productivity of labor.

A comment on definitions and postulates

For a century controversy has revolved about the definitions and postulates just described. In particular, the surplus value hypothesis, attributing all value increments of output over input to the action of living labor power, has been called arbitrary, inconsistent, and tautological. Without recounting past arguments in detail, it is imperative that our own view be stated clearly.

First, as for inconsistency, there is none. The idea that the value of the used-up inputs appears in or is transmitted to or is passed on to the value of the product is, it is true, merely a hypothesis. But it is one that is internally consistent. It is quite as logical to say, for instance, that C_i reproduces an equivalent of itself, or that V_i reproduces its own equivalent, as it is to say the contrary, that C_i does not do so or that V_i does not do so. If the denial (very often made) is internally consistent, so is the assertion. Marx's assertions concerning the productive nature of these respective capitals are primarily a specification of the meaning of terms that he uses in theorizing. They clarify the meaning that he attaches to terms such as "reproduces," "transmits to," "metamorphoses," among others. The reproduction postulate is merely a specification of the ordinary meaning of such terms.

By the same token, the definition of surplus value is logically consistent with the other definitions given. Surplus value is simply the value of the output over and above the sum of the reproduced values, of the C_i and of the V_i used up in producing that output. It is analogous to the marginal value or to the value of the marginal product of the ordinary economics, although set in the dynamic rather than in the static context. Like the definition of reproduction contained in the equations $C_i = C_o$ and $V_i = V_o$, the definition of surplus value as an excess above reproduced values is tautological.

The definitional system of the theory of reproduction is internally consistent, and the conclusion drawn with its aid and with the aid of the reproduction postulates is strictly logical: If $C_i = C_o, V_i \leqq V_o + S_o$, then $C_i + V_i \leqq C_o + V_o + S_o$ by the laws of algebra. The basic Marxian formula for the exchange value of a commodity, $C + V + S$, is thus *a strictly logical deduction* from reproduction postulates. This is, of course, as it scientifically should be. But what of the question of tautology within the definitional system? Is this to be held against the theory?

No science proceeds without definition of its terms and without specification of its postulates in the terms defined. The Marxian theory is not and cannot be an exception to this rule, and in Marx's own attention to these matters the finest standards of theorizing are reflected. All of this speaks for the system rather than against it.

There is, finally, the charge of arbitrariness to be considered. Is the surplus value postulate arbitrary? And what of the reproduction postulates? With respect to the latter, the simple fact is that men do reproduce their means of subsistence, their means of production and of consumption. As for the surplus value hypothesis, sometimes severely criticized,[6] we have already suggested the need for such a quantity in order to explain the existence of unproductive labor and unproductive consumption. Without arguing the issue further at this point, we conclude with this comment. Work on theory construction must always be permitted to proceed at least to the point where a number of historically significant propositions may be deduced from basic premises. As a matter of fact, the capacity of a theoretical system to generate testable theorems is regarded, even outside the Marxian philosophy, as a critical scientific attribute of the system. It testifies to the basic soundness of the system, including its root postulates, in this case the labor value–surplus value postulates. As may already be apparent, the Marxian theory possesses in extraordinary degree this capacity to generate useful theorems. We conclude that, because of its correspondence with historical evidences in general and because of its usefulness as an analytical engine for garnering new insights, the surplus value hypothesis may be regarded as an essential and viable part of any reasonable effort to understand the world we live in. In further illustration of these contentions, the scheme of simple accumulation carries us forward.

Simple accumulation

In explorations of economic and social formations of precapitalist epochs, the surplus product hypothesis leads to important discoveries. It helps with the identification of ruling or leisure classes sustained by its material assistance. But consider now surplus product in an alternative role, as a means of supporting productive rather than unproductive activity. In this capacity it appears as the element making economic expansion possible.

The role of the surplus in expanding a system can only be played if, to begin with, the surplus is materially constituted for its work of economic support. Rather than consisting of goods and services not useful technically for production – in simple reproduction, for example, of leisure class items such as decorative objects military paraphernalia, perfumes, amulets, and so on – suppose it to be composed of new additional means of production of whatever type technically appropriate (hoes, axes, knives, in a primitive agriculture; tractors, fertilizers, etc., in an advanced technique). Suppose, furthermore, that another portion of the surplus consists of additional wage goods over and above what the period reproduces of these; and these, too, are suited to the consumption needs of the labor force, enabling that force to reproduce itself. Now if the surplus in these respects materially matches the technique, and if, in addition, the surplus so constituted is put into motion, invested in support of additional labor power, then the input scale of reproduction of the following period of reproduction may be enlarged in the amount of the surplus. Economic expansion thus takes place on the input side.

Expansion may take place if the community produces a surplus properly composed of reproductively useful product so that an additional labor power, an amount of labor power above and beyond that previously used in reproduction, may be supported in more extensive work processes. In Figure 2.1 the sequence that unfolds on these conditions is easily followed. We assume, first, a given state of technique within the capitalist mode. This means the rate of surplus value and the value composition of capital are both fixed because both of these are determined by the prevailing technique. Second, unproductive consumption is zero. The whole of the surplus consists of reproductively useful product, and the whole is productively invested. Third, the wage goods and means of produc-

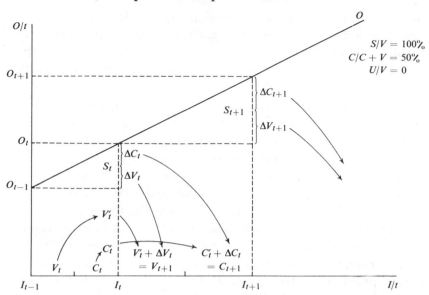

Figure 2.1. Simple accumulation (enlargement of the scale of reproduction by the productive consumption of surplus). When the surplus product $(S_t, S_{t+1}$, etc.) is composed entirely of product technically and materially suited to reproduction and when the additional wage goods and means of production are in the technically required proportion $(\Delta C/\Delta C + \Delta V = C/C + V)$, then the scale of inputs of the next period may be enlarged in the entire amount of the surplus $(\Delta C_t + \Delta V_t)$. This enlarged scale of productive input in $t + 1$ then becomes the basis for a larger output, O_{t+1}, given the rate of surplus value and the organic composition of capital. The same sequence holding for all periods, the circle of reproduction becomes the spiral of growth.

tion making up the surplus product bear the same ratio to each other in the surplus as in the original input capitals.[7] Fourth, let there be full employment: We assume for simplicity that the whole of the reproduced values of each period together with the new additional product to be utilized are put into motion subsequently.

Begin with period t. The constant and variable capitals used up in this period reproduce themselves, becoming a part of the total value of the output $(C'_t + V'_t)$. And we see that the surplus (S_t) consists of newly produced and additional wage goods (ΔV_t) and means of production (ΔC_t), both of the technically required varieties. What these imply for the activity of the following period, $t + 1$, is that production can take place on a larger scale than in period t. The input of wage goods, and hence labor power, in period $t + 1$ is $V_t + \Delta V_t$, so much larger than before. Similarly, the input of means of production of $t + 1$ consists of the reproduced values of the previous period (C_t) plus the additional means of production contained in the surplus (ΔC_t). Both V_{t+1} and C_{t+1} are enlarged in the amount of their proportionate share in the surplus S_t. The input scale of reproduction of I_{t+1} is greater than that of I_t by the value of the surplus product, S_t, and this enlarged whole serves as input for the second period of reproduction.

As the input of the second period $(t + 1)$ is greater than that of the first period, so, too, will the output be greater. In the second period the inputs C_{t+1} and V_{t+1} reproduce themselves of course. In addition, a surplus product again appears. If the surplus, S_{t+1}, is of the same *relative* magnitude as in period t, then the output of $t + 1$ is also enlarged. The essential value ratios being fixed by assumption – because the technique is fixed, the surplus remains a fixed fraction of the productive inputs, $C + V$ – the output is on an increased scale, just as the input is on an increased scale. This is what happens now for each successive peiod of reproduction. If the surplus of $t + 1$ is again productively consumed, consisting of new, additional wage goods, put into motion to support labor power, and of new, additional means of production with which that labor power works, then the scale of input of $t + 2$, and, hence, the scale of output of the period, will be correspondingly larger. Expansion is taking place. As Marx expresses it in a famous passage: ". . . the conversion of surplus value into capital is complete. From a concrete point of view, accumulation resolves itself into the reproduction of capital on a progressively increasing scale. The circle in which simple reproduction moves, alters its form, and, to use Sismondi's phrase, changes into a spiral."[8]

To recapitulate: The technique of production being given, the constant and the variable capitals will combine with each other in some proportion appropriate to the level of technique. The ratios of the values C, V, and S, one to another, will in fact all be fixed because within the Marxian theory these relations of the one to the other are governed by the technical requisites of production: ". . . the proportions which the expansion of the productive process may assume are not arbitrary but prescribed by technology."[9] *Simple accumulation is thus a case of wholly proportionate expansion featuring the enlargement in fixed ratios to each other of all exchange values throughout all periods of reproduction.* Even the period of reproduction is taken to be of fixed chronological length, as it, too, is governed by the level of technique. What happens under simple accumulation, the surplus being productively consumed, is that there is simply more and proportionately more of all inputs and outputs. This growth takes place because surplus value is converted always into new, additional capital so that scales of reproduction are correspondingly greater with each round. The circle of simple reproduction becomes the spiral of accumulation.

Population and economic growth

The theory of simple accumulation is simple in that it abstracts from technical change, a given state of technique being assumed. As a result, even though it lays the groundwork for handling easily certain problems of technical change, as we shall see, it is not entirely realistic. The theory does, however, make some matters quite clear. Among them is the important relationship between population growth and economic growth. The connection between these is quite readily apparent. If a surplus appears in the course of productive activity, and if it consists of what is technically required for production, all items properly proportioned to each other, then growth in the scale of inputs *can* take place. What is further required in order that it *should* take place is a volume of additional labor power in the amount required to utilize productively precisely these new additional means of production and of consumption. Without the hands to work it up (to use an old phrase), the additional social product can only be stockpiled, for it requires human energy in order to bring it to life in productive employment. This particular condition for economic growth, the growth of additional labor power, may be expressed this way. If an additional stock of wage goods and means of production (ΔV and ΔC) is created in a period, that stock may be used to support an additional labor power (ΔL). A growth in the labor force or an increase in the volume of labor power through its more intensive utilization is thus a precondition for the economic expansion of productive input in general. It follows that a growth of population may be a precondition for economic growth, if population growth is the only route by means of which the additional labor power required may be obtained.

Viewing the proposition historically, we see why the expansion of capitalism, especially in its early phases, was accompanied by a simultaneous growth both in volumes of commodities and of working people. The growth of population is the precondition for the growth of commodity production. The mercantile theorists of the seventeenth and eighteenth centuries understood this well, and they sought by every possible means, from the promotion of slavery and servitude to the direct encouragement of domestic population growth, to realize the labor power precondition for enlarging the economic and, hence, the political power of the nation-state. We can see, too, why until recently capitalists looked with enthusiasm upon the growth of population. It was seen as, and it was in fact, an essential element providing cheap labor for manning factories and plowing fields, for providing, therefore, the growth of profits at which the system aims. (Under simple accumulation the *rate* of profit does not rise, but *total* profits grow.) In contrast with the historical facts, and with their Marxian explanation, the Malthusian theory may be considered.

Thomas R. Malthus and his followers had seen population growth as following upon any release of the spring of sexual appetites. The release for biological reproductive capacities is provided by economic growth. In the Malthusian view, economic growth is not caused by population growth; rather, the reverse is true. The increase in numbers of the population is induced by the prospect of being able to afford a freer exercise of sexual instincts.

In this curious and "slanderous" (as Marx called it) theory, population growth follows upon economic growth, and the increase in numbers, in turn, causes the income per capita to decline toward the subsistence level once more. Unless, therefore, men and women exercise a moral restraint upon their appetites, the positive checks to population growth will set in: starvation, war, disease, and so on. One can see why such doctrines were powerful two centuries ago and why, as a matter of fact, the neo-Malthusian doctrines are still popular in some quarters. For one thing, according to this view, little or nothing can be done to help the poor. They can only learn to control their appetites. Failing this, they have only themselves to blame for the consequences. Such arguments have always appealed to the wealthy, but the trouble is that they are refuted by the evidences. As nineteenth-century experience has shown, the material standard of living rising with industrial accumulation, the population did not grow more rapidly, but, rather, more and more slowly. This evidence is consistent with the Marxian theory, but it is inconsistent with the Malthusian view.

The growth of population, to repeat, is a precondition for simple economic growth, and a growing population may be an asset rather than a liability for peoples just entering upon a process of economic expansion. This does not mean that economic growth is always contingent upon population growth. As economic development proceeds out of its early phases, as technical change takes place that promotes the growth of the system through the growth of productivity, population growth may decline. Moreover, it may be advisable to encourage its decline *as accumulation becomes complex* and technical change raises the productivity of labor. Before considering complex accumulation in any detail, however, there are still matters of principle that the theory of simple accumulation can help us to understand. The theory provides a good view of the principal determinants of the rate of growth of output.

The value ratios and the rate of profit (growth)

With the aid of the notions of constant and of variable capital, and of surplus value, the main determinants of the rate of growth – alternatively, the rate of accumulation or the rate of profit – may be defined and their functioning explained. Every scientific theory specifies the causal forces that bear upon whatever the theory seeks to explain. In the present case the principal determinants or independent variables are the rate of surplus value and the organic (value) composition of capital (ignoring for the time being the role of unproductive consumption). These variables are certain key ratios of the capital values previously defined.

The rate of surplus value, S/V, is the ratio of the surplus value to the variable capital used up in producing it. It reflects the important assumption that the productivity of social labor is the real source of all product. Apart from this, it reflects, first, the level of technique within which labor power is expended, and is higher when the technique is more sophisticated and lower when it is more primitive. The rate of surplus value or rate of exploitation reflects, second, the intensity with which labor is sweated within processes of production. If labor is paid by the piece, and

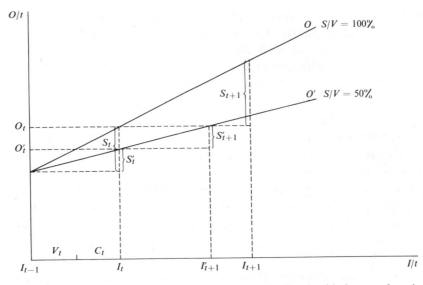

Figure 2.2. Simple accumulation (the rate of growth varies directly with the rate of surplus value). Shown are two growth paths, O and O', with differing rates of surplus value. If unproductive consumption is zero ($U = 0$), the whole of the surplus being productively consumed, the scale of inputs of period $t + 1$ may be enlarged the more greater the ratio of the surplus to the variable capital input (S/V), other things remaining the same. Note that the slope of the O line, which measures its rate of growth, is given by the ratio $S/C + V$, the rate of profit. The rate of growth or the rate of profit varies directly with the rate of surplus value.

as a result works more intensively, or if the workday or workweek is somehow lengthened, then the rate of surplus value may be raised.[10] The general effects of movements of S/V on the rate of growth (profit) are seen in Figure 2.2. If the rate of surplus value is 100 percent, the rate of growth is given by the slope of the O line (the value composition of capital is 50 percent). But if the productivity of labor had been less, the rate of surplus value, say, 50 percent, then a lower rate of expansion would have resulted (see the line O'). The rise in the ratio S/V increases the slope of the O line, raising the rate of growth; on the contrary, a reduction of the ratio pulls down the rate of growth.

The second primary determinant of the rate of growth is the organic or value composition of capital, $C/C + V$ (sometimes written C/V).[11] In the long run, as is true of the rate of surplus value, the main governor of this variable is the level of technique. The connection between them is this: The more sophisticated the technique, the more mechanized the process of production and the higher the value composition of capital. This

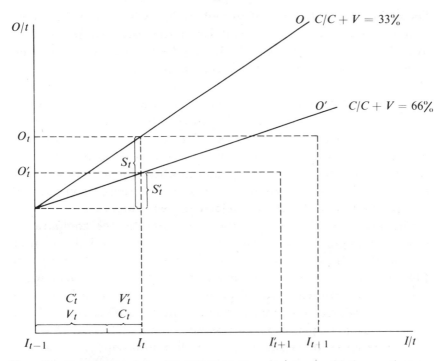

Figure 2.3. Simple accumulation (the rate of growth varies inversely with the organic composition of capital). Shown are two growth paths, O and O , rates of surplus value being the same but value (organic) compositions differing in the two instances. (Unproductive consumption is zero, and the surplus is productively consumed.) The greater the proportion of variable capital in the total input, the greater the surplus value and, hence, the greater the extension of the scale of inputs in the next period, $t + 1$. Other things remaining the same, the rate of growth or rate of profit will therefore vary inversely with the value composition of capital.

is because technical improvement substitutes congealed for living labor within the process of production. Production becomes more capital intensive, as the economist expresses it.

The relationship of the value composition of capital to the rate of growth of the system is an inverse one. The higher the value composition, the lower the rate of growth (profit); the lower the value composition, the higher the rate of profit (growth). Thus in Figure 2.3 we observe on the growth path O the value composition to be $25C$ and $75V$. If all of this is productively consumed, a rate of growth as shown by the O line (Figure 2.3) is generated. On the other hand, suppose the value composition had been $75C$ and $25V$, a more capital-intensive combination. Now the input yields only $25S$ with the same rate of surplus value, and the rate of growth is the lower rate as shown by the O' line. Other things

being the same, the rate of growth is low when the value composition of capital is high, and when the value composition is
low, the rate of growth is high. It may be helpful to perceive the
logic of this proposition by offering a general testimonial to it.
We observe, for example, that when expansion is proceeding in
less developed countries – as in the wake of a popular revolution,
most particularly – their rates of growth will be higher than those
in the more advanced countries. Not only does labor work to
produce an absolute surplus in the former case, so that rates of
surplus value are higher there than elsewhere (or may be so), but
the labor intensity of production where the organic composition
of capital is low accelerates the relative growth rate.

Or, again, to illustrate the theorem, consider the comparative
growth of England and of West Germany in the period just after
World War II, especially in the 1950s. The rate of growth of
English output averaged little more than 2 percent per year while
the German "miracle" yielded growth rates of three to four times
that.[12] Of course, the phenomenon is quite explicable, and the
superior German performance was not even a reflection of an in-
nate superiority of German over English philosophy.[13] The war
had resulted in the destruction of the largest part of the German
capital stock, and what remained was depleted or dismantled
and moved elsewhere, as to Russia. Thus for years after the war,
German production was labor intensive, or more so by far than
in England, and this circumstance accelerated the growth rate. It
is also important to note that for some time after the war the
retarding influence of an unproductive bureaucracy weighed
lightly on German backs, these burdens being carried by those
who had triumphed over the country in the recent conflict.[14]
More recently, the flotation of a conventional capitalistic circulatory superstructure has pulled German growth rates down to
quite unexceptional levels. The effects we observe are, in brief,
altogether to be expected within the framework of Marxian
economics, on the assumption that the circulatory apparatus of
capitalism is a principal haven of unproductive consumption. We
shall see later on that this is, indeed, exactly the case.

A third determinant of the rate of accumulation that we briefly consider is the period of reproduction. Like the rate of surplus
value and the value composition of capital, the chronological
length of the period of reproduction (t) is in the long run gov-

erned by the state of technique. The assumption is that not only the production but also the vending of commodities absorbs capital in support of this activity. In general, the more advanced the technique both of production *and* of circulation (vending of product), the shorter the period of time required to reproduce the social product, including the recovery of its exchange value in the monetary forms that capitalism requires (profit, in particular). The shorter this period of turnover of the social capital, the higher the rate of profit or of accumulation of that capital – and vice versa, of course.

The period of social reproduction is divided into two parts: (1) the interval of time required to produce the product (the period of gestation, as it has been called) and (2) the interval of time (period of circulation) required to transport it to market, sell it, and recover the monetary counterpart of its real value as a product of social labor. One can see, then, that a reduction in the length of time or, what is the same thing, of the volume of social capitals tied up in either productive or circulatory activity will allow the rate of profit and accumulation to be higher than it otherwise would be. Conversely, a lengthening of the period of reproduction, or in either of its component parts, will retard the rate of profit or accumulation. We return to these effects once again, but from a slightly different viewpoint, in discussing the economics of unproductive consumption. We turn now, however, to consider the rate of profit, the rate of growth, or the rate of accumulation, all of which are identical within a system of simple accumulation.

The rate of profit is defined as $P' = S/C + V$ and is conceived of as an average or general rate obtaining among a more or less large number of lines of production comprising the economy in its entirety. It is the surplus value divided by the costs of producing it[15] and thus corresponds to capitalists' own notions of profit rates, of net revenue divided by costs of production.

So defined, the rate of profit is equal to the rate of growth or of accumulation of the system. In Figure 2.1, for instance, consider any period of reproduction whatsoever. The rates of which we are speaking are all given by the *slope* of the O line, a slope that, as for any straight line (extending from the origin), measures its rate of growth. For period t, for example, the rate of profit, $S/C + V$, is measured by the ratio of S_t to the sum $C_t + V_t$ used up in its production. That this measures the slope of the O line will be obvious to the reader. In simple accumulation, then, although not necessarily so in complex accumulation, the rate of profit is equal to the rate of growth or of accumulation.[16] They are identical. This explains the Marxian assumption that the general rate of profit governs the rate of growth or of accumulation of capital. Profit is the fuel, and its rate governs the intensity and direction of movement of the entire order of accumulation. Its growth means expansion; its decline, contraction.

Complex accumulation: a sketch of the argument of Capital I

Like simple reproduction, simple accumulation is a skeletal model about whose frame the drapery of history must be wrapped in order that its abstractions should assume their full meaning. Used as such, in effect, as a vehicle for its own modification, the model helps give form to the data of social history. Indeed, it is one of the models used by Marx to explain the ascent and growth path of industrial capitalism and, also, the debris left behind in the rude passage of a mode of production impelled principally by profit considerations.

From this simple framework one may plunge directly into the argument of *Capital I,* at least that portion of the argument relating to the industrial accumulation and its consequences. To secure the theory for this purpose let us return again to the formula for the general rate of profit, $P' = S/V//C/V + 1$. This merely expresses in algebraic form the propositions just discussed, that the rate of profit varies directly with the rate of surplus value and inversely with the organic composition of capital. The higher the rate of surplus value, the more rapid its climb relative to C/V, the higher the rate of profit and, therefore, the growth rate. Alternatively, the higher the organic composition of capital, the more rapidly it grows relative to the rate of surplus value, the greater is the tendency for the rate of profit to fall. The general rate of profit, the rate of growth, is seen to depend upon the outcome of an interaction between the rate of surplus value and the value composition of capital.

Now in utilizing these simple principles to comprehend the argument referred to, we must take into account the principal additional factor of technical change. On the assumption of a continuing technical change the argument proceeds very simply and yet is governed by a close correspondence to historical events. In early phases of industrial accumulation, and especially with an incidence of rapid change in the period of industrial revolution, the rate of surplus value rises more rapidly than does the value composition of capital. With improvements restricted to certain lines of production – especially textiles, sugar refining, transport, and some others – the productivity of labor in these leading lines rises. Rates of profit rise, as does the prospect of their continuing increase. Of course along with the relative increase in the rate of surplus value goes a sweating of labor, a form of absolute exploitation facilitated by the urbanization of the population and the emergence of the factory system. These all combine to bring about sharp increases in the profitability of production and an acceleration of growth.

As noted, the incidence of science and of technical improvements deriving from it is typically restricted at first to limited fields within the capitalist economy. At first, only in leading lines is the tendency discernible for a higher value composition of capital. With the widening of capital accumulation among more and more lines, however, the great engine of accumulation (as Schumpeter called it) going at forced draft, the incentive for accumulation in its latest technical forms becomes widespread. The *average* value composition of capital rises, and this induces a profit crisis. Further, there are other cyclical instabilities; the engine runs unevenly. As prosperity advances, for instance, the price of labor rises while the industrial reserve army of unemployed is temporarily reduced. The rise in the price of labor affects profits adversely, and accumulation slackens. This combines with the rising value composition of capital to induce a crisis. With the subsequent crisis, unemployment rising, the price of labor is driven back downward once more. Finally, profitability is restored, and a renewal of accumulation takes place. After a longer or shorter interval of recession or depression, the process begins again.[17] While irregularity of the process is thus intrinsic to it, it is not this irregularity that is decisive for the long term. The long term is governed more decisively by the rate of surplus value in its relation to the value composition of capital, and we must return to look once again at this relation.

Technical change and the tendency for the rate of profit to fall

Looking casually at the formula for the general rate of profit, some have seen in it an indefinite possibility for the growth of profits as long as technical change continues. The numerator of the profit formula (S/V) is accelerated by the very growth of labor productivity accompanying technical change. As a result, it may be reasoned, even if the organic composition of capital grows and tends thereby to reduce the rate of profit, the growth of labor productivity and of the rate of surplus value that also results from technical change will raise the general rate of profit. Hence there is no reason for the law of the tendency of the rate of profit to fall to assert itself.

This view is not at all correct and is quite superficial. In the first place, it overlooks well-known phenomena that accompany technical change, especially a certain resistance to the *effects* of technical change, a resistance put up by both capital and labor, although for somewhat different reasons. With respect to labor, as is well known, the resistance to labor displacement by advancing technique shows itself in featherbedding, strikes, and forms of political opposition to the advance. While the rise of the rate of profit, or even its maintenance, depends upon capital's steadily displacing labor in production processes, labor struggles against displacement and measures its success in terms of the preservation of jobs as well as its standard of living.

More or less unsystematically at times, but without a real choice in the matter if profits are to be preserved, capital must intensify its opposition to labor's claims. Capital may desire to but cannot pay the costs of labor displacement without sacrifice of profit. It may be willing to finance the advance in technique, but it does not wish to extend the welfare system – what Marx with such prescience called official pauperism – to the point where labor will submit peaceably to its displacement from employment. The underlying opposition of interests forces a running struggle between these parties. Capital has no choice in its opposition to a real welfare system, one that would actually provide in an equitable and fair way a recompense to labor for its real costs of displacement. From the capitalists' standpoint, where is the net gain of lowering wage costs through technical advance and displacement, on the one hand, and raising wage costs through payment for all costs of displacement, on the other? There is none, and if the former raises the rate of profit, the latter as certainly lowers it. We see, however, that with the maturation of capitalism the question of social welfare becomes ever more imperative of solution. What the capitalists call socialism or the welfare state is born perforce of economic contradictions within the mode of production. The birth of this welfare capitalism, nevertheless, contributes to long-term stagnation by closing the gap between the rise in the rate of surplus value and the rise in the value composition of capital. We shall see later reasons why the conflict described must terminate in falling profits.

Finally, there are purely economic obstacles to accelerating the rate of surplus value, and hence profits, through technical change. Given a constant rate of invention and innovation, the rate of surplus value will tend to increase at a decreasing rate for reasons inherent in the generation of surplus value itself. The proposition we shall attempt to clarify here Marx states in the following terms:

Thus the more developed capital already is, the more surplus labour it has created, the more terribly must it develop the productive force in order to realize itself in only smaller proportion, i.e., to add surplus value - because its barrier always remains the relation between the fractional part of the day which expresses *necessary labour,* and the entire working day. It can move only within these boundaries. The smaller already the fractional part (of the working day) falling to *necessary labour,* the greater the *surplus labour,* the less can any increase in productive force perceptibly diminish necessary labour; since the denominator has grown enormously. The self-realization of capital becomes more difficult to the extent that it has already been realized.[18]

In order to perceive the boundaries, to grasp fully the constraints that limit the growth of the rate of surplus value and, hence, of profit, it is necessary to go back briefly to basic conceptions. The conception that underlies Marx's analysis is that of a workday (workweek, month, year, and so on) that divides into its necessary and its surplus labor time components. In the necessary portion of the workday, the workers reproduce the value equivalent to their own costs of reproduction; in the remainder of the day they produce a value in excess of this reproduction value, that is, the surplus value. The ratio of the surplus labor to the necessary labor is the same as the ratio of surplus value to the value of the variable capital. It is the rate of surplus value.

Suppose, now, a system of complex accumulation. Technical change is proceeding at a constant rate. In industries in which subsistence goods, labor's costs of reproduction, are being produced, productivity of labor is, at some point in time, at a certain level of development. Technical change continuing, however, the productivity of labor in these industries will rise. Now the question is, what is the nature of the relationship between the development of labor productivity and the rate of surplus value on whose growth relative to productivity (or, what is the same thing, to the value composition of capital) the rate of profit depends? Will the rate of surplus value rise in greater, equal, or smaller proportion than the growth of productivity brought about by technical change? To repeat, the assumption of Marx's critics has been that the rate of surplus value will grow either in increasing or, at least, constant proportion with the growth of productivity brought about by technical change. But is this assumption correct?

Were it even possible to reduce necessary labor to zero, the rate of surplus value would rise *at a decreasing rate* until the ratio of surplus to necessary labor had reached some quite high value, or until necessary labor had become a very small fraction of total labor. An example is offered in Table 2.1. Here we assume, to repeat, a constant rate of technical change and a periodic doubling of the productivity of labor. In period t, at the outset, surplus labor is zero and the whole of the workday is spent in reproduction of necessary labor (simple reproduction). Were the productivity of labor to rise above this reproductive level so that, say, half the workday is surplus and the other half necessary labor, the rate of surplus value would now be 1. Again there is a rise in the productivity of labor and a decline by one-half in the necessary portion of the workday: In $t + 2$ we see the ratio of surplus to necessary labor stands at 3, the rate of surplus value. The rate of surplus value has doubled (column 7). Now once again a doubling of the productivity of labor reduces by one-half the necessary portion of the workday, which falls from 2.5 hours in $t + 2$ (column 4) to 1.25 hours in $t + 3$. This again means a rise in the rate of surplus value, but at a reduced rate from the previous period: from 2 in period $t + 2$ to 4 in period $t + 3$, only a 133 percent increase over the previous period (column 7). The rate of surplus value is increasing at a decreas-

Table 2.1. *Technical change and the tendency of the rate of growth of the rate of surplus value to decline*

Period of reproduction (1)	Productivity of labor $(L_s + L_n/L_n)$ (2)	Length of working day (3)	L_s/L_n (S/V) (4)	S/V (S') (5)	$\Delta S'$ (6)	$\Delta S'/S'$ (7)
t	100/100	10	0	0	–	–
$t+1$	200/100	10	5/5	100	100	∞
$t+2$	400/100	10	7.5/2.5	300	200	200
$t+3$	800/100	10	8.75/1.25	700	400	133
$t+4$	1600/100	10	9.37/0.63	1500	800	114
$t+5$	3200/100	10	9.69/0.31	3100	1600	111 (approaches 100)

Note: In period t it is assumed that surplus labor is zero, and the productivity of labor just suffices for its own reproduction. Thereafter, surplus labor appears with the doubling of the productivity of necessary labor in industries producing its means of reproduction. Ultimately, technical change fails to accelerate the rate of surplus value (col. 7).

Since the surplus value on which profits depend is given by $S = S/V \times V$, the relative decline toward zero of productive labor cannot possibly be offset by technical change. The general rate of profit, therefore, tends to decline secularly.

ing rate, eventually leveling out to a constant rate of increase (in periods $t + 4$ and $t + 5$), while the productivity of labor continues to double. Productivity continues to grow relative to the rate of growth of the rate of surplus value.

Put this conclusion in a more directly relevant form. Does the rate of surplus value rise less rapidly than the organic composition of capital? This is the question on which the law of the falling rate of profit in part depends. We have seen that the rate of surplus value decreases relative to the growth of productivity; but productivity increases in proportion to the organic composition of capital. That is, the rate of surplus value tends to rise less rapidly than the organic composition of capital when technical change is proceeding at some constant rate. And this ultimately brings about the tendency for the rate of profit to fall.

We are assuming that it is possible to reduce by one-half the input of necessary labor with every doubling of its productivity. We assume, that is, a free displacement of labor power as changing technique requires. Even the kind of acceleration to the rate of surplus value that is theoretically possible (increasing at a decreasing and then a constant rate) can be achieved *only* if it is possible to effect regular required reductions in the input of necessary labor; *if,* that is, the value composition of capital can grow at some constant rate as demanded by the advance of technique.[19] In actuality, both the resistance of labor to displacement and the resistance of capital to covering the costs of labor displacement militate against even the limited acceleration of the rate of surplus value that is theoretically possible.

To be sure in early phases of capitalist development, technical change may yield a significant acceleration of the rate of surplus value. As time passes, however, and as the productivity of labor is developed with the reduction of necessary labor through technical change, the growth of the rate of surplus value itself stagnates. Its growth becomes resistant to the proddings of a changing technique. As Marx puts it: "The increase of productive force would become irrelevant to capital. . . ."[20] Indeed, it may be worth repeating here the most famous of all remarks on this subject: "The *real barrier* of capitalist production is *capital itself.*"[21]

Now we have seen a considerable part of the explanation of the tendency for the rate of profit to fall, a tendency that asserts itself "under certain circumstances and only after long periods." The tendency plays a primary role in engendering capitalism's most serious crises; it played this role in the past century, and it continues to play this role in the present century;[22] it plays it at this very moment. But while we have seen a large part of the explanation of the tendency, we have not yet seen all of it. There are other contributing circumstances to the periodic decline in the rate of profit and to the long-term secular stagnation and decline of the productive forces under capitalism. Certain of these will be taken up in the following chapter, where the theory of unproductive consumption occupies our attention. For the moment, by way of completing Marx's first approximation to the development of industrial capitalism, we may indicate the effects of capital accumulation upon the composition of the population, and from thence upon social relations.

The general law of capitalist accumulation

The course of capitalist development is erratic and uneven. Recurrent crises, the most serious of which are precipitated by the decline in the rate of profit, take their repeated and catastrophic tolls of unemployment and misery. Yet the whole movement, encompassing the periodic breakdowns so familiar to economic and social history, features also changes in the make-up of the population, including its class structure. Into these changes, too, the social scientist must inquire. This is an area of inquiry of great complexity, requiring a combination of historical and theoretical instruments in order to uncover what is hidden from direct view. In probing into this aspect of society Marx found useful the "law of the progressive increase in constant capital in proportion to the variable,"[23] the famous tendency for the value composition of capital to rise, whose effects upon the rate of surplus value and the rate of profit have just been examined. The rise in the value composition of capital influences the composition of the total population in quite definite if sometimes subtle ways.

It is not difficult to see that the relative decline in the variable capital input, the portion of total capital represented by living labor itself, would amount to what has been termed a "narrowing base of productive labor," a declining portion of the total population given over to *necessary* work of economic reproduction. This does not mean that the total numbers in the population that are

employed in the industrial substructure should not grow; it means
only that as a fraction of the total population the working population tends to decline. Marx stresses the relative decline of the industrial proletariat, the industrially necessary component of the
total population, at the same time marking the relative growth of
what he calls a relative surplus population, or, again, a consolidated surplus population, in connection with the general law of
capitalist accumulation of *Capital I:*

The greater the social wealth, the functioning capital, the extent and energy of its
growth, and, therefore, also the absolute mass of the proletariat and the productiveness of its labor, the greater is the industrial reserve army. The same causes
which develop the expansive power of capital, develop also the labour-power at its
disposal. The relative mass of the industrial reserve army increases therefore with
the potential energy of wealth. But the greater this reserve army in proportion to
the active labour-army, the greater is the mass of a consolidated surplus-
population, whose misery is in inverse ratio to its torment of labour. The more extensive, finally, the lazarus-layers of the working class, and the industrial reserve
army, the greater is official pauperism.[24]

With the accumulation of a social capital whose organic composition is rising comes an expansion of the industrial population,
whose growth declines relative to the total. Meanwhile, the
displacement of productive labor proceeding – irregularly and slowly, but proceeding nevertheless – the total population is growing,
finding the material means for its support in the expanding surplus.
Of course there is also a growing surplus population in the form of
the famous industrial reserve army, the army of short- and long-
term unemployed and partially employed. Thus there is a relatively
dwindling, reproductively necessary population on the one side,
and, on the other, a relatively expanding consolidated surplus
population, including the reserve army. The consolidated surplus
then consists of the various workers making up the industrial
reserve, plus all those in the population who are industrially
superfluous and who comprise a more general reserve that now
augments and now reduces the active army of employed labor. As
the general law indicates, the *tendency* is for this reserve to undergo
a secular expansion *relative* to the active labor army of the productively employed. This is Marx's first approximation to the changing
composition of the population under capitalism. From this base we
shall later (Chapters 10 and 11) extend a second and fuller approximation in order to replicate with theoretical precision the composition of the population of the advanced capitalism today.

Marx's first approximation, however, raises challenging questions. Most important among these is one relating, not so much to the development of the active industrial army, the army of productive labor whose relative decline may be seen in the diminution of the blue-collar population relative to the total, but to the make-up of the surplus population. What countertendencies to the general law has the development of modern capitalism produced? Has capitalism succeeded in forestalling the dire implication of the general law, the growing surplus and superfluous population? We observe, after all, the ominous expansion of official pauperism, the welfare order, of an unproductive reserve. On the other hand, what of the middle class of modern society? Does it not stand as a negation of the general law? Or does the middle class testify to its affirmation? To what conclusions are we led by a systematic extension of the analysis to a second approximation? Is the famous middle class perhaps the modern and most significant form of the consolidated surplus population? In whole? In part? Is there, in fact, a middle class? Or is it an illusion, an optical illusion, so to speak, of analysts unable to penetrate the mists enveloping our social planet? To the consideration of these central issues we turn as the development of the economics allows us to do so.

Without anticipating conclusions whose foundations are still relatively unexplored, let us say only that there are built into the mode self-regulating and self-limiting mechanisms of economic and social adjustment that stand as ultimate barriers to its further development. The famous theory of economic crises, crises tending to destabilize the system, deals with one of the instrumentalities through which capital arrives at its final assignments. There are other types of crises whose origins trace also to endogenous forces within the mode. Such a crisis is the accumulation of unproductive labor, an accumulation to which capital is very much addicted but which works to undermine even capital's very strong constitution.

3

Unproductive consumption:
its historical and
theoretical relevance

The scientific issue

It is a notable fact that, while the theory of the unproductive utilization of labor and resources – the theory of unproductive consumption or of unproductive labor – occupies a prominent place both in *Capital* and in the *Grundrisse,*[1] the subject has until recently received only cursory treatment by Marxists and still less consideration by students of the standard economics. For the latter this is not so surprising. In the philosophical folklore of economics, one must as a scientist avoid value judgments. Such judgments as may be required in order to distinguish between productive and unproductive employments of labor power, or between productive and unproductive uses of means of production and of wage goods (consumption) will, so they say, spoil irrevocably the work of the scientist. Whether or not a given activity falls into one or another of these categories has been taboo in scientific discourse. In orthodox economics, as a consequence, the blithe assumption has long been pervasive that all activity is productive. Indeed, it can be shown at the analytical level that the entire standard theory of production itself hangs upon the unraveling thread of this assumption.[2]

Consistent with its prohibition, modern economics does not face up to the issue. Marx, to the contrary, holding strictly to the classical tradition, recognized the inescapable need to confront the phenomenon theoretically simply because historical observation throws up so much evidence of its ubiquitous presence. Not only does capitalism contain within itself an inextricable element of unproductive labor and consumption, but within all socioeconomic formations there are indications of a need to strike some balance

67

between productive and unproductive forces. If, then, history confronts us with persistent evidences of the existence of unproductive activity, the true dictate of scientific morality is clear: It cannot be ignored. From the moral standpoint, in any case, whether to ignore or not to ignore the existence of unproductive labor is a value judgment forced upon all investigators and not merely upon those courageous or perhaps foolhardy souls who rise to the challenge. The orthodox denial of the propriety to inquire into the subject, because to do so is "unscientific," merely begs one to accept the value judgment implied.

The Marxist admits the value judgment involved but sees that the real issue lies elsewhere. The issue is at bottom not one of value judgment but of whether or not theoretically useful distinctions can be made (1) by giving adequate theoretical definitions of the variables unproductive labor and unproductive consumption, and (2) by showing their consequences not only within a general theoretical system but within historical processes themselves. The theory must conform in the end to the usual criteria of logical and empirical correspondence with historical reality. By these criteria, in fact, a very interesting theory of unproductive labor can be constructed, and the bulk of it is to be found precisely in the Marxian sources cited. Indeed, the theory is implicit in the scheme of simple reproduction already discussed. In that context, recall, unproductive consumption of the surplus could be viewed as a force helping to stabilize the reproductive order of society. But it may be a good idea, before returning to reproduction schema once again, to emphasize the kinds of evidences that underscore the scientific need for a general theory of unproductive labor. Among the many socioeconomic formations whose functioning leads to a consideration of roles of productive and unproductive labor, that of ancient Egypt is well known.

The Breasted interpretation

It is not very likely that James H. Breasted's exploration of the history of ancient Egypt[3] was either governed or appreciably guided by the Marxian theory of economic regression. This remark is not meant to detract from Breasted's capabilities as an investigator. His ability was beyond question of the first rank. The fact is that students of primitive, of antique, or of other formations are even today not usually informed concerning the fine points of economic theories; and this is not altogether unfortunate, as we have tried to indicate. It sometimes may happen that because of the student's semi-independence from school economics, the mind is freer to roam fruitfully, the generally informed imagination being superior, unfortunately, to that trained in the so-called economics. It is in any case difficult to accuse such a scientist as Breasted of rigging the data to suit his theoretical preconceptions, and his explanation of the rise and fall of the Egyptian empire constitutes one of those remarkable coincidences between an informed generalization and the inferences of formal theory.

In explaining the rise of Egypt much has been made, and rightly so, of the extraordinary fertility of the Nile and of the potential of the river for communication as much as for production: "The wealth of commerce which the river served to carry, it was equally instrumental in producing."[4] Yet this ecological condition, it must be remembered, remained essentially constant throughout Egyptian history. It is from the study of the human activities resting upon this ecological condition that the true explanation of development and decline may be drawn, Breasted tells us. That decline began around the thirteenth century B.C. and was completed some 800 years later. The expanding phase began perhaps a millennium and a half before the thirteenth century. One discerns at first an ascending phase when predynastic localisms are being dissolved, mines and quarries are being developed, public works in irrigation and transportation are being pursued, and a central government is being formed under Pharaonic auspices. As a result, by the first half of the third millennium (2980–2475 B.C.), "Art and mechanics reached a level of unprecedented excellence never later surpassed, while government and administration had never before been so highly developed."[5]

There is something more than simple primitive accumulation taking place within this period. The accumulation is complex, featuring technical change, and yet the productivity of social labor was high enough from the outset, apparently, to support the construction of a new bureaucracy with all its ceremonial works. The new accomplishments rest upon past achievements, and technical improvement, itself encouraged by the new bureaucracy, raises further the productivity of labor, permitting subsequent enlargement of scales of activity. In this expanding phase there are few indications that the temples and other incredible public monuments, or the bureaucracy itself, including the military, receive a disproportionate share of the material product; they themselves contribute to the general administration of productive affairs and receive little more than they return to the whole in terms of an enhanced pride and security, a higher morale for labor resulting from an enlightened direction of public affairs, and a greater accessibility to national and man-made means of production: "The age was dealing with material things and developing material resources. . . ."[6] The rate of unproductive consumption was not excessive, Breasted makes clear.

Both religious and military activities must have absorbed significant portions of social labor and product during the expansive phase, but as long as these contributed to the morale and security of those more directly engaged in material production they contributed to the strength of the productive forces and were at the worst no more than a minor drag upon the general rate of accumulation. The Scribe was justified in his opinion: "Twice great is the king of his city: he is as it were a place of refuge, excluding the maurauder. . . . Twice great is the king of his city: he is as it were a corner warm and dry in time of winter."[7]

But these conditions were not tenable in the following millennium. It is not merely that the power of Egypt's neighbors was growing, especially that of the Hittites; it is even more the result of a gradual triumph of unhealthy circumstances internal to the body politic, and here are to be found the reasons for the advancing decadence. There was, in particular, an ever-greater "mortgaging" (as Breasted terms it) of product to the priestly classes, an outcome of a conflict spanning several centuries among various claimants to the usufruct of the productive system. A wholesale competition among social classes for the surplus may in and of itself, of course, deflect resources from productive use. On the other hand, the emergence of a victor may portend a worsening of the situation as the rate of unproductive consumption rises. There was, of course, a development of a sacerdotal state in which social wealth was closely tied to the service of the priestly class at the very time that "Egypt should have been girding her loins and husbanding her resources. . . ."[8] Instead, she was "relinquishing her sword to mercenary strangers and lavishing her wealth upon temples already too richly endowed for the economic safety of the state."[9] The distortion in the distribution of resources worsened: "These extreme conditions were aggravated by the fact that no proper proportion had been observed in the distribution of gifts to the gods."[10]

The hegemony of "the insatiable priesthoods" was, as we have said, an inherited situation dating from the middle of the second millennium (1500 B.C.), so that a cumulative movement over some centuries preceded the final, critical stage. The undermining of industrial and technical skills by withdrawing the material means required for their support took place gradually, but, at least in retrospect, irresistibly, and one sees this in the artistic decadence that attends the process as well as in the neglect in maintaining the means of productive consumption built up over the centuries. Along with the internal deterioration, external threats were more and more dealt with ineptly, and the entire combination of unproductive forces became too much for the foundations to bear. The end came rapidly, and in the interval of but a few decades after Ramses III the kingdom settled quietly into the dust once more.

The decay of feudalism and the rise of capitalism

The fate of ancient Egypt is not held up as an object lesson from which we may infer the fate of modern capitalism; that fate is as may be, one might say. The case is presented to recall the need for a theory that would, in fact, confirm or refute the diagnosis offered, a theory of unproductive consumption that will facilitate inquiry into historical processes and, conceivably, assist in formulating measures for redressing balances between productive and unproductive labor when deterioration threatens. No serious student of history really doubts that the problem of social prodigality is a continuing and sometimes critical one. However, keeping our gaze still on more remote scenes, the period of transition from feudalism to modern capitalism in the West is, some say, highly instructive in these respects. Among the many students of the period, say, the thirteenth through the sixteenth centuries, Maurice Dobb is one of the finest. His *Studies in the Development of Capitalism,*[11] while guided by an informed awareness of Marxian theoretical possibilities to be sure, offers a reasonable and at the same time formidable interpretation of the transition period.

As a mode of production, feudalism differed in many important ways from its historical successor, capitalism. Its principal means of production was land; its principal producer, the serf. In contrast to modern capitalism, the serf's rights of access to means of production were set securely in the cement of custom and law: "The direct producer," Marx notes, "is here in possession of his means of production, of the material labour conditions required for the realization of his labour and the production of his means of subsistence. He carries on his agriculture and the rural house industries connected with it as an independent producer. . . ."[12] Under capitalism the access of the producer to means of production is by no means so assured. Those means become finally the private property of others than those who utilize them productively. Which is not to say that the "free" labor of capitalism is lacking in advantages, even from the producer's standpoint. Feudalism, for example, was a social order welded together through ignorance, superstition, political repression including force, while the awareness of the worker and his capacity to control his destiny were less developed than they are now. But why did feudal society give way to the market order of capitalism?

As the story is sometimes told, the decline of feudal society was hastened primarily by its ever deeper and more extensive contact with commerce and the money economy. However, as Dobb puts it, "There seems in fact to be as much evidence that the growth of a money economy per se led to an intensification of serfdom as there is evidence that it was the cause of the feudal decline."[13] Without summarizing the evidences offered in this connection, suffice it to say that Dobb concludes that the principal contributor to feudal collapse is a set of interacting circumstances featuring two principal aspects, a rather feeble development of labor productivity, on the one side, and, on the other, an intensifying demand for additional revenues, pressing down upon these intrinsically weak productive forces.[14] The feudal decline is promoted by an internal degeneration at least as much as from an external commercial penetration. It is the consequence of the destructive pressures of a rising scale of unproductive consumption, or of "overexploitation," to use Sweezy's term. As the scale of exploitation rises above what the generation of surplus labor can support, the encroachment upon the powers of serf labor, powers themselves only feebly developed, proves too much for productive labor to bear. The growing oppression of serf labor tracing to this twofold pressure culminates in a gradual disintegration of the system of social relations characteristic of the feudal mode of production. The mode itself gives way, or is gradually tranformed into something else. In the case of seventeenth-century France, in particular, we see in the court of the "Sun King" at Versailles the final flare-up of unproductive panoply accompanied by a decadence of the productive forces to which the king himself contributed. This was a spectacle, incidentally, that gave food for serious thought to whole generations of political economists, and to the liberals preceding Marx in particular, reflecting on the horrendous implications of an unchecked extravagance.[15]

Feudal society thus contained within itself the seeds of its own destruction. Dobb's analysis of this transition confirms again Marx's judgment of the general character of historical transformations. Speaking here of the process of economic and social decline in antiquity, in Greece and Rome, Marx writes:

> The aim of all these communities is survival; i.e., reproduction of the individuals who compose it as proprietors, i.e., in the same objective mode of existence as forms the relation among the members and at the same time therefore the commune itself. This reproduction, however, is at the same time necessarily new production and destruction of the old form.[16]

In the destruction of the old form of feudalism, unproductive consumption and its continuing reproduction on an extended scale made its contribution to the outcome.

It is worth noting again that the prospects for modern capitalism are not to be settled by ad hoc inferences from past to present, no matter how numerous past instances might be. The road that leads to secure answers to difficult questions is an intricate passage with twists and turns. Insofar as modern capitalism is concerned, perhaps the first of these comes with the question of whether some quota of unproductive labor is not an inherent and inextricable part of this mode of production, too. Beyond this turn are others that will lead finally to a reasonable assessment of the role of unproductive labor in contemporary society. Whether or not the rate of unproductive consumption rises inexorably under capitalist conditions of production, and whether or not this may be expected to undermine the old form in the course of time – these are problems to which we must, of course, return. For the moment, only the first corner is in sight: What forms of unproductive labor, if any, are inherent in the mode itself? This settled, at least as a first approximation, we can proceed to the formulation of theoretical principles bearing on issues of more distant consequence.

The circulatory establishment of capitalism

Among modern political economists Marx was the first to articulate a theory of the two spheres of social activity, of economic substruc-

ture and circulatory superstructure; and he was the first to consider
in full detail the interrelations between these. Under capitalism
these interrelations are antithetical; they express a fundamental opposition between the productive and the unproductive forces. At
first the productive and now the unproductive sphere gains the
ascendancy; economic and social progress waxes and wanes. This is
the overview.

Rather more familiarly, Marx saw the young capitalism in early
phases of its development as a mode pregnant with possibilities for
enlarging the force of productive labor through the advance of
technique and technologies. He saw also from the outset the prodigality and wastefulness of the mode, regarding unproductive
labor not merely as an incidental but as a constituent and integral
feature of the system. In regard to the prodigality:

The capitalist mode of production, while on the one hand, enforcing economy in
each individual business, on the other hand, begets by its anarchical system of
competition, the most outrageous squandering of labour power and of the social
means of production, *not to mention the creation of a vast number of
employments, at present indispensable but in themselves superfluous.* [17]

The clue to identifying the waste is contained in the phrase "a vast
number of employments, at present indispensable but in themselves
superfluous." Why "at present indispensable"? And in what sense
are they "superfluous"? What are the laws governing the development and rate of growth of these unproductive employments?

In the end, it may well be true that, as in the Egyptian case, some
priestly class mortgages the national income, tying it to a network of
dead-end consumptions. Whether or not this turns out to be the
case, it does appear inescapable that certain economic problems of
capitalism are and must be resolved in a distinctive and undoubted-
ly unproductive manner. Within the sphere of economic reproduction capitalism effects what any mode must effect, a continuing, if
somewhat erratic, transformation of real inputs into industrially
serviceable outputs. In the sphere of unproductive labor, the second
sphere, capital resolves its problems of circulation, that is, in the
broad definition of the term, its marketing operations. Within the
mode of production as a whole, all real values produced must be
transformed into their monetary forms, must be sold or realized.
These monetary forms are those in which profit and loss are reckoned and are the forms of reckoning preeminently characteristic of
this mode. These forms are also, then, means of purchase. These

money capitals, the floating powers to purchase that Marx refers to as latent or virtual capitals – monetary vehicles looking for commodities on which they may travel – must also be transformed into commodities as a precondition for their being put into either productive or unproductive use. Capitalism comprehends in its second sphere of circulation all activities of conversion of real into monetary values and vice versa, activities of buying and selling of monies and credits and of commodities themselves. These are all activities of a kind quite *necessary* to social reproduction under capitalism, but the activities of the circulatory sphere are nevertheless of a different order from those culminating in the direct transformation of input values into output values. The latter, the productive transformations, we might refer to as subjects of productive activity. The former, the unproductive transformations, have to do with the objects to which capitalism is dedicated, first and foremost the making of money profit by the appropriation of surplus value.

Historically, the broad division of social labor underlying the two spheres of circulation and of production began to expand in late feudal society when, for example, handicraft producers began to consign their wares to specialist tradesmen for disposition. But it is quite evident that marketing operations as specialized occupations have grown subsequently into an enormous and complex undertaking. Partly because of its vastness of scale, partly because of its signal importance in capitalism, the underlying differentiation in function is often forgotten. The difference is, however, of the greatest theoretical importance, and there is no real need either to confuse or to let slip from view the distinction between marketing and the productive operation. The fact that there is a specialized realm of buying and selling activity, necessary to but not the same thing as industrial activity, Marx seeks to clarify through a famous formula:[18]

$$M - C \ldots P \ldots C' - M' \qquad (3.1)$$

M is money and credit; C, commodities; P, the work processes in which production goes on; C', the enlarged volume of commodities emerging out of the productivity of labor; M', the larger money value realizable upon sale of the enlarged value of the output. The formula summarizes the interdependence of the two spheres.

The formula shows the two phases of circulatory activity already referred to, both connected with productive employment, but both conceptually and actually distinct from that productive activity. There is, first, the $M - C$ phase, a circulatory phase in which money capital is obtained for use in purchasing commodities either to be consumed productively or consumed unproductively, as the case may be. At the other pole, $C' - M'$, is the circulatory transformation of produced values back into commodities and, from thence, into monetary forms via the sale of output. This is the realization, Marx calls it, that is accomplished through the sale of the product. Finally, it shows the work processes, $P,$ in which the real transformation of production take place. In sum, capitalism features an array of layered activities performed by specialized divisions of social labor, activities that are at one level essentially marketing activities, some of which are preliminaries to productive, some of which are preliminaries to unproductive transformations, and all of which in real life proceed pretty much simultaneously with each other within a structured order of activities in general. These occupations of vending and buying of monies and credits and of commodities of every kind, the activities also of managing all of these operations – these absorb vast labor energies, principally of the so-called white-collar labor. As the accumulation of capital proceeds, changes in form and content and in interrelations of these spheres to each other take place in ways governed by laws of motion that we have as yet to specify.

There is no wish to belabor a distinction that will by now be obvious. Unfortunately, an excessive familiarity with the basic facts often leads one to underrate or overlook their significance. The division of social labor features two primary departments, and this must not be forgotten. Within the one are contained all of the activities of finance, of trade and commerce, whether in private or public sectors of the social economy. All of these are ancillary to production proper, and within the market economy are absolutely indispensable. But they are not to be confused with activities of farmers, shepherds, factory workers, and all directly employed in reproducing the means of reproduction and of subsistence consumed by all of social labor, productive and unproductive alike. For while the marketing activities are themselves ancillary to production, they require material means of support because they do not themselves converge directly upon the reproduction of those material means. This entire structure of social labor comprehends both productive and unproductive divisions and the structure as a whole reflects above all the intrinsic character of capitalism as a mode utilizing the mechanisms of money-market-commodity as means of circulating the social product. Because the latter work is unproductive in the sense defined, its material support must derive from the social surplus created by productive labor. Some portion of social production is of necessity dedicated to the support of work that is, viewed directly, only *contributory* to the main stem of productive activity and from this standpoint must be counted as unproductive no matter how *necessary* this work may be.[19] Another way of expressing this gives a yet sharper view.

The manifold activities of circulation require for the completion of whatever work they entail a certain passage of time. During this period of circulation, the labor engaged in performing its tasks demands material sustenance. The volume of material means so absorbed is obviously greater the longer this time period may be and smaller the more quickly the circulatory tasks are completed. While these energies and the material means of sustaining them are caught up in this circulatory work, they cannot simultaneously be engaged directly either in the maintenance or extension of the scales of productive input. Now certainly it is true as a matter of principle, true de facto in certain periods of capitalist development, that a shortening of the period of circulation, by reducing the volume of unproductive consumption, may help to raise the general rate of accumulation in the direction of its feasible maximum.[20] The contrary may also be true in principle, and, as we have already suggested, seems to have its historical expression: a *lengthening* of the period of circulation, or a relative increase in the volume of resources caught up in support of this activity, may reduce the rate of accumulation, promoting retardation and even economic regression.

The positive effect of the circulatory capitals in accelerating the rate of accumulation is well illustrated by the English experience. The industrial development that took place there from the sixteenth through the eighteenth centuries was significantly aided by the accumulations of money capital that were concurrently taking place. The profits of trade, domestic and international – and in the latter realm the slave trade was important – made available growing financial resources, latent money capitals for industrial deployment as technical progress made a complex accumulation ever more attractive and possible.[21] Even in the nineteenth century the consignment of circulatory problems by industrialists to financial and marketing specialists had significant positive effects upon profit rates and, hence, upon the general rate of accumulation. With the rising productivity of labor in transportation and communications, efficiency grew in financial and commercial activities and the farming out of circulatory operations by capitalists expanded enormously. With the advent of industrial capitalism periods of production and of circulation were shortened, and the rising rate of industrial growth both made possible and was itself accelerated by an extending investment in circulatory operations, unproductive though it was. These servo-mechanical interrelations among industry, transportation, communications, and commerce and finance, lay at the very heart of the unprecedented phenomenon of yesterday's expansion. Yet for all of the indirect effects of unproductive labor in stimulating profit rates and even real growth, unproductive labor remains unproductive. This must not be lost from view if what has happened subsequently is to be explained satisfactorily.

The overall effects upon the general rate of profit of productive in combination with unproductive labor, both enhanced in their effectiveness by a new and remarkable technical progress, were once highly stimulative. This is not the point at which to delve into the slowdown of accumulation that has since transpired, nor to attempt to evaluate it, but it probably correlates with a secular rise in the rate of unproductive consumption, a rise to some extent provoked by capital's very early success in farming out to circulatory entrepreneurs the work of vending the growing product; and, in addition, the work of circulation itself becomes more efficient as the scale of its activities grows larger, as Marx emphasized. But these positive features of an enlarged circulation are far from being the only ones attending the general advance. For example, as the scale of reproduction is extended, the problem of realizing its value in monetary forms becomes more difficult at the so-called macro- or aggregative level.

Since the collapse and depression of the 1930s the task of realizing the aggregate value of the social product has received a growing theoretical and administrative attention. The realization of the aggregate value has been solved through a very appreciable and continuing enlargement of circulatory operations aimed at maintaining an adequate growth of effective demand for the social product. Through a vast array of institutional devices – built-in stabilizers, governmentally supported markets for an enormous range of commodities of every kind, and especially military hardwares and softwares, instrumentalities for imperialistic penetrations and subjugations, domestic policing, and so on – demand has been artificially sustained.[22] Scientifically, it is a most interesting and challenging question of the extent to which economic laws of motion shape the emergence of modern state monopoly capitalism. One must consider how the laws of motion peculiar to this mode of production, taken always in conjunction with their countertendencies, culminate in a growing preponderance – if, indeed, they do – of unproductive over productive consumption. Is it not an endogenous build-up of unproductive labor and its consumptions that contributes most to the tendency for the general rate of profit to fall, to stagnation, to regression, and, incidentally, to collapse? To what conclusions does the theory lead us when taken in conjunction with historical evidences? In order to progress with these inquiries, a further spelling out of the theory itself is necessary.

The rate of unproductive consumption, U/V[23]

Theory is the net in which science ensnares the main facts of social history. Needless to say, it must be tightly woven so that what is relevant to our understanding does not elude us. In this weaving of the net, however, there is a point of diminishing returns. To weave more than is necessary is to strain out credibility; less than that risks the loss of what is important.

Let us begin with the concept of unproductive consumption previously used: any use of surplus product for other than the maintenance or extension of the scale of productive input. So defined, unproductive consumption amounts to any use of surplus product that does not figure in the process of basic economic reproduction. Social reproduction is another matter. For maintaining unproductive labor, and for extending the scale of its operations, an unproductive utilization of surplus product is quite necessary because all activity, including the unproductive, is a consumer of material means.

The rate of unproductive consumption may be defined with some precision; and it must be so defined because it has been implicit in the preceding argument and will reappear again and again in the course of this study. It is best defined with reference to the variable capital input so that it is formally parallel to the rate of surplus value, S/V. (The reason for this parallel will be clear in a moment.) The *rate* of unproductive consumption, U/V, is the ratio of unproductive consumption to the variable capital that yields the surplus. Just as the rate of surplus value shows the proportion of what may be productively *or* unproductively utilized out of current labor, or what is disposable of current labor, so the rate of unproductive consumption shows the ratio of what is destined for unproductive relative to what is available for productive use. The ratio of these two rates, the rate of unproductive consumption relative to the rate of surplus value, always shows the fraction of the social surplus being unproductively consumed: $U/V \div S/V = U/S$. The first, and in some respects the most important, point to be made in this connection is this. Whenever the rate of unproductive consumption is positive, the effect is to pull the rate of accumulation below what might be termed its "technically feasible maximum." Figure 3.1 will be of assistance to us in following the argument.

Begin with the line O, showing the rate of growth of a system in which the *rate* of unproductive consumption is zero, and, therefore, $U/S = 0$. The surplus is then productively consumable in its entirety in each period, and, assuming a full employment of all inputs, the line O represents the maximum, technically feasible, rate of growth. Given the state of technique, and hence rates of surplus value and of the organic composition of capital, the productive consumption of surplus expands the system as rapidly as possible.

But this path will no longer hold if the rate of unproductive consumption is positive and, therefore, some portion of the surplus product is unproductively consumed. Suppose the rate of unproductive consumption is 50 percent ($U/V = .5$). At the close of period t, then, one-half of the surplus, S_t, is used unproductively, in whatever forms may be peculiar to the mode of production and to the people in question. (The specific form, whether blowing chunks off the moon or building funerary monuments, or both, is of no concern at this juncture.) If this portion of the surplus, the amount U_t, is shunted aside in favor of unproductive utilization, then the input scale of period $t + 1$ must be reduced by so much: On the horizontal axis the input will now be I'_{t+1} rather than I_{t+1} (the latter when $U = 0$). If the input of the period $t + 1$ is thus smaller, and if the rate of surplus value and the organic composition of

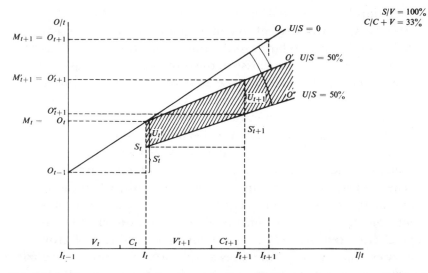

Figure 3.1. Simple accumulation: unproductive consumption and the retardation of economic growth. The line $O_{U/S = 0}$ shows the technically feasible maximum rate of accumulation, the rate that could be attained were unproductive consumption equal to zero, the whole of the surplus being productively consumed, the state of technique being given: ". . . if the velocity of circulation were absolute, i.e., if no interruption in production resulting from circulation occurred at all, then this coefficient (of the production process) would at at its maximum" (*Grundrisse*, p. 544). If, however, some given fraction of the surplus is unproductively consumed in work of circulation (for example, $U/S = 50\%$), then the scale of input of $t + 1$, instead of being I_{t+1}, will be only I'_{t+1}. Because of this reduced scale of input, the output of $t + 1$ must be correspondingly lower than it would have been had $U/S = 0$. The gross output of $t + 1$ will be only O'_{t+1} (as against O_{t+1}). With the same rate of unproductive consumption, the input scale of the following period will also be subject to reduction, since, again, only one-half of the surplus of the period will be available for productive consumption; and so on for each period as long as these conditions remain unchanged. With a fixed rate of unproductive consumption, the growth of gross output will follow the course of the line $O'_{U/S = .5}$. We see, first, that unproductive consumption pulls down the rate of growth of gross output, including unproductive consumption, below the technically feasible maximum rate. It is important to observe, second, that the rate of growth of *reproductively useful output*, of productive labor, given by the line $O''_{U/S = .5}$, is pulled down to a rate *below* that of the rate of growth of gross output. Note also that the less the growth of output, the less the increase in demand required to sustain it:

$$M'_{t+1} - M_t < M_{t+1} - M_t.$$

capital remain unchanged, then the output of $t + 1$ must also be correspondingly reduced *relative to what it would have been had the surplus been productively consumed in its entirety.* If we follow through this state of affairs for a number of periods, assuming a fixed rate of unproductive consumption ($U/V = .5$, for example), the result will be a general lowering of the growth rate below its technically feasible maximum. In other words, the system is on the growth line O' rather than O.[24]

A given rate of unproductive consumption pulls the rate of accumulation below its feasible maximum. An increase in that rate further reduces the rate of accumulation. On the other hand, a decrease in that rate relative to the rate of surplus value will permit the rate of accumulation to rise in the direction of the feasible maximum. Although the important relation of the rate of unproductive consumption to the rate of surplus value will be one thing or another according to circumstances, there are certain limits to the relation as far as the maintenance of economic reproduction is concerned. The upper rate of expansion is realized when the rate of unproductive consumption is zero; the rate of accumulation then reaches its feasible maximum. At the other limit, when the rate of unproductive consumption is equal to the rate of surplus value, the whole of the surplus is unproductively consumed, and simple reproduction results. Between these limits the real rate of growth of the system increases or decreases as the rate of unproductive consumption decreases or increases. This describes a general relationship between these two variables at the level of theoretical abstraction. What of historical actualities?

Again, the problem is too complex for any simple summarization, even when all relevant studies have been undertaken, perhaps. But at least one can point to two fields of application in which the principles discussed may turn out to be very helpful to inquiry. In the first of these, the principles will help us to understand a phenomenon that is otherwise most mysterious, the seemingly growing preference of capitalist investors for projects that raise the rate of unproductive consumption relatively. The puzzle is even more baffling when we consider that a rise in this rate lowers the real rate of profit and defeats the profit goals of the class as a whole. It would appear that while a relatively enlarged unproductive consumption lowers the general rate of profit, no connection between this effect and the expanded investment that brought it about is perceived by capitalists themselves. One reason for this may be that although retardation makes profits more easy to realize, it does this *because* of the very fact that it lowers the rate of growth. As a general rule, the higher the rate of growth, the higher the required rate of increase of effective demand that will permit a systematic realization of whatever values inhere in the growth of product. An increase in the rate of unproductive consumption, on the other hand, while it lowers the real growth rate of the system below the rate that might otherwise be attained, reduces also the required rate of increase in aggregate demand. This is seen in Figure 3.1, in which are compared the required increase in demand of $t + 1$ over period t when unproductive consumption is zero ($O_{U/S = 0}$) with the required increase in demand with a given rate of unproductive consumption ($O_{U/S = .5}$). It will be seen that in the latter case the required increase is absolutely smaller than the former.

The higher rate of profit implicit in the higher rate of growth that would take place were the rate of unproductive consumption low may never be experienced because of realization difficulties. Taken as a class, however, capitalist investors may have learned the hard way that when unproductive consumption approaches its maximum, there is never a shortage of demand for the social product. We refer, most obviously, to the lessons of wartimes, when the danger of realizing profits is at a minimum because of state prodigality, and to the lessons of peace, when collapse and depression seem to drive home the same conclusion but from the opposite standpoint. Better a bird in the hand than two in the bush is the kind of business maxim that supports the investors' preference for unproductive expenditures. We shall see that there are other important forces pointing toward a reinforcement of this extraordinarily antisocial preference, forces entirely built in to the exchange mechanisms of the capitalist mode.

But now, briefly, to the second field of application of the principles of unproductive consumption. A relatively lower rate of unproductive consumption permits a higher rate of growth and/or rate of profit. This suggests that if a people caught in the famous vicious circle of poverty are to break the circle, or, to use Sismondi's metaphor, to convert the circle into a spiral of expansion, it may be necessary to eliminate unproductive activities or somehow to convert to productive employment all of the labor power previously dedicated to unproductive pursuits.[25] This, after all, is a part of the process by means of which modern capitalism arose, and the reduction of unproductive consumption was part of what was at issue in the prolonged class struggles attending feudal decline and establishing the base for subsequent expansion. The transformation of unproductive into productive labor is one of the important undertakings to which socialist regimes in the underdeveloped context do, and must, pay close attention. As we shall see in discussing the transition of the advanced capitalism to socialism, it is also a task underlying some of the most important transformations leading out and away from the capitalist mode of production. But in regard to these important issues, while the pure theory of unproductive consumption is an invaluable aid in inquiry as to how to proceed, it is only an aid to the work to be done. Only a close and scrupulous study of history can enable us to identify with sufficient precision the *forms* of unproductive labor requiring conversion and, hence, to identify the means by which conversions may be undertaken.

Finally, we draw attention to a point about the *measurement* of social product, also easily grasped with reference to Figure 3.1. Given some rate of unproductive consumption, a portion of the social product is destined for unproductive utilization. In Figure 3.1, for instance, with $U/S = .5$, the scale of unproductive consumption is shown by the shaded area between O' and O''. On the other hand, the area beneath the line O'' shows the accumulation of the productive capitals, the growth capitals of the system. In other words, the line O' shows the growth of *gross* social product, including the portion unproductively spent. The line O'' represents the growth of *net*, real product only, the growth of what is productively utilized.

Were the economist to take the gross output as his economic indicator of growth and its prospects, he would be making a serious error. The real rate of growth is *less* than this, and its measurement requires subtraction of unproductive consumption from the gross product. The failure to allow for the rate of unproductive consumption in the measurement of growth rates is one of the most serious errors into which standard economics falls. With this failure, whose origins lie in the "scientific" effort to avoid the theory of unproductive consumption, the economist exaggerates the record of capitalist growth. He exaggerates the rate of expansion, especially when the rate of unproductive consumption is rising; by the same token, he fails to give fair warning of impending difficulties born of a falling rate of profit: economic retardation, depression, and even economic regression, whose nature we must now consider.[26]

The nature of economic regression

The retardation of the rate of accumulation by the rate of unproductive consumption points toward a slowdown in the growth rate and, ultimately, to stagnation. But as a matter of principle there is no reason why the rate of unproductive consumption should not exceed the rate of surplus value. What is the meaning of this

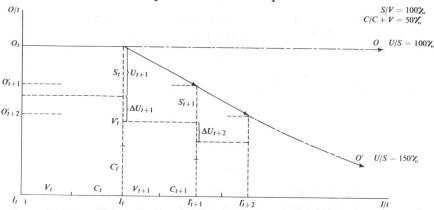

Figure 3.2. Economic regression: unproductive consumption exceeds surplus value ($U/S = 150\%$). The line $O_{U/S=100\%}$ shows the course of simple reproduction when the whole of the surplus is unproductively consumed, the rate of surplus value and the value composition of capital being given. Suppose, now, the rate of unproductive consumption to rise above this level, say, to 150 percent of the surplus. Out of the social product of period t an increment of unproductive consumption (ΔU_{t+1}) appears, and if this is not obtained from sources external to the economy, for example, through exploitation abroad, it can only derive from domestic product that would otherwise be destined for productive consumption. The increment of unproductive consumption thus reduces the productive input of $t + 1$ in the amount of this increment, and the scale of output of $t + 1$ is reduced, other things remaining the same. A (fixed) rate of unproductive consumption in excess of the rate of surplus value will culminate in a regression of scales of inputs and outputs as shown on the line $O'_{U/S=150\%}$. The continuation of such a course must culminate in the destruction of both productive and unproductive labor.

eventuality? How might it come about?

If the U/S ratio is greater than 1, because the rate of unproductive consumption exceeds the rate of surplus value, the question that remains to be answered is this: From whence comes the margin of social product by which unproductive consumption exceeds the value of the surplus product? If, for the moment, we exclude the possibility of obtaining the margin externally – a subject belonging in the discussion of imperialism – there is only one quarter from which the additional U can come. In Figure 3.2 a case of economic regression is shown. The unproductive consumption of each period is extended *by drawing upon the reproduced capitals of the previous period.* That is, for any given period, say, period $t + 1$, not only is the surplus product of period t unproductively consumed (U_{t+1}) but an additional increment of unproductive consumption (ΔU_{t+1}) as well. The result of this is to reduce the scale of inputs productively available in $t + 1$. Given this rate of unproductive consumption in excess of the rate of surplus value, in each period after $t + 1$, the general consequence is a reduction in scales of input and output as social product regresses along the line O'. Once unproductive consumption bites into not only the social surplus but also into capitals destined otherwise for economic reproduction, *the process of economic reproduction is itself impaired.* It is this kind of impairment, the result of what Sweezy called overexploitation, that culminated in both the decline of ancient Egypt and the collapse of feudal society. Does it also presage the collapse of modern capitalist society?

A hypothesis

The contemporary implications of the theory of unproductive consumption, not to mention its applications to the whole field of social history, are altogether too numerous and important to even attempt to recount them here. Some, to be sure, we shall consider by and by (see the discussion of stagflation in Chapter 8). For the moment, we merely sketch a hypothesis in regard to capitalist development, one whose specific application to capitalism and, more importantly, to the transition to socialism, will be argued in the sequel.

With the rise of modern capitalism, and up until sometime in the past century, the productive consumption of a portion of surplus product tended to predominate over other uses to which that product was also put. As long as the rate of unproductive consumption was less than the rate of surplus value, accumulation proceeded. Indeed, as accumulation became complex with the progress of invention and innovation, real growth could and did accelerate even with an accompanying enlargement of unproductive consumption in absolute dimensions. The scale of unproductive consumption rising, so, too, rose not only the scale of the capitalists' personal consumption but also the scale of capitalist investment in circulation. Unproductive labor could and did grow without impairing the expansion of productive labor, whose exploitation and accelerating productivity lay at the base of the entire movement. Under these circumstances the growth of the circulatory establishment seemed to be the cause rather than the effect of the expansion, and this illusion was quickly substantiated in economic doctrine. Marketing writ large became the hitherto undiscovered wisdom of the ages. The new, the neoclassical economics, emerged with the new circulatory order.

Hardly had these glories put in their appearance than the rate of unproductive consumption began its relative rise. In all of the countries of Western capitalism – and apart from sporadic accelerations associated with postwar interludes – there set in a more or less marked tendency to economic retardation, a tendency which has more recently become one of economic regression.[27] Even in some conventional measurements, retardation appears as a recurrent phenomenon; but with the relative advance of unproductive consumption, retardation has tended to regression. The seriousness of the latter tendency is indicated, *inter alia,* by an excessive depletion and depreciation of means of production (the capital stock), including the raw material and fuel resources of the modern energy crisis.

The tendency to regression complements and strengthens the tendency for the general rate of profit to fall. It reinforces the long-term movement toward economic decay that inheres in the relative rise of the organic composition of capital with the exhaustion of the stimulative force of technical progress already discussed. The entrance of the advanced capitalism into its degenerative phase places the rate of unproductive consumption in curious and deadly juxtaposition to the law of the falling rate of profit. The rise in the rate of unproductive consumption is best viewed as the consequence of a countertendency to the falling rate of profit. It expresses the effort of the capitalist to get out from under the decline in the general rate of profit through a more systematic expansion of investments that may be profitable in monetary terms but are unproductive economically and therefore undercut the monetary profitability that they themselves engender. Thus the extension of militarism, neocolonialism, official pauperism (welfare) and the extensive policing of domestic colonialism – these are especially favored forms of investment enterprise that, aimed at countering the tendency for the rate of profit to fall, yield in the long term quite opposite results. These activities only reinforce and strengthen the decline in real profitability. In the end, the expense of maintaining these investments becomes so great that capital even contemplates dismantling what it built up at such enormous cost – cost to labor, basically.

As for the economists, their chronic optimism with capitalist prospects traces, we see, to a failure to perceive the real forces tending to repress economic development, to their own misconception in respect both to the character and to the strength of these forces. Their misconceptions are magnified and crystallized by theories and methods of measurement (gross national product) that follow logically from the assumption that all activity is productive, but for reason of that very consistency lead to repeated confirmation of erroneous expectations.[28]

By way of gauging the magnitude of the expectational errors of the economists, it might be noted that less biased observers outside the science of economics have long been less sanguine at the prospects. Since the turn of the century a growing number of students of social affairs, including a few economists, have drawn attention to the signs of advancing decadence.[29] For the United States the rise of the U/S ratio probably dates to before the turn of the century, to the Gilded Age of Victorian exhibitionism; in England there was the insipid flowering of Edwardian insouciance; in Germany, a florid militarism; in France, the rococo festivals of the bourgeoisie after the reduction of the Commune. Everywhere, with allowance for national and cultural differences, came a spread of ostentatious consumption, a spread intimately connected with the extraordinary enlargement of a commercial, financial, and state apparatus of circulation and with the thrusts of a new militarism and a new imperialism. In the present century the process continues with the mushrooming state peddling the absurdities of its wastrel existence, with war and civil war blowing up again and again the flesh, blood, and resources of social labor. In the race between the development of the productive and of the unproductive forces, the latter have overtaken and passed their rival.

The tendency for the general rate of profit to fall now asserts itself more powerfully and with more devastating effect than formerly, partly because the countertendencies that arise do not really counter the decline, but instead reinforce it. This self-limitation of accumulation through the accumulation of unproductive labor is a vast subject on which, as yet, we have hardly touched. It will concern us throughout the remainder of this study not only for the sake of its political but for the sake of its scientific importance. Students of economics, for example, should view the theory as a scientific rebuke to the aridity and vacuity of standard economics, a call for an economics capable of identifying and offering remedies for the dissipation of social energies that underlies the advanced crisis. Theoretically, the demand is for a new social science. Politically, the system of war, of predation, of repressive and wasteful consumption, of aborted effort, demands measures whose discussion we must for the moment forgo.

Again, theoretical instruments are necessary for furthering analyses and furthering also our understanding of the Marxian economics. The time has come to consider the labor theory of value in its direct and pure form as an explanation of how definite quantities of labor power – labor power of definite *value* magnitudes – convey through processes of production and circulation definite values in exchange to all commodities comprising the main body of social wealth.

PART TWO
The labor theory of value

4

The meaning and measurement of value within the context of the labor theory

Value theory as a scientific imperative

In explaining the growth and change in composition of exchange values in capitalist development, the very meaning of exchange value was temporarily shunted aside. It must have been evident, even so, that the analysis always assumed the existence of certain values that, within the market economy, become manifest as prices in the course of their exchanges. Market prices and aggregate money values, such as aggregate demand, were assumed to approximate these values in exchange; long-run prices were "at their values," as Marx phrased it. Now even among the Marxists there are and have been many who would let it go at that; or perhaps deny the need for such assumptions. There are revisionists who, perhaps fearing that value analysis will throw open Pandora's box, have tried to keep the lid on, avoiding as much as possible formulations in the theory of value. Others, for the usual, and sometimes for unusual, reasons, have sought to discredit Marx's analyses of values. On the value as on other questions, however, we must plumb to the bottom and build from there, if that is possible. It turns out that the bottom is solid enough.

For Marx it was a matter of both scientific and political necessity, a matter of political economy, in brief, that the determination and measurement of values be analyzed. According to this conception of labor values, at a given level of development of the productive forces definite value magnitudes of exchange values are the real substance of the flows of inputs and outputs within reproductive processes. These values, in turn, are determined by the value of the labor power embedded in commodities in the course of their pro-

duction. They are a function of the living and of the congealed
labor power reproductively expended (on the assumption that the
thing produced is itself reproductively useful). Furthermore, these
exchange values, so determined, are in principle measurable in
units of labor time, man-hours, man-days, years, and so on. Given
that these claims can be shown scientifically, there is no need to flee
the labor theory. The theory is then something *more than* a revolutionary injunction, on the one hand, or a simple analytical tool, on
the other hand.[1] It points to a realm of historical reality whose comprehension is imperative as a preliminary to understanding all
economic and social phenomena.

The scientific claim is the one with which we are concerned here
and in the following chapter. If it can be substantiated, as we
believe it can, the implications are of the utmost importance. The
greatest theorists of the classical economics (of whom Marx was
one), indeed, some of the greatest social theorists the world has
known since the time of Aristotle, have been in agreement that the
explanation of values, including especially economic values, is
necessary as well as desirable. One *must* postulate some elemental
entity by means of which one may ultimately explain the portion of
the universe with which one is concerned. The point mass of the
Newtonian system, the molecule, the atom, the quantum – these illustrate the contention. From a simple, substantial postulate, scientific reasoning from the top down may proceed in accordance with
a proper regard for the rules of logic (including dialectical logic)
and observation. Marx summarizes this classical view:

The economists of the seventeenth century always started out with the living aggregate population, nation, state, several states, etc. . . . . As soon as these separate
elements had been more or less established by abstract reasoning, there arose the
systems of political economy which start from simple conceptions, such as labor,
division of labor, demand, exchange value, and conclude with state, international
exchange, and world market. The latter is manifestly the scientifically correct
method . . . the abstract definitions lead to the reproduction of the concrete subject in the course of reasoning.[2]

It is, therefore, no accident that Marx begins *Capital I* (Part I,
Chapter 1) with a discussion of the simple conceptions and the
abstract definitions. Nor is it by chance that he arrives ultimately,
in the course of reasoning, at the concrete subject. At the top as well
as at the bottom of the structure of explanation, there must be a
secure grounding in the stuff of social history.

As a second aspect of the scientific imperative, a good reason for value theory in economics arises because, since the commodities (the goods and services that are the material substance of inputs and outputs) are physically heterogeneous, a *numeraire*, or a par and equation, as Sir William Petty called it, will be necessary.[3] There must be a common denominator that reduces one and all to homogeneous entities whether for analytical or quantitative comparison. While conventional economics has virtually abandoned the search for a *numeraire*, this must not be permitted within Marxian science.

Finally, the need for a theory of value is logical. If one begins with the premise that the things that men value and the values that are implicit in their activities – and these are by no means coincident with each other – are to be scientifically explained, then premises that make references to values are unavoidable logically. If we are to draw from our theories statements about values, then our assumptions must relate to values directly in some fairly precise fashion. In the Marxian economics there is a further reason for value theory, intimately related to the foregoing. The purpose of defining a standard of value is to facilitate political evaluation. In contrast with the politically feeble stance of orthodox economics, political economy has always been concerned with the evaluation of social activities, and especially with those that are productive as against those that are unproductive. Is such objective evaluation no more than a contradiction in terms? Is it not more than a mere moral responsibility of the socially sensitive student of these subjects? Is it not true that a vital political economy concerns itself with questions of social survival rather than with the amorphous and languid social welfare? Is not objective evaluation an indispensable preliminary for strengthening and preserving social labor, "that general category of human material through which the community's technological proficiency functions directly to an industrial effect . . ."?[4] Surely the preservation of the productive forces can and must be an objective undertaking. It is an undertaking that can and must be informed by a reliable theory of value.

Subjective and objective (reproductive) utilities

At the top of the theoretical structure of the Marxian economics are postulates referring to two types of values of economic and social significance and to the general nature of their interrelationship. These are exchange values, governed by the value of the labor input, and use values, or utilities, as the standard economics refers to them. We begin with the latter not because they are the only variety of value taken seriously by the orthodox, however, but because, properly defined, they are fundamental to the Marxian theory of value as well. The importance of use values was certainly stressed by Marx,[5] although there has been a tendency in some of his disciples to play down their significance, presumably because conventional theorists make so much of these values in an effort to undermine the labor theory with which they are allegedly incompatible. But while it is true that the labor and utility theories of value have been portrayed as competitors because their respective adherents have been at hammers and tongs, at the theoretical level there is a certain necessary complementarity in the theories – properly interpreted, of course.

In regard to use values, first of all, there is no doubt that individuals assert preferences, make choices and selections among items they contemplate consuming, and so on. These preferences reflect the usefulness imputed to the commodity by its buyers, it is true. Further, the labor theorist may safely allow that, at least within certain social contexts, individuals do behave as if they were little "homogeneous globules of desire" (Veblen), moving under hedonistic impulses with a view to maximizing their "satisfactions." These contentions of neoclassical economists, of which so much is sometimes made by them as well as by their critics, are quite consistent with the labor theory of value. The trouble is that they by no means exhaust the subject of use values or their historical character as such. The advocates of the view that mankind is hopelessly hedonistic certainly understate the varieties of behavior and motivation that history reveals. Further, in their concentration on the subjective influences upon "choice," they fail to weigh properly, or fail to weigh at all, the objective factors affecting human selection. The determinants of selection include many influences not at all touched by free will, or anything remotely resembling it: levels of incomes and assets, class membership and economic interest, habit, ecological and other circumstances, and so on.

In addition to all of the preceding, there is another category of use values typically overlooked in standard economics. We refer to the utilities of goods and services that are technically necessary, technically serviceable for economic reproduction within a given technical framework, or at a given level of development of the productive forces. There is this category of what might be called reproductive utilities whose values in use are not at all subjective. The simple fact is that in their function as producers, rather than as the glorified consumers of the Keynesian world, people exercising a given technique will find imposed upon themselves, as a matter of objective necessity, a demand for certain tools, instruments, means of transportation, even certain foodstuffs, living conditions, educational and apprenticeship requirements, and a host of other essentials with respect to which no choice obtains. Not only particular tools and instruments are required by the level of technique, but the technical proportions that they bear to the individual and, more importantly, to the collective laborer, are also technically determined: The carpenter must have his hammer, the pressman his press, the doctor his dictaphone, and so on. In the demand for reproductively useful goods and services the state of technique fixes the selection. But the principle, we repeat, carries over into the so-called consumption of the consumer, who is sometimes a producer sometimes not. Our children require certain kinds and amounts of education and training for the work they must do. Our diets must be quantitatively and qualitatively balanced so that metabolic processes may service effectively our needs as producers. Thus much of what appears to the economist to be a matter of free choice may be, and most frequently is, a matter of constrained selections ruled by objective needs.[6]

The recognition of this category of utilities, together with the social priorities it implies, underlies the Marxian theory of value and, of course, the labor theory itself. The assumption is basic, and was recognized as such by Marx himself: "Nothing can have value without being an object of utility. If the thing is useless, so is the labor contained in it; the labor does not count as labor and therefore creates no value."[7] The forthrightness of this declaration belies the old allegation that Marxism ignores use values. The confusion underlying this allegation often may be traced to the failure of the critic to realize that Marx was preoccupied with a category of use values for which the neoclassical economists had found no use: the role of production coefficients in regulating demands for factor inputs has only recently intruded into standard economics. That much settled, what is the theory of exchange value that rests upon this base in reproductive utilities?

The labor theory of value explains, and makes possible the

measurement, of the exchange values of goods and services of given reproductive utility. The reproductive utility of commodities is, at least as a first approximation, a precondition to the explanation of values in exchange that are themselves explicated by the labor theory. In the explanation of exchange values *as a first approximation* the labor theory maintains that commodities exchange for each other in ratios determined by the value of the labor powers expended within each of them in the course of their production, and given a level of development of the productive forces.

One can, and no doubt should, approach the proposition just stated as an explanatory hypothesis. And yet, in view of the reproductive schemes already described, there is no point in being too coy concerning the scientific mileage to be had from a systematic utilization of the hypothesis in question. The hypothesis carries us a very considerable distance in the explanation of social history, and the present issue involves its own logical and empirical foundations rather than its usefulness for scientific inquiry. The labor theory must be looked at directly as well as indirectly, as previously, and although we come to this task very shortly now, there is one final consideration that may prevent one's seeing the scientific necessity for a labor theory of value. One may well ask why the values of commodities in exchange should not be explained in terms of their *relative usefulness* to those who demand them whether for production or for consumption purposes.

In response to this suggestion, two comments will suffice. First, let us note that differential utilities do exist, and their nature we come to in a moment; but these differential utilities bear upon the market *prices* of commodities rather than upon their values in exchange as defined by the labor theory. These are not at all the same thing even though, under certain conditions, the price of the commodity may serve as an index of its exchange value measured in units of socially necessary labor time. A more fundamental reply to the suggestion is that, if exchange values are to be explained by utility differentials, these differentials should also be economically explicable. Otherwise, one's explanation has an ad hoc character and is removed from the *value* postulates that social science so badly needs, as we have argued. Actually, if one pursues utility differentials with a view to explaining them, this is precisely what happens; that is, the theorist is forced by the very subject itself to proceed *outside* the realm of social phenomena in order to explain the differentials at issue. As it is an *economic* theory that we desire, this approach will not do. Let us examine this a little more.

The relative utilities of goods and services for economic reproduction – their objective utilities, as explained – are determined by the physical properties, the physical or natural characteristics of the objects themselves. Water is useful because it nourishes plants as well as men; it has physical properties that permit it to be used for the generation of steam power, for cooling engines. *Why* the usefulness is what it is can only be explained through biochemistry, physical chemistry, soil chemical analysis, and so on. Or, again, a diamond has definite industrial uses that render it more useful than steel for certain purposes. The determinants of these properties of both items are to be found in crystallography, however. Without multiplying uselessly examples to illustrate the case, let us simply say that the absolute and relative properties that make for differential utilities in industrial employment are governed by the state of technique, on the one side, and by the physical properties of the objects that figure within reproductive processes, on the other. In other words, the explanation of these utilities must carry the theorist outside the realm of social science. The search for an economic *numeraire* to explain exchange values of things reproductively useful must, therefore, proceed in some other direction. And there remains only the labor embedded in commodities in the course of their production that might serve the purpose. Once more, the Marxian premise: "If we leave out of consideration the use value of commodities, they have only one common property left, that of being products of labor . . . we make abstraction from its use value, we make abstraction at the same time from the material elements and shapes that make the product a use value. . . ."[8]

Thus while we are at last ready to begin to show how the explanation of values in exchange may proceed from labor value premises, the underlying assumption of given reproductive utilities should not be forgotten. Further, in order to simplify and at the same time make more systematic our presentation of the general Marxian theory of value, its labor as well as its use value components, let us assume that the exchange value of the commodity reflects also and proportionally its use value. In actuality, values in use and exchange values, measured in values of embedded labor, *may be* proportional to one another, the one being an index of the relative magnitude of the other. On the other hand, it will eventually be necessary to consider that this may not be so and that these values in use and in exchange may become quite disproportional to each other by force of circumstance. It follows that under certain circumstances market prices, because they are somehow related to exchange values, may or may not be indicative of use values as well. Interrelations among these values – among monetary, exchange (labor), and use values – being theoretically and, no doubt, historically, quite complex, our analysis begins with the simplest assumptions, among them the assumption that prices and values *are* all proportional to each other. Like other assumptions, this one will be modified when necessary.

Simple and socially necessary labor

The exchange values of economically useful commodities are governed by the value of labor power spent in their production, this labor power both of living and of congealed labor being utilized within a given technical milieu. Furthermore, the value magnitudes of the labor power inputs and, of course, those of the outputs as well, are in principle measurable in units of socially necessary labor time. One of the problems involved in supporting these claims is this. Note that, viewed in their material or substantial forms, the constant and variable capitals of social production are heterogeneous rather than homogeneous entities. This is true, moreover, whether one contemplates the varieties of commodities emerging from production processes or, for that matter, going into them as material means of sustaining them (means of production, wage goods), or whether one contemplates the different kinds and grades of labor power, the flows of low- and of high-powered labor comprising the primary energy input of reproductive activity. It is quite obvious that, if labor power is to comprise the *numeraire,* the common denominator by means of which all value magnitudes are to be gauged no matter how heterogeneous they may be, the different kinds and grades of labor power must themselves be reducible to units of some one kind of labor power, the *numeraire* of social labor itself. This is the famous reduction problem of the labor theory of value. It is, according to many critics of the labor theory, the principal stumbling block to the scientific pretensions of the theory.

   It is not enough by any means, as some Marxists have supposed, that one should always regard living labor power as a generalized and homogeneous expenditure of human energy whose mass has a value measured by the labor time required for its reproduction or, what may be the same thing, whose means of subsistence have a value measured by the labor time spent by this mass in the course of the production of those means of subsistence. While it might readily be possible to secure a statistic – so many billions of man-hours annually expended by this mass of labor power – purporting to estimate the value of its social product, that statistic would not in fact constitute the measure we seek. It would not for the simple reason that social labor is simply not a homogeneous mass, as such a statistic would presuppose. The grades and kinds of labor power comprising the whole work force of modern social economy are numerous, and, even within each grade, some heterogeneity does exist.

Granted all this, the extent of the heterogeneity should not be exaggerated. While within the different grades of social labor some workers are above and some below the average level of skill prevailing, there is, nevertheless, some average level of skills defining, in fact, the central feature of the grade itself. Also, if we consider all of the grades making up the labor force productively employed, there is a limit to the heterogeneity among grades in the sense that both at the top and at the bottom of the range of skills represented, certain limits may be seen. At the top the limit is set by the labor power marking the high tide of the advance of technique at a given historical juncture. At the bottom we find a grade of simple or unskilled or crude labor power, which, despite the sophistication of the structure taken in its entirety, is a kind of labor power that has not changed much qualitatively in modern times and perhaps is qualitatively what it has been over many centuries. (Men's psychological and even physiological capacities are not appreciably different from what they were millennia ago, we are told.) In any event, within the most advanced as well as within the least developed systems of production one observes ordinary or simple unskilled labor functioning at tasks that are socially necessary. Marx uses the term "simple" to designate this common and elementary expenditure of labor power sitting at the base of the hierarchy of required labor skills. The phrase "simple labor" designates the familiar force generated by the average simple laborer within this lowest strata of the working population: "It is the expenditure of simple labor power, i.e., of the labor power which, on the average, apart from any special development, exists in the organism of every ordinary individual."[9] Within a labor force consisting of several distinct grades of labor, there is always this substratum whose crude and unskilled exertions entail an expenditure of energy of the kind described: "Simple average labor, it is true, varies in character in different countries and at different times, but in a particular society it is given."[10] Standing at the base of the pyramid of social labor is the division of simple labor that the Marxian economics takes as the *numeraire,* the common denominator of all grades of labor power making up the entire hierarchy.

The hierarchy of which we have been speaking is that of the various grades of "socially necessary labor," the labor of those from ditch diggers and street cleaners to computer analysts, theoretical scientists, and so on, whose expenditures of labor energy are necessary to the process of *economic* reproduction. All of these are socially necessary grades, and simple, socially necessary labor is merely the socially necessary stratum at the bottom of the hierarchy.

This latter is a labor power in relation to which all other grades of labor are more or less high powered, perhaps more or less better paid, but *in no way* more socially necessary. In selecting simple labor as the *numeraire* of labor powers, the strategy is itself a simple one. It is by virtue of its position at the bottom of the labor hierarchy that the expenditure of simple labor may best serve as a standard for the evaluation of all labor power and of the social product in general. If the value of the labor power of simple labor can be gauged and if means can be found of converting the labor powers of the higher divisions and grades into man-hours of simple, socially necessary labor time, then a measure of a homogeneous value of social labor power and of social product as well – assuming the value of the product is no more than the value of the labor power expended in its production – may be at hand.

The par and the equation

The whole edifice of socially necessary labor that gives impetus to a given technique comprises skills and levels of skill, outputs of qualitatively different energies. Nevertheless, the labor value accountant, wishing to estimate the different value magnitudes represented by these various divisions, may simply regard the higher forms of labor as expending energies that are quantitative multiples of the value of the simple, socially necessary labor power. Suppose, for simplicity, the social economy employs only two grades of socially necessary labor power: (1) skilled (high powered) and (2) unskilled (simple). The man-hour expended by the former is some multiple of the man-hour expended by the latter. Given, for instance, the actual number of man-hours annually expended by skilled labor in economic reproduction, this number should be multiplied by the multiple or scalar (call it a) that tells us how many times a man-hour of skilled labor exceeds in value the man-hour of unskilled labor. If we know the magnitude of this coefficient, and if we know the man-hours of skilled and the man-hours of unskilled labor annually expended, then the value of the total labor power would be $V = aV_S + V_U$, in which V_S and V_U are raw-data statistics of man-hours annually expended by both grades of labor. Marx's contention is this, then, that $V = aV_S + V_U$ and the problem of the reduction of man-hours of skilled labor time into man-hours of simple, socially necessary labor time is, first of all, *one of devising a method for the quantitative estimation of the multiple or scalar, a,* in the equation for the total value of labor power. Provided our accountant can estimate the coefficient by which the man-hour of skilled or high-powered labor needs to be multiplied, he can then estimate the value of total labor power in homogeneous units of simple, socially necessary labor time. Hence we emphasize the importance of estimating the coefficient a and all the other coefficients for all grades of socially necessary labor above the base grade of simple, socially necessary labor. We must deal with this problem of quantitative estimation as a starting point for determining the quantifiability of exchange values in general.

But let us make a brief aside. Apart from the theoretical issue and that of direct quantitative measurement, it is evident that in the real world the reduction of labor powers does take place. The market assigns relative wage rates that may be taken as rough indices of differential labor values:

But how about skilled labor which rises above the level of the average labor by its high intensity, by its greater specific gravity? This kind of labor resolves itself into unskilled labor comprising it; it is simple labor of a higher intensity, so that 1 day of skilled labor, e.g., may equal three days of unskilled labor. This is not the place to discover the laws regulating this reduction. It is clear, however, that such reduction does take place.[11]

The man-hour of skilled labor, priced at its value, may thus receive a wage, say, three times the wage of unskilled labor. But the scientist cannot approach the problem of value differentials by taking wage rate differentials as indices. The labor theory of value must provide its *own* solution to the estimation of the relevant coefficients, and while under certain conditions the market may yield wage rate differentials that reflect the differing labor values involved, under other conditions it may not; and in any case the labor theory claims the capacity to make *independent* estimates of the value differentials involved. And how is this to be done?

In the course of efforts to measure the reduction coefficients, one principle should stand to the fore. It must be kept in mind that the production of labor itself is a process of reproduction. The output of the different grades of social labor consists of certain numbers of workers of various skills, while the input is likewise an input of labor powers of different qualitative kinds. Consider simple labor, for instance. The output of simple labor power is generated by a certain number of laborers regularly put into motion as productive labor. Within the processes in which simple labor power is itself generated by its producers, certain definite inputs are regularly required: of constant capitals that are the means of producing simple labor, for instance, schools, houses, hospitals; and of variable capitals, for example, the wage goods supporting the workers, who are themselves contributing to the production of the simple labor power, including simple labor itself. The simple principle to which we refer provides the main clue needed for the estimation of reduction coefficients and is stated by Marx in these terms: "The value of labor power is determined, as is the case of every other commodity, by the labor time necessary for the production, and consequently also the reproduction, of this special article."[12] The same principle applies to the value of any grade of labor. The value of a given quantity of this labor is to be estimated in terms of the labor time required to produce the material means of reproduction – the means of production and the wage goods – consumed in the production of any grade labor whatsoever. This is the solvent that dissolves difficulties standing in the way of empirical estimation of the magnitudes of reduction coefficients.

In line with the principle the estimation of the value of simple labor power is not difficult to devise. In making his estimate of V_U, the value of the simple labor grade alone, the accountant would need to gauge three things. First, he should gauge the total numbers of such workers annually required, say, for productive work in industry and agriculture. This is no more than an exercise in economic sociology for identifying and estimating the numbers functioning on the average within this division of technically minimal yet socially necessary skills. Second, the annual real-wage basket for reproducing this segment of the labor force would need to be identified and catalogued, taking into account both the means of production and the wage goods needed for the reproduction of this grade of labor. Finally, and with the aid of the foregoing information, an estimate could be made of the labor time required to reproduce this wage basket. This labor time, say, the man-years annually required for reproduction of this real-wage basket, is the direct estimate of the exchange value of this labor power. While one may see that such an estimate is not easily made, it evidently does not lie beyond the data gathering and processing capacities of modern estimators, as within the U.S. Bureau of Labor Statistics, for example.

These procedures, or perhaps less direct and more sophisticated procedures, would result only in an estimation of V_U in the equation $V = aV_S + V_U$. The estimate of the total value of labor power now requires an estimate of the a coefficient that will be used to multiply the raw man-hour data of V_S. Insofar as the latter is concerned, the raw data V_S is estimated in conformity with the same principle used in estimating V_U. The means of reproduction required for production of the given volume of skilled labor must be identified and an estimate made of the man-hours required for the annual reproduction of these means of production and wage goods. Now for reasons to be explained in more detail in the following chapter, this raw-data estimate of man-hours needed for reproduction of skilled labor may be decomposed into its simple labor power components, as Marx suggested, by taking the ratio of the raw labor times of V_S relative to V_U, provided that the raw-data estimate of V_S has been correctly made in the first place. The famous a coefficient, and all similar coefficients differentiating grades of skilled from simple labor, may be estimated by taking the raw-data ratios of which the ratio $V_S/V_U = a$ is but one example. What we shall see in the following chapter is, to put it briefly, that by using an input–output table of labor power flows we can make correct estimates of the raw-data ratios and, therefore, estimate the coefficients in the fashion suggested.

Supposing all this is feasible advice, its implementation would now provide the labor value account with an estimate of the value of total labor power in accordance with the formula $V = aV_S + V_U$ (the raw data V_S being multiplied by a, of course). There is still some way to go in estimating the values of commodities comprising the social product, because so far only V in the equation $W = C + V + S$ has been estimated. In estimating the other principal components of the labor value of the social product, we need not introduce any new principles. For both the C commodities and the S commodities, exchange values in man-hours, man-years, and so on, of simple, socially necessary labor time may be measured through analogous procedures to those outlined. The C goods, for instance, will have an exchange value whose raw-data labor time is given by the labor time required to be spent on the means of reproduction of the labor annually required to be spent in producing those C goods. That is, a certain volume of labor power (of different grades) will annually be needed to reproduce those C goods, and the value of the latter is measured in the raw *by the labor time required to reproduce the means of subsistence of the labor expended in* C *goods production*. It will be apparent that both V_S and V_U labor power is normally spent in the production of C goods, and given the raw-data man-hours annually expended in C goods production by each of these grades of socially necessary labor, we simply add together the value of simple labor power so expended (V_{UC}) to the value in units of simple labor time of skilled labor power so expended (aV_{SC}). Therefore, an estimate of the value of C goods, all in units of simple, socially necessary labor time, is arrived at. Supposing the surplus value to be composed of additional wage goods and additional means of production, the value of this surplus product may be estimated, once the physical volume of the surplus and its components are known, by direct comparison of the value of this volume of product with an identical volume of reproduced C goods and V goods, whose value estimation has already been discussed. Thus the aggregate value of the social product, $W = C + V + S$, has now been estimated by relatively simple procedures, and this value will be in units of simple, socially necessary labor time, the *numeraire* of the labor theory of value.

National-income measures and value categories

In the standard economics, as everyone knows, the value of the national product is estimated in terms of market prices at which commodities are sold; the value of the product is the monetary summation of what is annually produced (gross national product, or gnp). In the Marxian economics the common denominator of exchange values is not the market price but, as we have seen, the quantity of simple, socially necessary labor time required for reproduction. A brief comparison of these different accounting systems will help to strengthen our understanding of both of them.

Assuming a closed economy, measuring its social product in units of labor time, the value of the product is: $W = C + V + S$ in the Marxian formula. While the gross national product is valued as the aggregate of prices (i.e., prices times quantities) of the commodities composing it, under certain circumstances the monetary and real labor values would be directly comparable to each other. Were it the case, for instance, that market prices should all be proportional to the exchange or labor values of all individual commodities – that all commodities were to sell "at their values," as Marx expresses it – then the labor value and national income measures of value would be proportional to each other also. With prices at their values, for example, the total of wages and salaries (wage rates times quantities of labor employed annually) would give an estimate of V, the value of labor power in the Marxian formula. Similarly, if the money rate of depreciation of capital goods is proportional to the real rate of depreciation of these goods and if, also, the prices of raw materials, semifinished products, and so on, are at their values, then the sum of these will equal C. So money income measures could be used to estimate the values of C and V in the formula $C + V + S$. And what of S?

From the money value of the surplus product, when the product is sold at its value, all property income derives: rent interest, and industrial profit. The rate of interest governs the portion of the surplus value covering costs of reproducing financial and monetary services; it is the price of money capital. As will be seen in more detail when we examine the investment of social surplus in support of circulatory activity, the rate of interest is the means by which capitalists finance the replacement of constant and variable capitals together with their extension, and the means by which the profit of the finance capitalists is realized. The rate of interest is the price of money and credit, as economists put it, and is a price that covers the real value of capitals engaged in circulatory work plus the profits of financiers.

Rental income is also derived from the sale of the surplus prod-

uct. This portion of property income accrues to landowners by virtue of their monoply in landownership. Finally, there is industrial
profit, the profits of industrial capital, the residual from the sale of
the industrial product after payment of capitalists' costs of production. To summarize, when commodities sell at their values:

Exchange values	Money values
C	Depreciation of capital stock, cost of raw materials, etc.
V	Wages and salaries.
S	Profit or gross property income, breaking down into rent, interest, and industrial profit.
Gross value of product	Gross national product

Now if we subtract from the gross value of the social product the
C value, the value of all inanimate materials processed by labor
(machinery, raw materials, fabricated parts, and so on), the remainder, $V + S$, is the familiar national income of national-
income accounting: wages and salaries plus property incomes of
rent, interest, and profit.

These correspondences between Marxian and money values in
value accounting are more conceptual than actual. There are at
least two basic reasons why in the real world prices will in general
not be proportional to values and why, therefore, gnp data will not,
at least in unadjusted form, give estimates of labor values. First of
all, the law of unequal exchange works to cause deviations between
prices and values of particular commodities (see Chapters 6 and 7).
Secondly, the aggregate of money values may either be greater than
or less than the aggregate of real values, primarily because of the effects of unproductive consumption in causing aggregate price-value
deviations (compare with Chapter 8, especially the discussion of
stagflation). Finally, one should also mention the role of monopoly
power in occasioning particular price-value deviations. All of this
means that in using standard national income data as indices of real
values and changes in real values, the utmost caution is needed;
monetary statistics measure real values only when carefully processed, and ideally should be utilized for purposes of socialist
economic planning only when real-value data are unavailable and
otherwise as an adjunct to true-value data.[13]

Finally, it is important to remember that, whereas in the real
world prices and values are subject to forces of disproportionality,
and their relations may be disproportional over quite lengthy

periods of time, it is the flows of real values that are of basic importance; these are the flows that ultimately limit and control the pecuniary movements and their relations to each other. The money values of commodities move within definite limits set by their relations to the real-value flows from which they derive. This latter proposition is, it must be emphasized, one of the primary propositions of the present study whose truth we seek to demonstrate in a variety of contexts subsequently.

Let us return to labor value quantities, however. Our discussion of national-income measures has been pointed only to indicating the possibility of using them as surrogates for labor values in certain carefully defined contexts. The principal point of this chapter thus far has been, on the other hand, that labor value quantities are in principle *independently* estimable; we are not dependent upon monetary estimates for approximating their magnitudes – to the extent to which labor value accounting is a developed institution.

We conclude that there are no insurmountable obstacles to estimation of labor values embedded in commodities, including labor power itself, in the course of their production and reproduction. It is possible to estimate the multipliers or scalars, the coefficients that tell us by how many times a man-hour of a higher grade of labor power must be multiplied in order to reveal the simple labor power that the skilled laborer possesses. In practice, the obstacles to instituting a system of labor value accounting are many, and in order to surmount them in countries of the advanced capitalism some progress in the transition to socialism is first necessary. In the meantime, it is left to the ingenious theorist to compose for himself whatever data compilations and modifications he can in order to test the Marxian theory and in order to use it scientifically and politically. Not least of the obstacles to establishing a socialist system of value accounting is, therefore, a politically inspired resistance to the collection and processing of data relevant to the theory and to its use as an instrument of political economy. On route to establishing a socialist control over social economy, heavy going is to be expected at the scientific as at the political level.

The subject of the quantitative character of labor values, and of their scientific and social significance, is far too important to drop at this juncture. Not that definitive solutions to all problems can even be sketched in yet one further chapter on the subject; but in addition to looking into the possible use of input–output tables for estimating multiplier coefficients, we can advance in other ways the genetic claims of the labor theory as a scientific measure and a standard of value.

5

Value accounting, prices, and socialist planning

Input–output and value accounting

Under this formidable heading one might reasonably expect to find discussed some of the most abstract, complex, and at the same time purely scientific issues of economic science. If by purity is meant political purity, however, this is, quite frankly, not of our world. The Marxian economics avows its political impurity and seeks only to deal with it honestly, for instance, in determining whether or not exchange values measured in units of labor time can and should be used as guides to price planning. Evidently, this is a matter closely related to the old socialist ambition of eventually eliminating the market and its pecuniary categories of money and price, of merchandising and huckstering, from every department of social life.[1]

The project of an eventual eradication of the market and all its mechanisms has long been stoutly resisted by those opposing all administrative setting of prices, preferring instead the market system of free competition, and by those monopolists and their spokesmen who would themselves control prices with a view to reinforcing property claims in the furtherance of appropriate activities. So strong has the opposition been to socialist planning, in fact, that the very question of whether or not this planning can utilize effectively a system of labor value accounts has suffered from a lack of direct analysis, not to mention practical application. This is not surprising. While private property continues to be decisive, so, too, will all of its market categories, including its system of value accounting, and including, unfortunately, the economic theory of the pecuniary system as well.

But it is the socialist ambition that concerns us, and the scientific prerequisite to its realization, we have already seen, is that exchange values of different grades of socially necessary labor, along with the exchange values of all other commodities, be empirically estimable in other than price dimensions. They must be quantifiable in principle, if not always in practice, in units of simple, socially necessary labor time, through utilization of procedures placing no reliance whatsoever upon market prices as indices of value. As a result of this independence, whose realization requires the institution of a proper system of value accounting, the possibility is enhanced of doing away with market categories – supply, demand, price, money incomes, and all that – in the organization of economic and, hence, of social life. The possibility emerges of substituting for the market a planned allocation of real-value flows that will effectively realize social goals. Unquestionably more than value accounting is needed in order to accomplish a transition to a socialist economy,[2] and these comments on the possibility of the transition are not at all intended to exhaust this large and difficult subject. We stress only that the optimum balance of value flows that socialism requires, and that the progress of capitalism steadily undermines, can only be realized through a direct and informed knowledge of what the required flows are, what the given flows are, and what means of readjusting the latter will promote the former. This is where the need becomes apparent for a real-value calculus as an alternative to the pecuniary calculus that dominates the value data of contemporary capitalist economics.

Once more we are forced, therefore, to examine economic interrelations among inputs and outputs within the advanced economy, the relations referred to commonly as interindustry relations.[3] From the circumstance that at least some portion of the output of almost any given industry must be utilized as an input by other industries, an appreciation may be gleaned of the nature and extent of modern economic interdependence in production. In recent decades the study of interindustry flows has been promoted, not only within the planned economies of state socialism, but within those of state capitalism as well. Within the latter, too, the centralization of capitals has made possible and even necessary the development of planning mechanisms and aids and the institution of planning itself upon an ever-extending scale. Not that this is socialist planning – it is not, especially in that standards of value are utilized that have little bearing upon socialist planning. This is apparent in the use made by state capitalist planners of input–output systems. The tables utilized by these planners show either physical production interrelations – interindustrial flows of material quantities – or flows or money expenditures for interdependent inputs and outputs. In these dimensions input–output tables show the interlacings of product flows in a system in which each industry receives from virtually each other industry a portion of output that it utilizes in its own activity, an essential portion of its means of production or of the wage goods going to support its labor force. As a result of the pecuniary biases of input–output economics, the particular kind of economic interdependence that concerns us – the interdependency of labor power flows – has not had appreciable study. Nevertheless, this interdependence of labor powers in the course of their reproducing themselves may be brought into clear view with the aid of an input–output matrix properly constructed, and such a matrix, in turn, will lay the basis for the system of value accounting that will make feasible socialist price planning.

For the measurement of values in labor time units and, in particular, in the units of simple, socially necessary labor time that socialist planning requires, it is necessary to view in quantitative terms the system of economic interdependencies among the different grades of social labor power, however many of these grades there may be. That these grades of socially necessary labor are somehow intimately interdependent within the reproduction process the labor theory affirms most emphatically. It is the precise nature of this interdependence that the system of input–output interrelations helps us to see.

"Men make themselves," Marx was fond of asserting, and increasingly they do so through the medium of an extending network of exchange interrelations, and this principle applies to labor power itself. In Figure 5.1 a matrix of labor flow interdependencies is illustrated. Conforming with the usual matrix construction, this one shows on the horizontal rows the outputs of labor power of each grade, measured in units of labor time, being spent in servicing the reproduction requirements of each other grade of labor power. On the vertical columns one may read the inputs of each grade of labor power going into the production of a given grade of labor power. Assuming three grades of labor power, simple, semiskilled, and skilled (V_U, V_{SS}, V_S), we begin by explaining the meaning of the box entries, x_{11} . . . . . x_{33}.

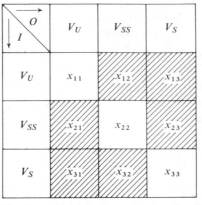

Figure 5.1. Input-output labor interrelations in the production of social labor (raw-labor time units). If we define $a = V_S/V_U$, then $a = \Sigma\, x_{13} + x_{23} + x_{33}/\Sigma\, x_{11} + x_{21} + x_{31}$; and if $b = V_{SS}/V_U$, then $b = x_{12} + x_{22} + x_{32}/\ x_{11} + x_{21} + x_{31}$, and so on. Thus, empirical estimates of the coefficients are easily made.

The entry x_{11} in the first row shows the value of simple labor power spent periodically by simple labor in its own reproduction, as may occur directly when an unskilled waitress serves lunch to a hungry workman; x_{12} is the value of simple labor spent periodically in the production of semiskilled labor, as when the window washer cleans the secretary's window; x_{13} is the value of the cleaning lady's services in cleaning the doctor's office. As these are labor times expended by simple labor, they indicate directly the exchange values of the quantities of labor expended. Now, reading a column by way of illustration, take the column V_U. We find that x_{31} is the labor time spent by skilled labor in contributing to the production of simple labor; x_{21}, the man-hours spent by semiskilled labor in the reproduction of simple labor power; and, again, x_{11}, the labor time spent by simple labor in servicing its own reproductive needs. It is evident, now that, *except for the entries of labor times spent by simple labor,* all entries of labor power flows are *raw* entries showing only labor times expended and *not* measuring directly the exchange values of the flows simply because they are raw and unreduced labor times obtained by direct observation of some data-gathering agency.

We illustrated the matrix with reference to flows of labor power spent directly by each grade of labor. According to the labor theory of value, the reproductive needs of social labor encompass not merely its own direct servicings but *all* of the means of production and wage goods that are necessary to its production and maintenance. That is, the production of any grade of labor power is mostly roundabout, consisting of production of the material means that labor requires for its reproduction. When we gather the data to be used for estimating exchange values, therefore, it does not suffice to estimate merely labor times spent directly by labor. The value of labor power, like that of any other commodity, is measured by the labor time required for the reproduction of this special article, or, *what is the same thing,* by the labor time required to produce the means of production *and* the means of consumption that are its material means of reproduction. This is the primary principle that needs scrupulous observance in compiling a raw-data labor flow matrix.

In estimating x_{11}, for instance, what is desired is the labor time spent annually by simple labor in producing its own means of production and of consumption; x_{13}, for instance, is the labor time spent by simple labor annually in producing means of production and means of consumption for the reproduction of skilled labor, and so on. Or, again, x_{21} is the labor time spent annually by semiskilled labor in producing means of reproduction (means of production and wage goods) required for the reproduction of simple labor power; x_{22} is the raw labor time spent by semiskilled labor in the production of its own material means of reproduction, and so on. The point is now clear. The construction of a matrix such as that of Figure 5.1 requires first of all an *identification* of the material means of reproduction peculiar to the production of each of the grades of labor power. Given the peculiar items comprising the reproductive wage basket of each grade of labor power, the raw-labor times spent periodically by each grade of labor power in producing each particular wage basket may be estimated by any competent data-gathering agency.

What the raw-data matrix will show when filled in, then, is the allocation of labor times periodically expended by each grade of labor in producing its *own* means of reproduction (which will appear on the main diagonal of the matrix) and in producing the means of reproduction of each other grade of social labor. A matrix so constructed will then reveal in raw-data terms (with the exception of the simple labor power entries) the relative magnitudes of the different labor time flows and their distribution within the structure of social labor as a whole. The significance of this distribution is considerable, as we shall see.

Value flows in the matrix of social labor

The labor times expended by grades of labor higher than simple labor are not indicative of the values of the labor powers concerned. Nevertheless, the raw-data matrix provides the means of estimating whatever reduction coefficients may be needed for the conversion of raw-data units into simple socially necessary labor times; while the matrix entries are not in reduced units, the matrix provides the means of making the required reductions. The principle permitting us to see how the raw matrix is to be utilized for this purpose is the one previously alluded to: "The value of labour power is determined, as is the case of every other commodity, by the labour time necessary for the production, and consequently also the reproduction, of this special article."[4] It is a matter of determining the relative *cost* differential of the man-hour of high-grade labor relative to the standard man-hour of the simple labor. The matrix permits an estimation of this multiple by the following technique.

Take, for example, the a coefficient, defined as the number of times the man-hour of skilled labor exceeds in value the value measured by the cost of that labor power – the value of the man-hour of simple labor: $a \equiv V_S/V_U$.[5] Now in the terms of the matrix entries, e.g., those of Figure 5.1, the ratio $a \equiv x_{13} + x_{23} + x_{33}/x_{11} + x_{21} + x_{31}$. By dividing the algebraic sum of the labor times of column 3 by those of column 1 we obtain the estimate needed. Similarly, if we define $b \equiv V_{SS}/V_U$, the relative cost of the man-hour of semiskilled to the man-hour of simple labor, our estimate of the coefficient $b \equiv x_{12} + x_{22} + x_{32}/x_{11} + x_{21} + x_{31}$ is likewise easily obtained. These are, in this particular case of three grades of social labor, the coefficients required for converting all of the raw-labor time data of Figure 5.1 into units of simple, socially necessary labor time. The coefficients are the multiples by which the raw-data entries for semiskilled and for skilled labor must be multiplied in order to reduce raw- into simple-labor time units. Of course direct observation of row 1 entries are already in units of simple, socially necessary labor time. The conversion into reduced, simple units of the data remaining in rows 2 and 3 is illustrated in Figure 5.2, in which the b and a coefficients are used to convert the raw observations into homogeneous, simple units. In this way, techniques of empirical estimation may bring into statistical view the underlying reality that so many have failed to comprehend, and will no doubt continue to fail to comprehend no matter what empirical technique

$\begin{smallmatrix} O \\ I \end{smallmatrix}$	V_U	V_{SS}	V_S
V_U	x_{11}	x_{12}	x_{13}
V_{SS}	bx_{21}	bx_{22}	bx_{23}
V_S	ax_{31}	ax_{32}	ax_{33}

$$V = V_U + V_{SS} + V_S$$
$$V_U = x_{11} + bx_{21} + ax_{31}$$
$$V_{SS} = x_{12} + bx_{22} + ax_{32}$$
$$V_S = x_{13} + bx_{23} + ax_{33}$$

Figure 5.2. The converted matrix of labor value flows (units of simple, socially necessary labor time). With the aid of the raw data of the matrix of Figure 5.1, suitably processed, it is possible to construct an empirical portrait of the historical labor flows of a given period, all flows measured in units of simple, socially necessary labor time and, therefore, indicative of exchange value magnitudes as postulated by the labor theory of value. Since it is possible to observe directly the exchange values of simple, socially necessary labor power (row 1 of Figures 5.1 and 5.2 are the same), it is only a matter of multiplying the raw-labor times of rows 2 and 3 by the coefficients that reduce the man-hour of complex labor to the man-hour of simple labor, the man-hour of the former being so much greater than that of the latter. The ratio of the costs of reproduction of the high grade to the simple labor, as explained in connection with Figure 5.1, provides estimates of the coefficients *a* and *b* as defined. These are then used as multipliers to convert the raw data as compiled by statistical agencies.

puts before them. We refer to the indubitable engine of labor energy expenditures that, since men left behind them the foraging stage of their transitions, has been the principal vehicle of their sustenance and of all their advance. The underlying reality of contemporary reproduction is exposed by empirical estimation, which merely puts into usable, scientific form the substance postulated by the labor theory of value. This estimation justifies at this level, incidentally, the underlying assumption of *Capital I:* "For simplicity's sake we shall henceforth account every kind of labour to be unskilled, simple labour; by this we do no more than save ourselves the trouble of making the reduction."[6] A somewhat further scrutiny of labor flow matrices will help to drive home their significance.

Without attempting to test with actual data any appreciable number of provocative generatlizations, we can make some generalizations that seem relatively safe and obvious. In regard to the distribution of actual labor value flows within the advanced capitalism today, for instance, a converted matrix, if available, would show no doubt that the great bulk of simple, socially necessary labor values expended in the reproduction of labor power fall to the lower right (southeast) about the main diagonal of the matrix. Moving to the northwest along the diagonal, we would observe the opposite tendency. The concentration to the southeast quadrant of the matrix reflects the heavy emphasis of the advanced capitalism upon the reproduction of the more costly, high-powered grades of social labor. These are the grades technically required for producing and implementing the advanced technique; they include also, as we shall see in analyzing later on the economic character of the expanded white-collar population, those grades of labor required by capitalism for circulating or for managing the circulation of the social product. In sum, the precipitation of simple labor power to the southeast along the main diagonal reflects the technical and circulatory needs of the mode of production. Conversely, the lighter distribution of simple labor values to the northwest in the matrix shows the corresponding de-emphasis on the reproduction of simple labor power in its rudimentary forms.

The current distribution of simple labor power described is, of course, the outcome of a process of capital accumulation that extends far into the past. If we had annual data of the type shown in Figure 5.2 extending back over a century or more, then we would be able to observe statistically the shift in values of simple labor power from northwest to southeast along the main diagonal. This is the shift in the value composition of the labor force that underlies the shift in occupational structure of the labor force as shown in Table 5.1, which reveals the general drift toward relative enlargement of white-collar relative to blue-collar workers in the total, a shift in the composition of the working population whose economic significance we shall explain in connection with the analysis of the class structure of advanced capitalism. For the moment, suffice it to say that the movement of the center of gravity to the southeast on the main diagonal is not necessarily indicative of capitalism's uninhibited tendency to development of the forces of productive labor. As suggested before, the multiplication of more expensive divisions of social labor, and the relative growth in the numbers of workers within them, does not confirm a relative growth of productive relative to unproductive labor and it *may* even signify the con-

Table 5.1. *Changing occupational composition of the U.S. labor force (in percent)*

Occupational group	1910	1920	1930	1940	1950	1960	1967[a]	1975[a,b]
Managers, officials, and proprietors (except farm)	6.6	6.6	7.4	7.3	8.8	8.5	10.1	10.4
White-collar workers	14.7	18.3	22.0	23.8	27.7	33.8	36.0	38.1
Professional and technical	4.7	5.4	6.8	7.5	8.5	11.4	13.3	14.8
Clerical	5.3	8.0	8.9	9.6	12.3	15.0	16.6	16.9
Sales	4.7	4.9	6.3	6.7	6.9	7.4	6.1	6.4
Blue-collar workers	38.2	40.2	39.6	39.8	41.2	39.5	36.7	34.0
Craftsmen and foremen	11.6	13.0	12.8	12.0	14.5	14.3	13.2	13.0
Semi-skilled	14.6	15.6	15.8	18.4	20.9	19.7	18.7	16.9
Unskilled	12.0	11.6	11.0	9.4	6.8	5.5	4.8	4.1
Service workers	9.6	7.8	9.8	11.8	10.3	11.7	12.5	13.8
Private household (e.g., maids)	5.0	3.3	4.1	4.7	2.5	2.8	2.4	
Other service	4.6	4.5	5.7	7.1	7.8	8.9	10.1	
Agricultural workers	30.9	27.0	21.2	17.4	11.8	6.3	4.7	3.6
Farmers and farm managers	16.5	15.3	12.4	10.4	7.5	3.9	2.6	
Farm laborers	14.4	11.7	8.8	7.0	4.3	2.4	2.1	
Total[c]	100.0	100.0	100.0	100.0	100.0	100.0	100.0	100.0

[a]Data for 1967 and 1975 refer to employed persons only.
[b]Projected figures.
[c]Individual items are rounded independently and therefore may not add up to totals.

Sources: Michael Reich, "The Evolution of the United States Labor Force," in Edwards, Reich, and Weiskopf, *The Capitalist System*, Englewood Cliffs, N.J.: Prentice-Hall, 1972, p. 178, Table 4-I. Data for 1910–1940 from U.S. Dept. of Commerce, Bureau of the Census, *Historical Statistics of the United States, Colonial Times to 1957*, Table D 72–122; data for 1950–1960 from U.S. Dept. of Commerce, Bureau of the Census, *U.S. Census of Population, 1960*, Table 201; data for 1967 and 1975 from U.S. Dept. of Labor, *Manpower Report of the President, 1968*, Tables A-9 and E-8.

trary, a growth of unproductive relative to productive labor. What, indeed, the movement does signify can only be determined by an extension of this analysis of labor values into an analysis of the developing class composition of the population, an extension that cannot be undertaken at this juncture. Whether the shift in values of simple labor power, whether the growth in their absolute magnitude, indicates a development or a fettering of the productive forces of social labor remains to be determined by precise empirical measurement as well as by more general evidences of tendencies of the advanced capitalism. But the progressive allocation of labor energies into the extended reproduction of the advanced forms of labor power makes ever more imperative an objective assessment of the functions performed by these advanced forms, of the utilities and disutilities generated by the energies expended. Until we can take up this subject at some length, we shall remain with the question of the feasibility of value accounting.

Once more let us recall that in the estimation of exchange values of graded powers of labor the groundwork is laid for the estimation of all of those exchange values of commodities composed of labor power inputs whether of congealed or of living labor. It is virtually certain, however, that in estimating values of congealed labor in the forms of means of production, raw materials, and so on, the accountant will encounter special obstacles to measurement that will force him to utilize much of the experience long garnered in gathering and processing data of relevance to conventional economics. Without attempting to foresee these difficulties, their resolution must be effected while keeping in view the general principle used in estimating the value of living labor power: The value of the commodity may be decomposed into the value of the labor power spent in its production, and the latter, in turn, into the simple labor time cost of its reproductive maintenance. With reduction coefficients in hand the commodity value can be gauged no matter how many grades of labor are expended in its reproduction. Finally, the accountant must recall that all exchange value unproductively expended is to be counted as a deduction from the social product in the estimating of its net value. This does not affect the estimation procedures for gathering the information needed but, rather, their ultimate utilization.

We conclude that there is no theoretical reason why the labor theory of value cannot be given a direct, statistical implementation, whether for the scientific testing of the theory in econometric undertakings or for providing an empirical basis for political implementations, as will be specified in discussing problems of the transition to socialist economy.[7] The devising of estimation procedures should pose no greater difficulties than are presently involved in national income estimations, in construction of price indexes and other economic indicators. At this procedural level the system of labor value accounting is as feasible as any other; but it is the potential superiority of the system for purposes of social control that remains to be argued.

Labor value accounts in history and theory

The social significance of labor value accounting is, perhaps, no more self-evident than its empirical feasibility. Even within the so-called communist countries, accounting rests for the most part upon other than labor value premises, and pecuniary and physical quantities dominate their social bookkeeping. Nor should this observation be taken as a call for eradication of these alternative and supplementary systems of measurement and account. Only insofar as the market has become a socially redundant instrument of economic organization can its statistical categories be safely dispensed with.[8] On the other hand, as the socialist advance succeeds in raising the level of development of the productive forces, and especially in raising the level of administrative technique that obviates the need for the market, the need for an extended system of labor value accounting proceeds apace: ". . . after the abolition of the capitalist mode of production, but still retaining social production, the determination of value continues to prevail in the sense that the regulation of labor time, and the distribution of social labor among the various production groups, ultimately the bookkeeping encompassing all this, becomes more essential than ever."[9] Quite clearly, if there is a recession of market categories, and hence of the forces of supply and demand that make money prices and incomes so important and useful as economic indicators, another system of bookkeeping is needed. Let no one suppose that in such a situation the ascendancy of labor value accounting would be an historically unprecedented event. Accounting systems far less sophisticated from a theoretical standpoint than the one whose feasibility we have discussed, but resting upon the regulation of labor time all the same, have already sufficed for social purposes, and, above all, for the purpose of maintaining just and proper economic relations within the community.

In a medieval Japanese village, for example,

the principle of exchange is people and days. Thus, if a household A has two people at work on household B's field for two days, household B is expected to provide its equivalent on A's fields – this may be three people one day and one person another day or any other combination to equal two people working two days. . . .

When four or five families work together in one *kattari* group, the figuring is on the same basis. This requires a book to check days and workers.[10]

Here we find even the account book in which entries are reckoned in labor time. Such devices are by no means peculiar to the Orient, although they do not always function in such an obvious manner. In Europe of the Middle Ages (as in connection with the corvée), among the American Incas, in ancient Egypt, among many African tribes, and elsewhere, more or less articulate systems of labor value accounting, more or less visible customs presupposing the importance of labor time balances in exchange, appear as central features of social organization. In addition to formalized accounting practice seen in many instances, however, customary practice often reflects a social recognition of the importance of a reciprocal exchange of labor services. Among the iron workers of Dahomey, a smith will accumulate the scrap iron he requires and keep it until it is time for his fellow smiths to convene in order to work it into hoes and other tools. The smiths then proceed to work up each man's collection of iron.[11] Or, again, social customs may reflect the overall need to stabilize the flow of labor power inputs, and intertribal relations may allow for the importing and exporting of manpower in order to ensure a stabilization of economic reproduction.[12] The testimonials of history and of economic anthropology to such institutionalization of labor powers are numerous, and in all likelihood more pervasive and characteristic of social organization than is yet acknowledged. There is no doubt ample precedent for labor value accounting in historical annals and even in current practice within noncapitalist modes of production.

From early days of theoretical reflection on such phenomena, reason for social practice of the type referred to has been evident to discerning students. Scientific efforts to understand the real basis of social interrelations, and to put the principle of exchange reciprocity upon a sound practical footing, extend back at least to Aristotle and his *Nichomachean Ethics*.[13] With acumen and skill the great philosopher subjected the exchange of work to an analytical eye. He sought, apparently, a general answer to the question, what ratio of work being exchanged by different kinds of productive labor is best calculated to hold the workers together in society by ensuring an equitable and necessary satisfaction of their respective needs? Whatever this ratio might be – and it does exist – there is a need to determine it. It must not only be specified but honored in practice, for "Justice is the bond of men in states." Not the least remarkable feature of his analysis lay in this perception of the possibility of putting economic justice into a scientifically and politically tenable formula.

Thus Aristotle argued that when work is being exchanged among workers or among divisions of labor of the same grade, as between his prototypical builder, on the one side, and his shoemaker, on the other, the general rule is that equal work must flow between the parties to the exchange. In modern phraseology, equal-exchange values are the rule under the circumstance that the parties are qualitatively similar workers, that is, qualitatively of the same grade of labor. He saw also something of the greatest practical and scientific importance, that an exchange of work between equals was *not* the typical case of exchange. As Aristotle puts it, "there is nothing to prevent the work of the one being better than that of the other. . . ."[14] Within this more general situation he did not succeed in providing the formula expressing the equalization of unequal work, the formula of what he called proportionate requital or, simply, reciprocity. But he saw unmistakably the importance of having a formula, and he believed in the possibility of its formulation. He believed, in other words, in the possibility of equating the work of men qualitatively different in the exercise of their skills. This conception of the problem of equilibrating social interrelations through economic and scientific means we now recognize, on the basis of our discussion of the labor theory of value, as virtually identical with Marx's own conception. Marx's proposal that all grades of labor be reduced to units of simple, socially necessary labor fits in precisely with what Aristotle, too, saw to be a precondition to the establishing of equitable and just exchanges. There is also a certain family resemblance in the way in which these theorists would utilize the exchange formula, once derived. Aristotle, for example, speaks of the set price that conforms to the reciprocity formula, a price administratively fixed, perhaps.

Without surveying the slow development of the labor theory of value, suffice it to say that with the rise of modern capitalism there is a resurgence of concern that the new prices of the price-making markets should be just and equitable prices. Aquinas' analysis in the *Summa Theologica* very much reflects this concern. By the late eighteenth century the opinion had become widespread that the markets of free competition tend to yield these natural prices, and with Adam Smith's *Wealth of Nations* there came a demonstration that, on the average and in the long run, the forces of free competition would push prices to their natural and, by implication, just levels. With Ricardo, the proposition that prices tend to proportionality with exchange values, the latter measured by the labor embedded in commodities in the course of their production, received a relatively precise expression.[15] This, in turn, was taken as conclusive scientific demonstration that competition tends to yield the best of all possible worlds. Subsequently referred to, especially by Marxists, as the law of value, this proposition of the classical liberal economists that prices tend to be proportional to values may be given a precise form within the Marxian theoretical economics. Where W is the exchange value of a commodity, and P is the market price (in the sense of money expenditure for the commodity), and with the subscripts $(1 \ldots n)$ numbering the different commodities being exchanged, the law of value reads:

$$P_1/W_1 = P_2/W_2 = \ldots P_n/W_n \qquad (5.1)$$

This is the proportionality of prices to exchange values that, the classical liberals thought, would tend automatically to come about through the working of the simple and natural system of liberty of Smith. In this formula there is a balanced reciprocity in exchanges between sellers and buyers, and the market thus appears as the primary agency for realizing the age-old dream of social justice for each and all engaging in economic exchanges.

And yet, among the value theorists prior to Marx it was Ricardo himself who was most troubled by the thought that the market system might not work precisely in the manner forecast. He was inclined to remember what others, and as usual his followers, were inclined to forget, that there are qualitatively different grades of labor employed within production processes and they are employed in quite different proportions in relation to the inanimate means of production with which they work, the tools, machines, and raw materials with which they combine in productive activity. With variations in what Marx termed the "organic composition of capital" from one work process to another, and with qualitatively different labor powers engaged within those processes in consequence of the varying techniques utilized, will the pricing mechanism of competitive capitalism succeed in equalizing in a just and equitable fashion the qualitatively different work being exchanged? We are back again at Aristotle's problem of the proportionate requital in a system in which men are *not* equal. Ricardo seems to have doubted that the same law of value (5.1) would hold under the condition that work is unequal, that organic compositions of capital and, therefore, the grades of labor utilized, are unequal.[16] Ricardo's famous pessimism in regard to the functioning of competitive capitalism may in part have been the consequence of his awareness that, if the law of value is not a general solution to the problem of equity in exchange, the whole question of the virtues of capitalism as a mode of production is thrown wide open once more.

The liberal faith in the beneficence of competition was tied very closely to the contention that competition would, at least in the long run, yield an optimum set of prices. It was precisely at this contention of the liberal economics, however, that Marx, perceiving the essential weakness of the argument, sought to direct his attack. For one thing, even if one assumed the law of value to be operative under capitalism, granting for the sake of argument that prices would tend to be proportional to exchange values over the long term, still it might be possible to show that the accumulation of capital would yield recurring economic crises, crises whose causes were operative despite, or even because of, the functioning of the law of value. This is the strategy of *Capital I*, it will be recalled, where on the assumption that the law of value holds, and with capital accumulation and technical change proceeding, the general rate of profit tends to decline as the average organic composition of capital rises. This strangles the drive to accumulate. Further, the changing composition of the population seems to point toward a gradual attenuation of class struggle (the general law of capitalist accumulation).

For another thing, there is the possibility to be considered that, technical progress continuing and with it a developing variety of grades of socially necessary labor, the law of value may not hold even under more or less competitive conditions. This is the realization that informed so much of the argument of *Capital III*, as we shall see in detail in the next chapters. The thrust of the argument we need not wait to describe, however. Marx saw that the law of value could not prevail in anything like its simple form (5.1) because, under conditions of technical change, differing organic compositions would emerge among different lines of production. Ricardo's suspicion is verified and justified by Marx, who shows that the long-run market prices (his famous prices of production) will not tend to be proportionate to exchange values but will deviate from exchange values in a definite and highly significant manner.[17]

The implication of Marx's analysis of unequal labor is, in brief, that the long-run tendency of competitive capitalism is to disequilibrium between prices and values and that this disequilibrium contributes in its own way to undermining the mode of production itself. Marx's solution of Aristotle's problem of unequal labor confirms Ricardo's concern for the future of capitalism. The relations of price to value that define a system of equitable reciprocity cannot in the long run prevail within the market economy, and, indeed, Marx's analysis may be said to confirm Aristotle's own conviction that a system geared to money making is destined to disintegrate: "For it is by proportionate requital that the city holds together."[18] This entire issue is of such consequence for the analysis of capitalist development that it must have more extended treatment than we can give it immediately. We leave it, therefore, for just a moment.

Price, value, and the economist

Enough of the labor theory of value has now been described and explicated that the crucial character of the theory itself must be evident. We begin to see that it offers avenues to establishing still more securely the empirical bases of the Marxian economics, and it does so in those terms of *value* that must be an integral part of any scientific enterprise worthy of the name. In other words, the theory defines a standard as well as a measure of value and thereby opens the way to an objective evaluation of economic and social processes and of the roles played by group and class participants within those processes. In view of the empirical and political potentialities of the theory, its abandonment by mainstream economists of this and of past century is either wholly incomprehensible or wholly comprehensible; incomprehensible, in their abandonment of the potentialities referred to; comprehensible, in their flight from the responsibilities, scientific and political, that the theory might impose upon those who understand it.

The political circumstances of recent decades, including the revolutions that have wracked the underdeveloped world, have fostered as their byproduct the rise of schools of Marxian economics. They have forced and are continuing to force a tardy recognition of the Marxian economics throughout the whole of the

globe. Yet the great hiatus of interest in the labor theory of value and in all of its implications, so many of which still await scientific elaboration, remains something of a mystery. In neither the conventional nor the Marxian economics are all practitioners either fools or scoundrels as they sometimes charge each other with being. There is something to be explained here.

There are doubtless many sociological and political reasons for the reputed collapse of the labor theory, a fall that is no more than a preliminary to its present rise, in fact. The explanation most often given by Marxists is that the triumph of capitalism ground out of the general ideological universe those strains of thought inimical to the interest of the dominant bourgeoisie. There is a very great deal to be said for this thesis that does *not* imply a craven servility on the part of the bourgeois economist, but only the latter's underestimate of the ideological distortions and repressions accompanying the evolution of the mode of production, an underestimate of the variety and strength and subtlety of those forces contained within the circulatory superstructure. When, in fact, we come to discussing the class structure of contemporary society, we shall see the extraordinary way in which the school economics of today reflects the ruling class interest in new forms of labor power useful for its purposes. One reason often given in explaining the collapse of the labor theory and the rise of utility theories in the past century will not do at all, however. This is the claim that the labor theory is not the great engine of analysis that the orthodox theory has always posed as being; attached to this assertion, typically, is the minor bill that the Marxian economics tends to metaphysics,[19] a bill that has been drawn up with the help of the vulgar Marxists as often as not.

In reviewing the reproduction schemes and suggesting the range of their historical applicability both as explanation and as tools of investigation, in reviewing also the labor theory of value in its empirical and heuristic aspects, we have intended to reveal the vacuity of old criticisms of the Marxian economics. What is to be explained is not the collapse of the labor theory of value but the collapse of those whose scientific responsibilities might have led them to develop that great underdeveloped country of theoretical Marxism were it not for the intrusion of other business. The rejection of the Marxian economics by Western economists cannot be explained through the scientific aridity of Marxian premises but through the economic and sociological situation of the economists themselves in

relation to the functioning of a mode of production that they insist on viewing as the immutable portion of an otherwise evolving universe.

There is doubtless truth in the observation of John Maurice Clark that Marx's pungent commentaries offended Victorian sensibilities; Marx's comparison of vacillating conceptions of value with Dame Quickly's not knowing "where to have it" was hardly reassuring. But in any event, what incentive did the post-Marx generation have for pursuing his uncomfortable ideas? And without the insights into historical processes offered by the labor theory, how could they have foreseen the developing chaos of the twentieth century? How could they have foreseen the obsolescence of their theories or the renaissance of the labor theory that has come with the revival and resurgence of the Third World? How could they see, either, that China, a mere bone of contention among imperialist nations, would one day shrug off her oppressors and, at a critical juncture, fall back upon systems of labor value accounting reminiscent of ancient practice yet effective in their modern application?

None of this is to say what cannot in truth be said, that in socialist countries economic planning generally proceeds upon the basis of labor value accounts and an articulate Marxian economics to organize the accumulation of capital so as gradually but steadily to weed out the market and its categories. But the opposite cannot be said truthfully either, that the science has made no contributions to the proceedings. Robinson reminds us of a most important instance: "But Marxism can claim the credit for saving the planners from believing in academic economics. Imagine the present state of Russian industry if they had regarded their tasks as the 'allocation of given resources between alternative uses' instead of 'the ripening of the productive powers of social labor' by investment, exploitation and education."[20] At the same time, some considerable progress is seen in both the East and the West in the direction of planning by labor value criteria.[21] This is seen in action in the instituted practices of the Chinese communes and in the planning of labor power allocations in postrevolutionary contexts. It is evidenced also by the growing number of theorists who are aware of the scientific and political potentials implicit within the labor theory in its Marxian formulation.

Thus far the scientific utility of the theory has been stressed again and again. The theory is useful for the construction of laws actually

reflected within historical processes and for perceiving the countertendencies to which the operation of those laws gives rise. It informs the data-gathering and processing activities of science and promises guidance on an empirical basis to planning the development of the productive forces. Contrary to the view of the labor theory as a device for propaganda and exhortation exclusively, a view held by some Marxists and by the many non-Marxists who see only its political function, is the view of the theory as a self-contained apparatus for social planning.

With the empirical bases of the theory established, we can now launch upon the work set aside for a consideration of value theory, the work of explaining directly capitalist development. With a measure and a standard of value in hand, the pricing system of the so-called competitive capitalism can be realistically appraised, its real role in capitalist development can be objectively determined, especially with respect to what economists are fond of referring to as the allocation of resources. The Marxian theory does offer an explanation of that allocation, and of the role of prices in effecting it; but this explanation is not of some ideal and equilibrium distribution of scarce means among alternative uses, but of actual patterns of deployment of labor power and of means of production as historical observation reveals them to have been, together with an evaluation of those deployments through an application of the labor value standard.

6

The transformation of values into prices of production

What is an explanation of prices?

One of the half-truths one hears of the Marxian economics is that it offers no explanation of prices. Even when the critic grants that the theory of capital accumulation is interesting and perhaps important, he asks hastily the question, "But what of prices?" Typically, the query is rhetorical. He stands ready and eager to cast his own theoretical pearls before the Marxian swine.

This charge against the economics rests upon a number of misconceptions. One of these is that modern pricing theory is the private property of the standard economics. But Marxists, too, have contributed to its creation and have found its theories useful for certain purposes. Marx himself utilized theories of supply and demand whenever he found it necessary to do so, and here and in successive chapters we shall do likewise without hesitation whenever the facts require that we do so. A more important misconception of the critics is that no *historical* explanation of prices can be scientific. The point here is that, unlike standard theory, the Marxian theory does not seek to explain prices alone but seeks their explanation in relation to exchange values and use values – all within the historical context. It seeks to explain the development of price-value relations in the real world, especially as they unravel with the rise of capitalism out of feudal society and as they subsequently evolve into those relations peculiar of the present state of affairs.

Always, however, the theory underscores the existence of a world of labor values more fundamental than, but related to, the world of pecuniary values. The interrelations between these spheres are not only complex but of the very greatest social significance. While the

131

economics of textbooks thus features a static and one-dimensional
theory of price – a theory whose premises, to be sure, reflect in some
degree the actual structures of existing markets – the Marxian
economics probes into the interrelations of price with other, fundamental phenomena. As an introduction to the latter theory, a
few words of contrast with the standard tradition will help to throw
into perspective what is scientifically as well as politically involved.

Probably the most famous theory of price within the standard
repertory is the general equilibrium theory of the neoclassical
school, a school that claims as its forebears the classical liberal
economists of the eighteenth and early nineteenth centuries.[1] The
equilibrium theorist traces his antecedents to the French
physiocrats and their *laissez faire, laissez passer;* to Smith in
England and to Ricardo (especially the latter's nonsocialist
followers). The theory was rendered mathematically by Leon
Walras in the 1870s, and in detailed linguistic form by Alfred
Marshall during the Edwardian period. It remains to this day a
primary scientific exhibit of school economics.

In general, the theory asserts that under conditions of perfect
competition the price-making markets of capitalism will yield in the
long run a set of prices of commodities that balances or equilibrates
in some presumably optimal fashion the supplies and demands for
each and every commodity in production and in consumption.
Given the varied preferences of the consumers of the final bill of
goods, given a certain technique, a certain mobility in occupational
and geographic dimensions of the factors of production (land,
labor, and capital), market forces of supply and demand will in the
long run allocate available social resources in such a way as to
reflect both the relative intensities of consumer demands for final
products, on the one hand, and, on the other, their relative costs of
production. It is commonly alleged that this balancing of utilities
against costs is carried out by the market through establishing a
system of competitive prices that will maximize the former or
minimize the latter. The long-run equilibrium thus entails an optimum allocation of resources or would yield this result given that
the forces of competition had sufficient time to work themselves
out.

This theory rests upon a mélange of assumptions, some dubious
and insubstantial, some reasonably sound and valid. Those of the
dubious category have sometimes been modified and incorporated
into theories of imperfect or monopolistic competition, theories

rather more in correspondence with market realities. From the Marxian standpoint, what is interesting about the general equilibrium theory is its postulation of a general system of interdependent and competitive interrelations within the capitalist order. Although reality does not at all function the way that the theory says that it should, it does function, and this poses the question of why it functions the way that it does. A good way to begin with the issue, then, is to consider precisely those assumptions that are substantial and to combine them with others that are equally so. And with at least two assumptions of the general equilibrium theory one could hardly quarrel: (1) that entrepreneurs seek to maximize profits and (2) that there is a tendency, a result of competitive forces, for rates of return upon invested capitals to move to equality among all lines and branches of production in the long run. These propositions are plausible, and it is only their peculiar combination with historically invalid propositions that leads to the irrelevant conclusion of a general equilibrium of optimal prices.

Indeed, the assumption that there is a tendency for rates of profit to equalize among various lines and branches of a competitive economy figures quite prominently in the Marxian theory of price-value relations. From this premise, in combination with some others equally substantial, Marx, however, drew conclusions quite at variance with the famous tendency to general equilibrium. What conclusions one must accept depends upon what premises one must take as bases for one's reasoning.

The extraordinary way in which the tendency for profits to be equalized works within the theory of general equilibrium is as follows. Assume a free entry and egress of capitals among all branches of production: no monopolistic or state interventions either to block or assist the entrepreneur in his quest for maximum profits. Should the rate of profit on money capitals invested in one sector be higher than in another, there would then follow a movement of capitals from the sector of lower to the sector of higher return. This withdrawal from one quarter and reinvestment in another would lead to an increase in supplies of commodities in sectors where rates of return were higher, and reductions in supplies in sectors where rates of return were lower. The former increase drives down the market price, pushing down formerly high rates of return; the latter raises the market price and raises formerly low rates of return. These movements everywhere continue until rates of return are equalized among all lines of production, whereby the incentive for further movement is destroyed and equilibrium ensues. With rates of return equalized, the new allocation of resources will reflect the new supply-and-demand conditions.

From this premise of a tendency to equalization of rates of profit, one may come to quite different conclusions, however. By combining it with other premises, one must interpret its mode of operation somewhat differently. There is no real need to prejudice historical inquiry with the loaded language of "freedom of entry and egress," for example.[2] The actualities of competitive history remind us that the tendency for rates of profit to equalize may involve entries and egresses that are effected by fraud or chicanery; by political connivance, coercion, or, even, amicable if conspiratorial agreements of one kind or another; and by force and violence in the limit. The choice of premises must be governed by reason and knowledge of what is what. The fact is that, in actuality, the devices by means of which entrepreneurs work for their cut of profits are as numerous as the looters themselves. Furthermore, the preferred instruments and devices of profit equalization may change from one period to another according to circumstances – according to what technique brings to hand and to what the public will, or may be forced, to bear.[3] The exploration of economic and social history demands that we not prejudice our viewpoint with preconceptions concerning either the actual or the ideal modes of competition. There is little doubt that in some sense of the term "competition" tends to equalize rates of profit; but it does not follow from this if one selects premises with due respect for history that a tendency to general equilibrium is the result. What tendency or tendencies can we legitimately infer? Whatever answers may be given to this question, it is certain that our explorations must be governed by assumptions that have a historical justification. But in bringing into view Marx's answers to this question, some little further theoretical comparison will be helpful.

The equalization tendency and terms of exchange[4]

Smith and Ricardo, the greatest of the classical liberal theorists prior to Marx, both contemplated the possibility that in the long run prices would gravitate toward their natural or normal levels. The natural level itself was thought to be governed by the quantity of labor embedded in commodities in the course of their production. Further, it was supposed that the movement of prices toward coincidence with exchange values, themselves controlled by embedded labor, would be brought about through the equalization of rates of profit or, more precisely, through movements of market prices that would have this effect. They suppose, in other words, a law of value to be operative within the market economy, a law akin to the law of gravity, defining the levels toward which the price of each and every commodity would move. The movement of prices to their natural level would be socially beneficial. The grand design of prices would be fair and just because of the proportionality of prices to values that were themselves socially significant, above all the values of men's labors. The exchange of commodities, including their labors and the product of their labor, would in the long run take place upon terms that would do justice to all. In this embryonic form the classical liberals before Marx were predicting a tendency to general equilibrium, albeit sometimes, as with Ricardo, with some misgivings.

If we now put this proposition of a movement toward equilibrium in the terms of the labor theory of value, we can devise a bit finer specification of the entire theory. Let us suppose a three-sector economy in which competition has done its work. Prices have been set by competition so as to equalize rates of profit within and among all branches of production. Let us also suppose rates of surplus value to be the same within each department of production, and each department is at a similar level of technical development: Value compositions of capital are everywhere the same (not an unreasonable assumption, as long as all branches of production are relatively undeveloped and value compositions are low everywhere). This system of production is, moreover, an interdependent one; firms in each branch export some portion of their outputs to firms in other lines of production, retaining, perhaps, some portion of what they produce for their own internal consumption. Under these conditions the classical result will obtain. The long-run profit-equalizing price of each commodity is proportioned to the exchange value of each commodity, that is, to its natural value, where the latter is measured by the labor embedded in the commodity in the course of its production (in units of simple, socially necessary labor time, of course).

Table 6.1 shows the possibility. Assume at the outset that the price of the input is proportioned to its exchange value (column 7). The social average rate of profit, or the general rate, is 45 percent,

Table 6.1. *The equalization of rates of profit and of terms of exchange by equilibrating prices*

Dept.	Inputs $(C+V)$ (1)	S/V (2)	Outputs $(W=C+V+S)$ (3)	P' (4)	P (5)	$\dfrac{P_i}{W_i}$ (6)	$\dfrac{P_x}{W_x}$ (5) ÷ (3) (7)	T (7) ÷ (6) (8)
I	$90V+10C$	50%	145	45%	145	100	100	100
II	$90V+10C$	50%	145	45%	145	100	100	100
III	$90V+10C$	50%	145	45%	145	100	100	100

and in each branch these rates are equalized, $S/C + V = 45$ percent. There is, we see, one market price for each commodity that will yield the average money rate of profit. If (column 6) competition sets prices of 145 for the product of each branch, then the price will be proportioned also to the output of each branch (column 8), just as it is proportioned to the value of the input of each branch (column 7). And this is the point. Within this system of reproduction, given the price-value ratios of the *input,* and given the profit-equalizing tendency, there will tend to appear a similar price-value ratio for *output.* Further, because the outputs of each period are destined in an interdependent system to become the inputs of the following period, the price-value ratios of the inputs will always tend to be equal to the price-value ratios of the outputs. Both inputs and outputs of labor power are flowing in and out of production processes at prices that conform to the law of value. Or, as we express it in column 9 of the table, the *terms of exchange* among branches are equal throughout. This equalization of terms of exchange described in fact a large part of the classical liberal claim that long-run, free competition is a just and equitable system. It is a system of equal exchange, they believed.

To see this let us define the terms of exchange of any department, firm, or economy:

$$T \equiv \frac{P_x}{W_x} \div \frac{P_i}{W_i}$$

$$(6.1)$$

For any given branch, its terms of exchange are the ratio of the long-run market price received for the unit of value that it exports (P_x/W_x) relative to the market price that it pays for the unit of value that it imports (P_i/W_i). The overall significance of the ratio lies in the circumstance that it measures relations of exchange within an interdependent order of production, an order in which each producing unit exports a portion of its output in order to provide inputs to others, just as each imports its necessary inputs in order to produce, itself, the commodity that it exports. This is the essence of economic interdependency: the interdependency of input and output values in reproduction. What does it mean to say, then, that terms of exchange are equal throughout?

As long as prices are high enough to cover costs of reproduction of each and every branch, the equality of each branch's terms of ex-

change with each other branch's means that for all producers prices
per unit of value exported are the same and prices per unit of value
imported likewise. Each producer and each branch is precisely like
each other producer in each other branch, sharing and sharing
alike in both the costs and the gains of economic reproduction.
Reproduction in conformity with the law of value implies an
equalization of terms of exchange throughout an interdependent
order. This is why the alleged tendency of competition to equalize
these terms through establishing prices that equalize rates of profit
was a jubilant and joyful claim of the old liberal political economy.
It is therefore important to express this tendency with precision, as
in the following equation:

$$\left(\frac{P_x}{W_x} \div \frac{P_i}{W_i}\right)_1 = \left(\frac{P_x}{W_x} \div \frac{P_i}{W_i}\right)_2 = \ldots \left(\frac{P_x}{W_x} \div \frac{P_i}{W_i}\right)_n \qquad (6.2)$$

in which the subscripts x and i refer to exports and imports, and the
subscripts $1 \ldots n$ refer to the economies, departments, or
branches within an interdependent system.

The historical transformation

This liberal vision of an order of mutually reciprocal and beneficial
exchange is in itself an old one. As we have seen, it resembles the
Aristotelian dream of mutual reciprocity, a dream that the liberals,
however, attached to the progress of free competition under
capitalism. The latter see the equalization of terms of exchange
permeating social as well as economic relations according to the
degree of development of the system of liberty itself. This view of
the world was not too carefully explored by the liberals, at least in
comparison with its subsequent spelling out, and at certain junctures it was so unclear that not even the liberals themselves were
fully aware of all the assumptions underlying their theories.[5] As a
rule, they failed to realize how very special are the conditions under
which capitalist production and exchange would yield an extending
division of labor mutually and reciprocally advantageous to all parties intermeshed within it. As our example reveals, one assumption
in particular they failed to appreciate: the assumption that value
compositions of capital would remain equal throughout all departments of production. But before exploring the implications of this,
a few words about the transformation of values into prices that

equalize rates of profit, that is, prices of production, Marx calls them, considered as a historical rather than a purely logical transformation.

Whatever the situation as regards value compositions of capital in more recent times, in early phases of capitalist development, a tendency of prices to be proportioned to exchange values is discernible. In a passage packed with the fruit of historical study, Marx expresses his view of the precapitalist universe of exchange interrelations:

> . . . it is quite appropriate to regard the values of commodities as not only theoretically but also historically *prius* to the prices of production. This applies to conditions in which the labourer owns his means of production, and this is the condition of the land-owning farmer living off his own labour and the craftsman in the ancient as well as in the modern world . . . the evolution of products into commodities arises through exchange between different communities, not between members of the same community. It holds not only for this primitive condition, but also for subsequent conditions based on slavery and serfdom, and for the guild organization of handicrafts, so long as the means of production can be transferred from one sphere to another only with difficulty and therefore the various spheres of production are related to one another, within certain limits, as foreign countries or communist communities.[6]

Within the precapitalist world, commodity exchange is limited; above all it is limited in that land and labor are not yet enveloped by market mechanisms. In this world, an exchange of socially necessary work does take place and often in ratios of exchange in which labor time governs more or less decisively. Again, in feudal society a variety of institutional and administrative devices is geared to the labor time standard, as in calculation of the worth of time spent in the corvee or in other exchange between lord and serf. With the decline of feudalism the mutation of dues from labor time to monetary forms does not depart from the underlying labor standard. Prices set by the market are now, as in the view of Aquinas, considered to be just only when in conformity with labor time criteria. Thus the craftsman in feudal society, and even well into the early stages of capitalist development, still regulates his price by his work. Alternatively, his work has a value that is being transformed into prices still proportional to labor times.

As markets encroach steadily upon spheres of production internal to the receding feudal order, as price-making markets envelop handicraft production, for example, the money prices attaching to commodities still conform to traditional standards. This was the rule both within and among crafts, within and among local communities being tied together within the interstices of a spreading market apparatus: "What competition achieves, first in a single sphere, is a single market value and market price derived from the various individual values of the commodities. And it is competition of capitals in different spheres which first brings out the price of production equalizing the rates of profit in different spheres."[7] It is only with the maturation of capitalism that profit-equalizing market prices are established, for these require a considerable mobility of all commodities, a considerable interdependence within processes of production, or, what comes to the same thing, a considerable extension of the social divison of labor: "The latter prices [of profit equalization] require a higher development of capitalist production than the first one."[8] The price of production is an outcome of a historical transformation of values into prices, a transformation accompanying the rise of modern capitalism.

The famous transformation of values into prices is not primarily a logical problem, as it is widely assumed to be,[9] but a historical process whose developing interrelations of price to value are to be explained and their implications assessed. The transition from feudalism to capitalism features a transformation of values, a conversion of traditional ratios of exchange into new, monetary forms, and an establishing of ratios between these values and these prices, which are themselves subject to continuing evolution within the new market order. With the infiltration of markets and the spread of commodity exchange a network of market prices gradually appears, and at first the members of the network are proportioned to the labor time ratios that preceded the advent of the market and yet remained fundamental to exchange within the context of the law of value. For a long time the resulting proportionality of prices to values was the rule rather than the exception.[10]

Beginning with the seventeenth century, however, and with the gradual but continuing progress of technique tracing to the new science of mechanics, the price-value relations that the market had imposed upon precapitalist foundations began to change once more. All of the changes that now took place were not simply the consequence of unbridled greed and "the nasty business of money-getting," as Martin Luther referred to it. They traced rather to the sophistication of technique and its influence upon the value composition of capitals.[11] While we postpone just a moment longer how the emergence of new technical conditions in practice alters the structure of price-value relations, the evolving technique does make a contribution to the uneven development of the social economy. In the first place, the technical advance affected ever more processes of production to which the technology of the machine industry was applicable: sugar refining, textiles, and, later, mining and other branches of manufacturing. These advances heralded a continuing revolutionizing of social relations between the industrial entrepreneur and the working class, and above all the making of the modern proletariat. Then, with the industrial revolution, the revolution in social relations reached its nineteenth-century climax with full-blown cadres of industrial and financial capitalists in social and economic predominance relative to the industrial workers. In the second place, the incidence of science remained for some time upon industrial rather than agricultural sectors, the science of mechanics being further advanced than that of agronomy and related disciplines.

With the acceleration of a complex industrial accumulation, however, the tendency for rates of profit to equalize becomes increasingly pronounced, and the vaunted mobility of capital is extolled by political economists of the old school. There is an accompanying sophistication of all forms of capitalist competition to facilitate the equalization tendency. But while the tendency to equal profit rates becomes ever more pronounced, the unevenness in development throughout the whole economy by no means disappears and in fact becomes more pronounced with the acceleration of industrial accumulation – and this for reasons having as much to do with the functioning of the competitive pricing system as with the biased incidence (so to speak) of natural science. The unevenness of capitalist development is a continuing, if increasingly bizarre, phenomenon, and it will be seen to be a consequence, too, of the structure of price-value relations that emerges in the development process.

With new technical and market conditions, and with the industrial accumulation proceeding, the transformation of values into prices becomes regularized and the very presence of underlying values is further buried under the mounting fetishism of commodities, pointed to by Marx. The resulting concealment of real values beneath the superficialities of price-quantity transactions hides also the fact that *relations* between prices and exchange values are shifting. If in early phases of the 500-year transition from local to world market, market prices tended to correspond with

traditional rates and terms of exchange, then in later phases the
simple law of value, while remaining in some sense of the phrase an
operationally effective governor of some basic price-value relations,
began to be superseded by new rates and terms of exchange. Looking to their own immediate past, Smith and Ricardo saw – or
thought they did – an even and proportional distribution of prices
relative to values, as in the old handicraft era. For the future, they
saw no decisive reason why, under free competition, a continuation
of the old terms of exchange should not be expected. But they failed
to recognize the profound economic, technical, and cultural differentials being sponsored by the new order. They failed to see that
a differential advance of technique, and the response of the pricing
mechanism to it, would make an equalization of terms of exchange
the exception rather than the rule. In actuality, when the liberal
economics was in its ascendancy, the economic basis for a trend to
equilibrium exchange was steadily melting away under the heat of
industrial accumulation. The primary transformations of values into prices now being completed, the rise of machine industry on an
extending scale effected a secondary transformation in relations between prices and exchange values. The new relations tended to
disproportionality, one that traced to differential levels of technical
development in the first instance, and to the resulting inequalities
in exchange that foster and extend ever further those differentials.

Prices of production and the new terms of exchange

In England, by the end of the eighteenth century, certain effects of
the spreading system of markets upon social relations had become
most serious. As Thompson notes, "the final years of the 18th century saw a last desperate effort by the people to recover the older
moral economy as against the economy of the free market."[12] No
small part of the troubles of the working people in this chaotic
epoch is traceable to the drive of capital for a free and untrammeled mobility in its exploitation of social labor. The English
triumph in the Napoleonic Wars meant victory for English capital,
too, and henceforth it moved domestically and internationally with
remarkable ease and fluidity, equalizing rates of profit through
widening spheres of economic and geographic space. At the same
time, the expansion was accompanied by movements in terms of exchange that tended to divorce prices from even an approximate correspondence with exchange values within an extending division of

social labor. To see why terms of exchange now move in new directions we must return to theory.

While a simplified model will suffice to show why the alteration in underlying conditions of production brings alterations in terms of exchange, this model need not, and, indeed, must not be removed from the principal historical circumstances of the day. Its point of departure will therefore be historical in that it assumes economic interdependency among producers whose prices are at first proportional to exchange values for reasons previously explained. Therefore, in Table 6.2 we shall assume (column 2) that at some juncture in the system of economic reproduction prices are, or have been, proportional to exchange values, productive inputs being bought and sold in accord with the law of value, and terms of exchange tending to equality.[13] But with the accumulation of capital continuing and, in particular, technical change proceeding in the leading sectors, organic compositions of capital will come to differ among the various departments comprising the interdependent system. In our simplified model, then, subsequently differing values compositions of capital in the six departments are shown in column 1. What we shall discover is that the first consequence of the uneven incidence of technical change is an alteration of the original price-value relations that is of the utmost significance for exchange.

The tendency for profit-equalizing prices to appear is still assumed and is in fact more powerful than ever.[14] Rates of surplus value are the same throughout. And now the long-run prices of production will begin to deviate from the exchange values underlying them. Given that market prices for commodities of each department are still prices that equalize profit rates, the general or average rate of profit to which each department conforms is shown in column 6. The real rates of profit in each department will differ from their respective money rates because, organic compositions varying from department to department while rates of surplus value are the same, the magnitudes of the surplus values emerging from each department will also vary. However, there is one set of prices for each commodity of each department that will equalize rates of profit for each, sharing out as it were the total surplus value or total profit so that each department receives its proportionate share of net proceeds. In this case the profit-equalizing price is 122.[15] If each department sells its output at this price of production, its cost of production being 100 (column 1), then rates of profit are

Table 6.2. *Inequalities in terms of exchange established by equilibrating prices*

Dept.	Inputs (%) $(C+V)$	$\left(\dfrac{P_x}{W_x} \div \dfrac{P_i}{W_i}\right)_{T_{t-1}}$	S/V	Outputs $(W = C + V \div 5)$	P' (%)	P' (%)	P	$\left(\dfrac{P_x}{W_x}\right)_t$	$\left(\dfrac{P_x}{W_x} \div \dfrac{P_i}{W_i}\right)^I_{T_t^I}$	$\dfrac{P}{W}$
	(1)	(2)	(3)	(4)	(5)	(6)	(7)	(8)	(9)	(10)
I	$95C + 5V$	100	100	105	5	22	122	122/105	100	>1
II	$85C + 15V$	100	100	115	15	22	122	122/115	110	>1
III	$80C + 20V$	100	100	120	20	22	122	122/120	114	>1
IV	$78C + 22V$	100	100	122	22	22	122	122/122	116	$=1$
V	$70C + 30V$	100	100	130	30	22	122	122/130	124	<1
VI	$60C + 40V$	100	100	140	40	22	122	122/140	132	<1

Note: The price that equilibrates rates of (money) profit for all departments (col. 7), is a price such that all products except those of department IV, where the value composition of capital is of the social average, sell either above or below their value: the P/W ratio (col. 10) is either greater than or less than 1. On the assumption that terms of exchange are on a par at the beginning of the period of reproduction (t), as in col. 2, the equalizing price results in new terms of exchange which are shown in col. 9 where terms of exchange for each department in its exchanges with department I are calculated. Department I's terms of exchange are progressively more favorable the lower the value composition of the department with which it exchanges. Conversely, departments with lower value compositions experience declining terms of exchange in their trade relations with department I. Given a network in which each trades with all, the distribution of terms will on the average favor the advanced over the retarded. In the real world, where interdependency is often not that advanced, or where trading patterns are shaped by other than purely economic influences, terms of exchange of the less developed may not be so unfavorable as indicated and those of the advanced economies less favorable than shown.

everywhere equal at 22 percent. A comparison of these equilibrium prices with the exchange values of the outputs of the different departments reveals a regular pattern in the *deviations* of prices from values.

Where values compositions of the input capitals are above the social average of value compositions (in Table 6.2, department IV is of the social average), where, in other words, the productive technique is more capital intensive, the market price in the long run will be greater than the exchange value of the commodity. On the other hand, where the value composition of the input capital is below the social average composition, the price of production will be less than the exchange value of the commodity. Only where the value composition of the input capital is equal to the social average does the old law of value strictly hold. In this average case the price of production is proportioned to the exchange value of the commodity, as in the original instance (law of value). Otherwise there is a remarkably regular pattern of deviations of prices from values that emerges with the uneven development of the economy, and it is a pattern whose causes and implications are worth exploring further in slightly different terms.

With the equalization of profit rates through long-run prices of production that yield this effect, those prices of production will no longer everywhere be proportioned to exchange values in accord with the law of value. Some prices will continue in their old relation to values, and this is the case whenever the branch is of an average level of technical development and where, therefore, its value composition of capitals is of the social average. Otherwise, deviations appear, although these deviations are quite systematic: Prices rise above exchange values for more developed lines and fall below exchange values for less developed lines. Departments I, II, and III fall into the former category while departments V and VI fall into the latter category. The old law of value, which declares a *universal* proportionality of prices to values, is therefore broken! To be more precise on this important point, one can see that value continues to exercise a decisive influence over the structure of prices taken as a whole, but that influence now exercises itself differently than it did formerly. While prices tend approximately to be proportional to exchange values in the average case, the prices of commodities produced under either above or below average technical conditions tend to disperse themselves around this average in a systematic way

– and in governing this dispersal the average value composition may still be thought of as exerting a decisive influence on the whole – rising above exchange value where the value composition is high, and falling below value where the value composition is low. In other words, the exchange value of the social average departments' products must be viewed as a kind of center of gravity about which the price-value planets disperse themselves, swinging about the center in ever-widening circles. We shall see later, that the widening swings of prices vis-à-vis values are subject to limits, that the law of value finally asserts itself and, in the phase of economic crisis, pulls back on outlying planets, bringing prices back into a more proportional relation to values. But for the moment it is the explosion rather than the implosion with which we are concerned.

Under new conditions of industrial expansion in which an uneven development of technique characterizes the extending system, prices and values tend to move into new constellations, tending to move systematically away from the old value base with its general proportionality of prices to values. In this process, accumulation proceeding more or less rapidly and forcefully, prices and the rates of profit that they equalize may *appear* to be in equilibrium, competition equilibrating the extending scales of economic and social reproduction. But prices relative to exchange values are something else again, and what the new relations of prices to values portend within this extending system can best be understood through the notion of terms of exchange. In general, the old tendency to equal exchange gives way under new conditions to a tendency to unequal exchange.

In Table 6.2 again, it will be observed, we have lined up the departments of production from I to VI according to the value compositions of their capitals. They range from the most developed branch of production (I) to the least developed (VI). If we compare for each branch the price of its output relative to the exchange value of that output, and if we bear in mind that this output is being exported within an interdependent system, we see that this ratio of price to value of what is exported is higher the higher the value composition of capital and lower the lower the value composition of capital (column 8). In order to show the implication of this uneven development of the productive forces, suppose we calculate the terms of exchange with all other departments of production of, say, department I (column 9). We see that the terms of exchange or

terms of trade of department I with each other department now differ, but these terms, too, differ in a quite regular and systematic
way. In general, the terms of exchange of department I are higher
the less developed the department with which it trades. Uneven
development is thus generally characterized by unequal terms of exchange. But before pursuing the historical significance of this
generalization, a more specific rendition of it is necessary. If we
rank our departments of production from I to n according to their
levels of technical development, from highest to lowest value compositions of their capitals, and if we take, further, the ratios of the
prices of their *inputs* to the exchange values of those inputs at the
beginning of a reproduction period as a base 100 (prices proportional to values), then at the close of the period of reproduction, as
a consequence of the establishment of profit-equalizing prices, the
terms of exchange for each department will conform to the following law:

$$\left(\frac{P_x}{W_x} \div \frac{P_i}{W_i}\right)_{\text{I}} > \left(\frac{P_x}{W_x} \div \frac{P_i}{W_i}\right)_{\text{II}} > \cdots \left(\frac{P_x}{W_x} \div \frac{P_i}{W_i}\right)_n \qquad (6.3)$$

(The subscripts x and i refer to the department's export and import
prices and exchange values, and the departments are, to repeat,
ranked from I to n, from highest to lowest levels of technical
development.) This is the law of unequal exchange. It is the law of
price-value relations as these emerge in the process of capitalist
development, especially in its phases of expansion.

A tendency to unequal exchange inheres within a system of
capitalist exchange that is competitive in that prices that equalize
profit rates tend to be established in the long run. The tendency to
unequal exchange, like the famous tendency for the general rate of
profit to fall, is one of those contradictory impulses inherent within
the mode of production itself, asserting its effects, "under certain
conditions and over the long period." These (6.3) are the new terms
of unequal exchange that attend the uneven development of the
capitalist economy and that, in their turn, make their own significant contributions to the extension and perpetuation of inequalities
characteristic of capitalist relations of production. This last remark
is, of course, interpretive of the law, and raises the whole question
of the significance of the tendency to inequality in terms of exchange. What is the nature of a universe in which prices relative to
values are subject to a torsion-like tendency to dispersion? This sub-

ject we pursue more intensively in the following chapter, but some intimations of a proper response to the question may be appropriate now.

The key to understanding the meaning of the tendency to unequal exchange is contained in the concept of terms of exchange, and that concept, in its turn, realizes its full import within an interdependent system of generalized commodity exchange, within, in other words, a capitalist economy in an advancing state of economic and social development. Within this order, input–output interrelations extend progressively, and the level of interdependence of each branch upon each other branch is very high. Each branch obtains its productive input from a considerable number of other branches and transmits its own output in exchange to service the input requirements of other, dependent branches like itself. Nevertheless, the exchange that interdependence entails proceeds upon quite different terms for its various industrial and other branches comprising the order as whole. That is, for any branch the price received for its output per unit of value exported may be greater than or less than the price per unit of reproductive value that it imports. (There is, of course, the average branch whose terms of exchange will be equal terms only if it exports and imports among all other branches so as to realize this equality.) On the whole, more developed branches will export to less developed branches and import their inputs from the latter. Conversely, the less developed will export to the more developed and import from the more developed branches with which they exchange. This is on the whole the main tendency, and, as a result capitalists in the former, more developed branches will enjoy relatively favorable terms of exchange, the price per unit of value exported by them being greater than the price paid per unit of value imported by them. The former branches reproduce themselves, therefore, whether on an extending or stationary scale, at a relatively lower cost or greater profit, and tend, as a result, to accelerate their rate of growth vis-a-vis those branches with which they exchange. The less developed branches, on the other hand, having unfavorable terms of exchange, reproduce themselves at a greater cost or a lower rate of profit, and their development is by so much retarded. While the former associate with the latter to their growing financial and real advantage, the latter become subject to growing deterrents to their own development.

Before coming to consider more concretely some typical manifestations of unequal exchange, recall once again the situation of England at the time of the Industrial Revolution. That revolution fed some fires of accumulation at the same time that it banked some others. Given the then incidence of the science of mechanics, it was unavoidable that leading sectors in the advance should have been industrial and capitalism became industrial capitalism. But if the laws of unequal exchange fostered a continuation of this unevenness throughout all spheres of British imperial exchange, they did so not merely because mechanical science and innovation were the peculiar genius of the English people. Rather, they did so because the industrial lead brought in its wake a general transformation of price-value relations through all branches in all the countries and regions falling within the embrace of British capital. With the passage from mercantile to industrial accumulation the pricing mechanism of capitalist circulation reinforced and strengthened for a time the British lead. At home advancing industrial sectors made a relatively retarded agriculture subject to relatively unfavorable terms of exchange; abroad, whole nations and peoples fell similarly under the imperial hegemony for economic as well as political reasons. The mechanism of capital accumulation was then, as it is today, a highly discriminatory apparatus that twisted terms of exchange so as to favor the advanced and impede the relatively retarded. Still today this feature of capitalist relations of exchange shows itself again and again wherever accumulation is proceeding. Within all of those quarters of the global economy in which the capitalist mode holds court, hierarchies of economic inequality follow from the expansion of trade and exchange with the accumulation of capital. Capitalism remains today incapable of generating a process of balanced and equitable growth.

Conclusion

In response to the brashness of Marx's critics and to the perennial question, "What of the Marxian 'theory' of prices?" no Marxist need stand silent.[16] There is no need to bow down before logical abstractions removed from the historical process, meanwhile lamenting the Marxian "deficiencies" in scientific levitations: "Unfortunately, some Marxist economists have never understood what is involved in the transformation of values into prices of production and have continued to treat it as a real process with important consequences for the functioning of the system."[17] Our investigation of the unorthodox theory of price-value relations underlines the differences between ahistorical and historical theories. The transformation of values into prices turns out to be not at all what Marx's critics have supposed it to be, an issue of pure logic in a septic science, but an explanation of evolving economic and class interrelations in the context of capitalist development.

At the same time, standard theories of perfect and of monopolistic competition are not to be viewed as wholly competitive with Marxian explanations. So far as the former have relevance to the real world, they are simple ancillaries of the Marxian explanation rather than alternatives to it. They are complements to a more general explanation of development and in this role may provide useful and even necessary amplifications in regard to the detailed functioning of particular markets at particular junctures. But as we shall see in the sequel, the development of various market forms is largely a response to, rather than a cause of, unequal exchange.

The Marxian economics gives conventional theories of supply and demand a real role to play in the explanation of social history by fitting them into a larger system. Above all, that economics relieves the economist of that awesome and impossible responsibility of asserting a meliorative trend to the course of capitalist development. It relieves him of the noxious task of denying history by denying the possibility of its explanation, and so frees him to legitimize whatever is scientifically useful in the standard repertoire. It places standard theory within a setting in which the main trend is away from a metaphysical assertion of static balance and toward a truly evolutionary theory of economic and social relations, one that is entirely and scrupulously respectful of the observed data of historical processes.

None of this should be interpreted as a suggestion that the Marxian theorist is an easy rider through the lanes of social history. Not only is the theory in need of a continuing articulation in order that we be able to ascertain its points of difficulty – of real rather than of imagined difficulty, preferably – but a spelling out of details is necessary also in order to facilitate an exhaustive application of the theory to the explanation of all of the phenomena on which it may throw light. Indeed, it is to the contemplation of problems of application of the theory that we now turn. While it is our hope that the exercise of the theory in Chapter 7 will give us a new and improved view of economic and social relations of certain kinds, it is always possible that the effort to use the theory will reveal its inadequacies or, if not that, then those junctures at which some modification of the theory is necessary. To date, the playing around with the Marxian theory by standard theorists has brought no embarrassing impasse to light.

Appendix to Chapter 6:
a note on the logic of transformation

It is not enough, of course, that a theory conform to observable evidences. It must also be logically consistent, conclusions following from premises in the wake of a logical transformation of some kind: a mathematics, a syntax, or a formal logic. Whether or not Marx's transformation of values into prices conforms to this requirement has long been argued.

Dispute on the issue traces to the latter part of the past century, to Boehm-Bawerk's *Geschichte und Kritik der Kapitalzins-Theorien* (1884) and his *Zum Anschluss des Marxschen Systems* (1896).[1] While Boehm's assault covered virtually all conceivable objections that might be raised against the labor theory, he noted in particular an inconsistency between the analyses of *Capital I* and *Capital III*. In the former, as we know, Marx assumed prices to be proportional to exchange values, while in the latter he argued that they tend to disproportionality – hence the inconsistency claimed by Boehm.

In *Capital I* Marx abstracts from differing value compositions of capital; ratios of *C* to *V* are assumed everywhere equal, and with rates of surplus value everywhere the same there is no inconsistency in assuming prices to be proportional to all input and output values whether of individual branches or in the aggregate. However, in conformity with his method of successive approximations, Marx proceeds in *Capital III* to drop the assumption of uniform capital-labor ratios. Having investigated in *Capital I* the implications of capital accumulation on the assumption that the structure of individual prices does not influence the development process, he wishes in *Capital III* to assess the implications of differing value compositions on the structure of prices and of values – with the results we have seen. It is obvious that his inquiry simply utilizes different models at different junctures, in strict conformity with the method of approximations, and with the object of coming to a general analysis of the whole. (*Capital III* is subtitled *The Process of Capitalist Production as a Whole.*) Failing to perceive the methodological principle at work, Boehm mistook models resting upon different assumptions for an inconsistency in reasoning. But where else does the issue of logic enter in to transformations?

We have seen how competitive theorists since the days of Smith have viewed history as a beneficent process for the vindication of competition through a movement toward general equilibrium. The logic of this argument is much touted; its consistency with labor value premises at a certain level of abstraction further confirms the logic of the argument. But is it logical to assume the converse? Is there an inconsistency in the theory that competition tends to an ultimate disequilibrium between prices and values? Again, this is a logical question. The problem of showing that the price-value theorem – prices of production falling above or below exchange values depending upon whether the value composition of capital in a branch is above or below the social average – is logically consistent with a competitive, interdependent economic system has been the subject of study by Winternitz, Seton, and Morishima, among others.[2] In showing the consistency of the theorem with the reproduction system, Seton's work is noteworthy.

Seton begins by representing an economy of interdependent flows among n branches by a set of equations such as:

$$k_{11} + k_{21} \dots \dots \dots \dots \dots \dots k_{n1} + e_1 = O_1$$
$$\dots \dots \dots \dots \dots \dots \dots \dots \dots \dots \dots \quad (6.1\,A)$$
$$k_{1n} + k_{2n} \dots \dots \dots \dots \dots \dots k_{nn} + e_n = O_n$$
$$s_1 + s_2 \dots \dots \dots \dots \dots \dots \dots \dots = s_n$$

Within this matrix each of the k entries represents the usual output – input quantities measured in units of labor time, *measured in units of labor time, each of which* may be broken down into its constituent elements of capital (C) and wage goods (V). The remark is occasioned by the fact previously noted that, in actuality, a given product rarely falls uniquely and exclusively into the class either of C or V commodities. Rather, products serve dual functions in use. If sector 1 produces corn, for example, a part of the product may serve to feed animals (C) and a part to feed labor (V). So it is with other sectors, so that an output, O_n, must be viewed as a congerie of the two basic types of capital values. In any case, the equations of the preceding matrix are merely a generalized representation of the values of social reproduction over a period of time, and their solution may be obtained if the number of equations is equal to the number of unknowns.

One may then incorporate into the equations the assumption that competition tends to equalize rates of return upon money capitals. The value entries of (6.1 A) will be multiplied by the prices (p_i) for which they sell, on the left-hand side of each equation. Each is then equated with the equalized cost ratio, ρ , multiplied by the money value of the output of each sector: $\rho\, O_i p_i$. The system of equations then appears as:

$$k_{11}p_1 + k_{12}p_2 \dots\dots\dots\dots\dots\dots\dots\dots\dots\dots\dots\dots\dots k_{1n}p_n = O_1 p_1$$
$$\dots\dots\dots\dots\dots\dots\dots\dots\dots\dots\dots\dots\dots\dots\dots\dots\dots\dots\dots\dots\dots\dots \quad (6.2\mathrm{A})$$
$$k_{n1}p_1 + k_{n2}p_2 \dots\dots\dots\dots\dots\dots\dots\dots\dots\dots\dots\dots k_{nn}p_n = O_n p_n$$

To focus upon interdependency in its simplest form, the input – output entries representing surplus ($\Sigma\, s = \Sigma o$) may be dropped out if simple reproduction is assumed in its simplest form.

Seton then represents the system of flows in (6.2A) with a matrix of cost-input coefficients, K_i. This matrix is obtained by dividing each entry in (6.2A) by the value of the total output of the sector. In terms of prices prevailing, the matrix of production coefficients will then appear as:

$$(K_{11} - \rho\,)p_1 + K_{12}p_2 \dots\dots\dots\dots\dots\dots\dots\dots\dots K_{1n}p_n = 0$$
$$K_{21} + (K_{22} - \rho\,)p_2 \dots\dots\dots\dots\dots\dots\dots\dots\dots\dots K_{2n}p_n = 0$$
$$\dots\dots\dots\dots\dots\dots\dots\dots\dots\dots\dots\dots\dots\dots\dots\dots\dots\dots\dots\dots\dots\dots\dots \quad (6.3\mathrm{A})$$
$$K_{n1}p_1 \dots\dots\dots\dots\dots\dots\dots\dots\dots\dots\dots\dots\dots + (K_{nn} - \rho\,)p_n = 0$$

The consistency of this scheme of equations requires the vanishing of their determinant, $/\,K - \rho\,I/\ = 0$. With consistency so determined, it only remains to be seen whether or not the price-value theorem can itself be derived from the system. Seton's treatment of this part of the transformation problem is worth more attention than will be given it here. Suffice it to say that Seton demonstrates the consistency of the theorem with the system just shown (6.3A). He concludes: ". . . the internal consistency and determinacy of Marx's conception of the transformation process, and the formal inferences he drew from it, have been fully vindicated by this analysis. . . ."[3] This conclusion, obviously, gives little comfort to the critics of Marx's logic. Seton's analysis of the price-value theorem shows that, even though output prices become input prices, and output values become input values, these interdependencies may be logically consistent with the theorem. Seton is the first to show this with the apparatus of modern mathematics, and his demonstration is still unchallenged within the framework of assumptions that he utilizes. Seton himself draws attention to the restricted character of his assumptions, so that his proof may conceivably not suffice for all reproductive schemata in which the accumulation of capital is proceeding.

Marx, too, was aware of the fact that each period of reproduction establishes new terms of exchange among buyers of productive inputs in relation to the sellers of thos inputs.[4] There is a need for a more elaborate analysis of the development of relations of prices to values extending over a number of reproduction periods precisely because the deviation of price-value ratios of outputs from those of inputs within a period means that in the succeeding period the price of the input will deviate from what it had been in the former period. Because the outputs of one period become the inputs of the next, the deviations of prices from values also undergo a progressive development – and within this dynamic process of extended accumulation does the price-value theorem hold logically?

It is in the direction of answering this last question that Anwar Shaikh has carried on the analysis.[5] He has thus far shown that in an iterative sequence of shifts in price-value relations the shift in terms of exchange that takes place within the *first* of a number of successive periods well characterizes the resulting movement as a whole; that is, the price-value theorem describes well the movement of a sequence of iterations of price-value relations. As Marx says of his own analysis, "Our present analysis does not necessitate a closer examination of this point."[6]

There thus appears no very crucial logical problem of transformation to this juncture in the study of Marx's economics. And since the publication of *Capital III,* as the studies described suggest, there has been altogether too much attention paid to the logical and far too little to the historical issues. Now why has this been the case? I would suggest that it is because the historical meaning of the price-value theorem carries with it a political economy that strikingly contradicts the hopes of the bourgeois economist for a "meliorative trend" (as Veblen described it) toward competitive equilibrium. Some work by economists suggests the propriety of this interpretation.

Two essays have been offered by Paul Samuelson, a Nobel Prize winner whose elementary textbook has been basic to the education of several generations of students of economics.[7] While declaring, on the one hand, that "I am abstaining here from appraising the fruitfulness of the exploitation hypotheses," he declares, on the other hand, that economists should "take an eraser and rub them [the value schemes] out."[8] While there is an apparent inconsistency in these statements – labor value schema are the basis of the Marxian theory of exploitation – an examination of these writings suggests that it is the deviation of prices from values that our logicians find both incomprehensible and disturbing. This is confirmed by certain conclusions of Morishima, who also calls for a Marxian economics without a labor theory of value.[9] The theory with its troubling dualities, as Morishima regards them, is scientifically troublesome because prices and values persist in their disproportionate relationships. Add these objections to what Baumol calls the quantitative limitations of the labor theory of value, and the case against the labor theory would appear to be complete.[10] What all of the standard critics of the theory thus have in common is an incapacity, or perhaps a refusal, to relate the labor theory of value to the real world, whether through its logical *or* its quantitative manipulation. This incapacity they justify by referring to one or another assumed defect of the theory rather than to their own ideological limitations. This, we know, is an old problem of the bourgeois economist.

That ideological bias continues to infect the standard economics the younger generation of economists has come to realize. The real transformation problem is transforming the bourgeois mind with its equilibrium preoccupations. In criticizing Samuelson's theory of international trade, H. G. Johnson puts his finger upon the real issue. In this theory of trade the possibility of an equilibrium exchange in conformity with a comparative advantage mutually advantageous to both parties remains central to the economist's argument, despite the fact that in reality terms of exchange move in ways suggesting the presence of exploitation. Johnson says of this theory:

Despite its analytical flexibility objection can legitimately be brought by the practical, policy oriented economist against the Heckscher-Ohlin, Samuelson model [of international exchange] on two major grounds: that its assumption of perfect competition, which includes costless access to knowledge, ignores the role in international trade and investment of the large industrial corporations and the associated phenomena of monopolistic competition; and that its analytical formulation of growth problems leaves as exogenously determined and indeed extraneous the very aspects of economic behavior that are of most practical concern, especially the propensity to accumulate capital per head and the rate of technological advance.[11]

It is, in fact, these very aspects of accumulation that Marx is dealing with and that point, we have seen, to a persistent, disequilibrating movement of terms of exchange. No wonder the economist seeks to exorcise by logic what appears to him to be at best a specter, but that is in reality a material universe moving to undermine and destroy his preconceptions.

PART THREE
Relationships between prices and values

7

Unequal exchange:
price-value relations,
irregularity, and instability

The development of economic interdependencies

The commodity exchange out of which, under certain conditions, the capitalist mode of production itself develops, has its historical origins in the exchange of surplus product between communities.[1] In early trade, what changes hands is what each party finds superfluous to its own economic reproduction, the excess of use values that it produces.

With the emergence of capitalism, exchange comes to encompass on an extending scale items that are industrially and reproductively vital to the communities or to the segments of communities (for example, the town and the country) involved. However, even as recently as the seventeenth and eighteenth centuries, this system of productive interdependencies was still in its infancy. At that time, economic relations between Western Europe and the peoples of Asia and of Africa were still largely relations of the more ancient form – the obvious exception to this, from the standpoint of the latter parties, being the slave trade, in which a vital commodity was exported – and did not feature a notable sacrifice of what was reproductively vital to their own productive consumption.[2] With the industrial and commercial expansions of the past two centuries, under the political auspices of the capitalist nation-state, the composition of trade begins markedly to shift. The division of international labor, like the division of domestic labor, involves an extending interdependence of industrial and agricultural elements required for economic reproduction.

Apart from the extending interdependence, what is especially noteworthy (and familiar) are the imbalances that attend it and a

161

certain instability and an irregularity of the movement that brings
it. In irregular but powerful pulsations the interdependence of productive structures is brought forth; for example, the dependence of
the advanced capitalism upon Third World imports.[3] On the other
hand, while shortages of productive capacity and a terrible retardation in development of the productive forces are still to be found
within even the advanced capitalism – particularly in the more exploited divisions of social labor – these deficiencies are most marked
and pervasive within the less developed countries with which the
former trades. In sum, the extension of interdependence globally
and domestically has been, and continues to be, uneven and irregular, and while these features of the process are most apparent
in the situation of the less developed countries, these irregularities
and unevennesses are everywhere an integral part of one general
organic interrelation. Any proper explanation at the global level
must, in other words, encompass the local phenomena as well.

In explaining the movement, we find that the law of unequal exchange is especially important. The law, we have seen, asserts a
tendency of terms of exchange to move in favor of the more advanced productive forces – more precisely, in favor of those controlling the more developed forces of social labor – and to move
against the technically retarded laborers and, to a lesser degree,
against those controlling the more retarded forces. Within a system
of capitalist relations of production, the law of unequal exchange
yields a torsion effect upon terms of exchange that, on the one
hand, accelerates accumulation for those whose terms are favorable
or rising, while repressing accumulation of those economies whose
terms are unfavorable or falling. One might say simply that the
relations between prices and values that the law predicts show a
recurrent tendency to cut the pie in favor of those who have already
had more than their share.[4] The unbalanced growth that follows is
one overall effect of the general exchange, given the relations of
production to which we have referred. Another is the familiar irregularity, the expansion followed by collapse and contraction.

In the generation of this uneven pattern of capital accumulation,
the law of unequal exchange, like other Marxian laws, is seen to
yield certain countertendencies. The processes of capitalist exchange themselves work to undermine the political and organizational relationships that are predominant during periods of general
expansion. The process of expansion contains barriers to its con-

tinuation, but since efforts to overcome these barriers will be made, the crisis brings in its wake policies and practices that may or may not succeed in restoring eventually the forward movement. The law of unequal exchange, in other words, yields effects against which the organism moves in an effort to contain and neutralize its own malignancy, in order to continue its growth. These aspects of capitalist development may be seen in action at various levels and in various spheres.

Uneven development: industry and agriculture

Rather than begin with the subject of international relations, however, we go back to the domestic, national setting. Since the industrial revolution recurrent movements of terms of exchange, favoring the technically advanced and repressing the relatively retarded of industrial society, have been an important part of the history of industrial-agricultural interrelations. All of the capitalist countries, and some of the socialist ones too, have experienced scissors movements of prices of industrial relative to agricultural products.[5] Apart from wartime, a persistent tendency appears for prices of industrial products to rise relative to those of agriculture during periods of general expansion. The price per unit of value received by industry from agriculture falls, while the latter experiences an unfavorable movement in its price-value relations.

This movement of terms, an aspect of the general scissors movement of prices, adds impetus to the industrial accumulation by providing industrial departments with cheaper foodstuffs and other raw materials for its labor force, thus holding down costs and raising profit rates. Viewed from the other side, the same movement of terms represses accumulation and discourages technical innovations, even when the latter are available, by imposing financial stringency and hardship upon farmers. For agriculture, as the law predicts, the price relative to value received from industry rises at the same time that agricultural income declines relatively. Agricultural indebtedness increases. By the same process of squeezing, the repression of agriculture forces labor out of rural areas, thereby enlarging urban pools of cheap labor and hastening the urbanizing and the proletarianizing of the population. The overall result is the long-familiar imbalance in development of these broad departments of social reproduction. While the movement of terms favoring industry encourages industrial competition and, accompanied by profit-equalizing market prices, transfers surplus value from agricultural producers to industrial capitalists, at the same time the acceleration of industrial accumulation does not benefit industrial labor proportionately. The gains of industrial labor lie in the increased employment attending the expansion rather than in a rise in the material standard of living. When real wages begin to rise as the expansion proceeds, the rate of profit soon tends to fall and crisis ensues.

The power and perversity of the market forces at work are well known by socialists, too. The economy in transition to socialism is fully vulnerable to their operation. In the Soviet Union after the Revolution, planners sought to establish a pricing structure equitable in its terms both to industrial and to agricultural producers; but the necessity of retaining market structures as organizational and distributive agencies sometimes negated, and invariably complicated, their efforts to promote a balanced exchange and growth of both departments. Within capitalist countries, also, the dialectical tendency shows itself in the irresistible need to counter politically the main disruptive effects of the movement of terms of exchange. The downward drift of capitalist agriculture in the absence of remedial measures is toward depression and a misallocation of resources, and these tendencies, unless reversed, work to undermine demands for industrial produce. This consequence of the law has in the past brought reconstruction and reform in the wake of depression and in conformity with the capitalist principle of ex post planning. Agricultural price parities, income supports, acreage allotments, and so on, aim at restoring prosperity, but typically they encourage the foliage while leaving the roots of the problem untouched. The malfunction is endemic and is the consequence of a whole system of interrelations of agriculture with other sectors. The trouble lies in the terms on which interindustry exchanges develop within the context of certain relations of production.

Value interrelations and the general instability of exchange

The history of industrial-agricultural interrelations suggests a connection between terms of exchange and economic instability at large. In fact, the essential character of the problem of economic instability under capitalism may be more easily described if we apply the exchange dichotomy theorem to relations between those departments of production charged with the reproduction of constant capitals, on the one side, and, on the other, those departments engaged in the reproduction of means of consumption or wage goods. This is merely a broader and more comprehensive division of departments of economic reproduction than the one previously described between industry and agriculture. In conformity with his methodological principle of approximations, Marx himself approaches this problem in *Capital II* by first specifying the conditions required for an exchange equilibrium.[6] If we pause to reproduce his analysis, it will be easy to see why in general exchange between department I (means of production) and department II (means of consumption) must inevitably be disruptive of production equilibria.

Assume a system of simple reproduction in which, of course, the whole of the surplus is unproductively consumed. In department I the constant capitals are produced; in department II, the wage goods. In department II, also, the luxury goods for unproductive consumption by the capitalists are produced. Because I produces only capital goods, while it requires both wage goods for its labor force and luxury goods for its capitalists, it must obtain these from II in exchange. Similarly, because II produces only wage and luxury goods, it must obtain its means of production from I through exchange. So I must produce the means of production it requires for its own use plus whatever additional amount II requires. II must produce wage and luxury goods for its own use plus whatever additional amounts of these I requires. Now what is required for an equilibrium exchange?

Everyone agrees, demands must equal supplies throughout. This means that the supply of each department's output must be equal to demand for it. With respect to means of production, for example:

$$C_1 + C_2 = C_1 + V_1 + S_1 \tag{7.1}$$

And for department II, whose supply must also equal demand:

$$V_1 + S_1 + V_2 + S_2 = C_2 + V_2 + S_2 \tag{7.2}$$

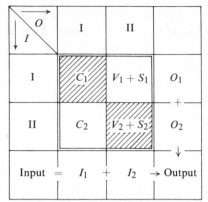

Figure 7.1. A two-department interdependent system. This tableau of simple reproduction shows the stability condition as an equalization of values exported to and imported from each department, the condition being that $C_2 = V_1 + S_1$. In row I are shown the outputs of department I: C_1 is the constant capital produced and retained for use in department I; $V_1 + S_1$ is equal in value magnitude to that constant capital that department I must produce for export to department II, to be used in the latter as means of production. In row II, department II must have a constant capital, C_2, to use as productive input, and to obtain this it ships to I a value of wage and luxury goods of equal magnitude. Each department thus imports value magnitudes equal to its exports in an equal exchange. The figure shows that this means that the values lying outside the main diagonal of the matrix must be equalized. In simple accumulation, the two-sector balance equation for equal value exchange reduces to: $C_2 + S_{C_2} = V_1 + S_{V_1}$. That is, the value of constant capital required in department II to maintain and to enlarge its capital stock must be equal to the value of the wage goods plus additional wage goods required for use in department I but produced in department II. In capitalist exchange between the two departments, prices must be proportioned to these values in order that values move at proper equilibrium rates between I and II. Hence $P_C/C_2 + S_{C_2} = P_I/V_1 + S_{V_1}$.

Simplifying, we see that these equalities reduce to one simple equation, the one adduced by Marx:

$$C_2 = V_1 + S_1 \qquad (7.3)$$

The economic meaning of the equation is simple (see Figure 7.1 and note). The equation says that in order for an equilibrium exchange to take place between the two departments, the value of means of production that I exports to II (C_2) must be equal to the value of the wage and luxury goods that II produces for export to I ($V_1 + S_1$). Equal values are thus exchanged between the two. It will further be evident, on a moment's reflection, that since these values are bought and sold at money prices, an equilibrium exchange requires that market prices be proportioned to their values. That is, if the law of value is to be observed and equal exchange is to take place, actual market prices must relate to values in precisely the way that we have previously described. Denoting the price of I's product by P_c and the price of II's by P_v, the equation of equilibrium exchange is:

$$\frac{P_C}{C_2} = \frac{P_V}{V_1 + S_1} \tag{7.4}$$

The equilibrium condition for an equal market exchange is that the price relative to the value that I exports to II must be equal to the price relative to the value paid for what I imports from II. Putting it more broadly, and in the theoretical terms explained in the previous chapter, their respective terms of exchange must be equal; these terms will be equal to each other when for each sector prices are proportioned to values exported and imported.

An equality of price-value ratios of exports and imports among interdependent economies or departments is precisely the equal exchange called for by the simple law of value. However, we have already established that this equality cannot be realized under certain circumstances. Under certain conditions the transformation of values into prices of production does not proceed in such a fashion that equal terms result. Instead, exchange among interdependent economies may yield ratios of prices to values that deviate above and below the social average ratio in a regular and systematic way; and this, in turn, makes unequal exchange inevitable. The only question to be answered, therefore, so far as exchange between departments I and II is concerned, is whether or not equal exchange is possible between these departments. In actuality, the accumulation of capital, coupled with technical change, destroys the conditions of equal exchange and makes for an unequal exchange between the two critical departments.[7]

In the development of capitalism an equal exchange between departments I and II proved finally to be impossible, and this inequality, in turn, accelerated the accumulation of means of production (I) and retarded relatively the production of means of consumption (II). Initially, improvements in terms of exchange for I resulted from higher value compositions of capital that were themselves the consequence of technical improvements rendering more capital intensive the production of means of production. Wage goods sectors, on the other hand, tended to lag behind means of production in their technical development; only in more recent times have there been really significant technical accumulations in these departments generally, and in agriculture in particular. As these conditions would suggest, periods of rapid accumulation have hitherto seen terms of exchange moving in support of the former and against the latter, accentuating and extending the sectoral imbalances between these principal departments in a highly unbalanced process of expansion. With the very inception of industrial accumulation, then, terms of exchange foster a forced draft accumulation of constant capitals under capitalism as the exchange mechanism itself, in conjunction with capitalist competition, transfers surplus value from sectors of lower to those of higher organic composition. But it is not only unbalanced growth that follows from unequal exchange. The growth becomes unstable as well.

The movement of terms in favor of department I production leads to overproduction in all industries and branches whose value compositions are above the social average. In early phases of expansion, incomes of enterprises in department I rise with the improvement of their terms of exchange, stimulating production of means of production beyond the amounts required for equilibrium exchange with department II. In relation to the production of wage goods, unequal exchange pushes in the opposite direction; too few wage goods are produced for an equilibrium exchange with department I producers. Overproduction in the former is matched by underconsumption and retardation in the latter. The law of unequal exchange in this way contributes to the evolution of periodic crises in exchange relations between these departments of production, crises that play an important role in laying the groundwork for general economic collapse when the general rate of profit moves into decline.

Uneven development: international trade

In international exchange disparate movements of terms of trade become marked and, ultimately, highly disruptive of exchange relations over long periods.[8] Periodic deteriorations and disruptions of international exchange are nothing new to the capitalist scene, and the current crisis in these relations merely repeats on an extended scale the kind of situation with which students of trade were already thoroughly familiar in the past century. The statement of a Venezuelan statesman is, indeed, of a kind often made in the past *and* in the present century by leaders of less developed countries referring to their experience with their more developed trading partners:

We have repeatedly pointed to the impoverishment of our countries as dependents of the North American economy. Before the energy crisis and before petroleum prices reached the levels at which they stand today, the raw materials produced by our countries were purchased year after year at prices which were never in proportion to or in equilibrium with the prices of the manufactured goods which our countries require for their development and which have been purchased largely in the United States. . . .[9]

The present somewhat misleading division of the world into rich and poor countries reflects, but does not altogether describe, the divisions encouraged by the law of unequal exchange. This law ensures that within the less developed countries most departments will experience on the average unfavorable terms in their exchanges with countries the majority of whose departments of production will experience better-than-average terms. It is not the famous – or infamous – law of comparative advantage that determines commodity flows and their relative rates of exchange. The strains of a mutual harmony of interest, sung so sweetly by economic apologists, are now and again drowned out by the noise of exchange inequalities and inequities.

Even before economic collapse turned attention elsewhere, distortions in terms and patterns of trade became so acute that they aroused inquiry into the matter. Called during a period of healthy expansion, the UN Conference of Trade and Development noted that between 1950 and 1963:

The slower growth in the quantity of exports of the developing countries and the adverse movements of their terms of trade were largely the reflection of the present commodity composition of their trade, consisting, as it does, predominantly of the exchange of primary products for manufactured imports whose relative positions in world markets have undergone significant changes. World trade in manufactures has been increasing at an annual rate more than twice that of trade in primary products.[10]

The adversity encountered by the developing nations in international exchange is in large measure the consequence of a chronic distortion of terms of exchange. For approximately the period under UN consideration in the report referred to, Pierre Jalee offers these estimates of terms of exchange (1958 = 100):

	1954	*1958*	*1965*
Developed capitalist countries, total commerce	97	100	102
Third World, total commerce	109	100	95
Third World, commerce with developed capitalism	112	100	93

There is much empirical confirmation of the impression of the victims of exchange that there is a pillaging of the Third World going on. Jalee summarizes his data:

In its exchanges with the developed capitalist countries, the Third World, therefore, lost ground to the extent of about 19%. In other words, to obtain the same manufactured product in 1965 as in 1954, the Third World had to sell a 19% greater volume of primary products. And it had to increase production by more than 19% in order to make any commercial headway at all.[11]

Jalee's manner of expressing the tendency is precisely in conformity with the law of unequal exchange, for it is not only through relative price movements but through the relative values of commodities being exchanged that the process of exploitation takes place. Exploitation is a multidimensional phenomenon.

While differential development of the productive forces yields inequalities in exchange, the continuing accumulation of capitals under these conditions may serve only to enlarge and extend the original unevenness. For departments technically advanced, either export prices rise per unit of value exported in relation to the price paid per unit of value imported; or, the value of exports declines per unit of money paid in relation to the unit of value imported; or both, in varying degree. But however unequal exchange shows itself, it involves a deterioration of terms of exchange on the underside and their chronic improvement on the upper side. In international as in domestic affairs, therefore, countertendencies are certain to appear.

The tendency to unequal exchange was especially powerful in the 1960s when the accumulation of capital was still running strongly. As terms moved dialectically between the advanced and the retarded, however, antithetical reactions emerged. Financial crises, debt crises, came periodically to threaten exchange relations as chronic imbalances in trade flooded some countries with currencies of those running chronic deficits. Threatened breakdowns brought new international conventions (still continuing), summoned legislators and statesmen to thrust their hands into sagging dikes, fluttered the economists' dovecotes, and conjured up visions of old crises that they thought had vanished from the new world of the Keynesian economics.

As in countering domestic depression, programs of reform and reconstruction are advanced, especially in financial-monetary realms where basic truth is thought to reside. Subsidies to the monopolists become popular once more, as well as tariffs, rebates, credits, and loans – the old gamut of bureaucratic inventions is trundled out in an effort to prevent a complete breakdown. New markets are diligently cultivated – to date with indifferent success in the largest of them, Russia and China – and always in the background the rumblings of actual and prospective trade warfare and the rattling of old arms as armaments industries are revived. Capitalist planning again shows its ex post character, in harmony with the principle that an ounce of repair is worth a pound of prevention. While the tendency to unequal exchange contributes much in the period of upswing to undermine the exchange order and establish the prerequisites for general collapse,[12] much of what then happens depends upon whether or not the tendency of the rate of profit to fall overpowers, or fails to overpower, the force of such rising countertendencies. Crises are less serious when the tendency for the rate of profit to fall is out of phase with some of its own elements such as the tendency to unequal exchange. On the other hand, when the main conjuncture points toward depression, the decline in the general rate of profit becomes decisive and the forces of instability exert an overwhelming influence.

Uneven development: social labor

Finally, the inherent imbalance and instability of capitalist exchange assert themselves in the production and exchange of labor power itself. The most important thing to be remembered in this connection is that the reproduction of the variegated grades of social labor power is also an interdependent process. This is so most obviously in that the economic means of subsistence that the different grades require for their reproduction are a joint or cooperative product of all of the grades of productive labor; in varying degree, all branches of productive labor participate in the creation of the material means of their own reproduction. Of only slightly less importance for understanding the law of unequal exchange as it works itself out in this realm is the fact that a structure of differential wage rates attaches itself to the different kinds and grades of social labor.

In the view of conventional economics the differential wages received by social labor in its different grades reflect above all the differential costs of producing these grades of labor; some of them being more and some less expensive, the structure of wages will disperse itself accordingly. The implication of the neoclassical theory of wages is that differential wages are by no means unjust and inequitable merely because of wage differences. As long as wage rates are proportioned to differential costs of reproduction, or as long as the law of value governs the structure of wages, while men may be unequal they are paid in conformity with their reproductive needs and, hence, are justly paid. A view such as this is still widespread in school economics.

The contention that wages gravitate to their natural levels has long been questioned, however. Even by the middle of the past century the astute observer John Cairnes was so disturbed by what he regarded as excessive discrepancies in wage disbursements that he sought a new explanation for the wage structure, and his theory of "non-competing groups" attempts to account for these discrepancies.[13] In this theory, discrepancies are shown to be the consequence of preexisting *social* discriminations affecting different groups of workers. In the old liberal theory of wages, wages would tend to proportionality with costs of production of labor provided there was a free mobility of laborers among different occupations. It is this free mobility that social discrimination prevents, whether the latter is based on race, nationality, sex, religion, or some other bigotry. Discrimination cuts off the tendency of wages to proportionality with costs of production of labor by reducing mobility. As a result, wage rates become disproportional to these costs.

So Cairnes introduced into liberal theory a most important factor that early liberals had assumed competition would naturally eradicate. By the mid-nineteenth century it was clear that competition would not only fail to do away with discrimination but that it would accommodate itself to old ailments, renewing their importance in the modern social context. To some extent, Cairnes' theory and the Marxian theory cover some of the same ground and are certainly concerned to explain the same important phenomena. However, the theory of unequal exchange offers a somewhat different view of the differential wage structure and the role of discrimination within it.

First of all, Cairnes' theory seems incapable of explaining the secular movement of wages toward *growing* disproportionality, and this movement may be observed to take place within the wage structure during periods of rapid accumulation. Secondly, even if we grant social mobility, and were capital able to realize this happy state, the structure of differential wages would still tend to an excessive distortion because of divergent movements of terms of exchange among all grades composing the division of social labor. In sum, the law of unequal exchange explains both the extent and secular movement of wage differentials. While it by no means denies the existence of social discrimination as an important factor in the general wage situation, it tells us that in this, as in other areas in which the law is operative, systematic deviations of wages from the values of labor power are only to be expected.

In the production of the various divisions of social labor, we are well aware that different ratios of *C* to *V* are utilized. As a rule, the value composition of the productive capitals varies directly with the level of training and skill of the laborer being produced. The doctor requires for his production a host of expensive educational and apprenticeship instruments – laboratory equipment and facilities, books, recreation and housing, an extended education and training – all consumed over a long period and most typically increased in volume with the inception of an active work career. Much the same might be said of many grades of skilled labor, while semiskilled labor is likewise expensive to reproduce. Unskilled labor, on the other hand, even today has minimal costs of reproduction, and these are labor rather than capital intensive. It needs, and for the most part gets – when it gets anything at all – a short apprenticeship and a mediocre education that hardly encourages an active mind. Education is catch as catch can, and housing, food, recreation, and all of the vital services are kept to a minimum standard.

Under these conditions it is hardly surprising that the law of unequal exchange should spread to its outer limit the structure of wages and salaries. Even where differentials can be minimized, as under socialism, differentials there will be; but nothing as compared with the capitalist structure. At the upper limit under capitalism they are far in excess of the exchange value of the advanced grades of technical and administrative priority; at the lower limit they are far below the exchange value of the labor power, and reproduction of the latter is a precarious business for the worker, while on the lowest social levels capital seeks to cut off entirely the process of the workers' reproduction. In general, the familiar torsion effect of the market system twists price-value relations throughout the spectrum. It should not be surprising that while the doctor can afford the housemaid, the latter keeps her troubles to herself. This is, after all, the main tendency.

The excessive and continued spreading of wages and salaries in extended reproduction of course gives rise to countertendencies. For labor power of the simpler grades, money wages decline relative to exchange value, and this occasions sporadic and sometimes desperate efforts by the worker to secure a minimal subsistence. The ruling class, for its part, is from time to time confronted with the need to act in order to keep the bottom from falling out altogether. Minimum wages, unemployment insurance, social security, and a handful of welfare services – all of these varying in scope and content according to national tradition – these prove the need of capitalism to counter the antisocial tendencies of the inherently irrational system. Official pauperism is brought about in considerable part by distortions of the wage-price structure that reinforce the tendency to surplus labor, while this semisocialization of minimal services itself evidences the tendency of the uninhibited competitive market to destroy those grades of social labor in numbers in excess of those that capital requires for its purpose. Thus the ruling class finds it politic to modify the natural system of liberty with its absurdly distorted wages, while the worker is forced to press for socialism. The present compromise, the welfare state, seeks to reconcile the opposing interests but promises to satisfy the needs of neither party. Within this state of affairs, what is the role of social discrimination?

Everywhere, it is safe to say, social discriminations are an obnoxious feature of the social landscape. But are they a function of the mode of production itself? In answer we say simply that it is not the ethnic, racial, religious, sexual, or political condition that gives rise to economic discrimination; rather, it is the converse. Economic discrimination encourages and fosters social discrimination in whatever forms are in keeping with the national tradition and experience.

Capitalism takes all varieties of social discrimination serviceable to its ends, refurbishes and systematizes them, and presses them into catering to its own requirements. In this sense, capitalism may be said to be the cause of discriminations that may, in some instances, have their roots far in the distant past. The most immediate instance to come to mind is the slave trade with its concomitant racism, but the continuing subjugation of women with its sexism, the Jew with its attendant anti-Semitism, are also to the point. While it is true that capital needs free labor that it can employ at profitable prices, those prices are the more favorable the more intense is competition among workers seeking employment. Mechanisms of discrimination have their monetary value, for they encourage workers to compete on racial, ethnic, or other bases. This is not all, however. The mode of production itself maintains competition in all its forms as a basic institution, but in what sense of the term is competition in bigotry basic to capitalism?

Given that capitalist society is class society – and this is built in to its relations of production – given, further, that the division of social labor demands a segregation of the working population into socially necessary divisions, then some principle or principles of discrimination are required in order to populate each division and in order to effect the main segregations required by relations of production in general. In other words, capitalism demands not only a division of population according to industrial function of the worker, but it demands an overall segregation between those who appropriate surplus value, that is, the capitalists, and those who produce it. This division of social labor, a division necessary and peculiar to the mode, must be obtained by a practice of segregation that separates the total population into higher and lower class divisions as the maintenance of relations of production dictates. What Veblen called "invidious distinctions" are thus constituent elements in the organization of capitalist relations of production.[14] They serve to track the population into its primary class compartments. While this is true of all of the various national capitalisms, since it is true of capitalism in general, it also allows full play for local and national prejudices in contributing to the overall result.

The accumulation of capital is much more than a simple quantitative accumulation of population; it involves qualitative segregations within the expanding population also. The required segregation of the population is carried out more quickly and at lower cost if capital avails itself of ancient prejudicial attitudes and practices that amount to a kind of free overhead capital, means of organizing for profit that facilitate the exploitation of labor for all those who enlist their assistance. The fact that social discriminations exist are, like air in processes of combustion or like the natural fertility of land, a contribution of nature to the required result, in this case the segregation of the population at minimum cost to the entrepreneurs. In assisting in the segregation of labor power, social discrimination simply joins hands, as it were, with the law of unequal exchange. The latter works to encourage the production of a labor force of differentiated skills in the following manner. By paying the technically and administratively advanced grades of labor at rates in excess of exchange value, the market mechanisms of capitalism stimulate the production of these grades of labor by making them more attractive to the young, on the one hand; on the other, by pulling surplus value out of labor of less expensive grades and transferring it to advanced sectors for overpayment and, hence, overproduction of advanced grades, the market cruelly represses the production of labor power of less skilled and educated workers. And this, of course, is precisely the effect of social discrimination. Social discrimination, by intensifying competition among laborers and all candidates for employment, helps to ensure that the victims of discrimination should stay on the lower rungs of the ladder of social wages, while the subjects of discrimination move onward and upward into advanced categories. This is why the fruits of social discrimination disperse themselves into ranks of superior and inferior throughout the occupational and wage hierarchy.[15]

Therefore, Cairnes perceives but half the truth. Social discrimination only partly explains the structure of differential wages. The other half of the truth is that capitalism perpetuates and even nurtures discriminatory attitudes and practices in view of the necessity of reproducing a stratified and specialized labor force geared to the military mode. The modern ghetto is built and maintained by capital's need to accumulate a hierarchically ordered and segregated population conforming to circulatory and to productive needs.

Class interrelations and unequal exchange

In discussing to this point the various realms in which the law of unequal exchange is operative, reference has been made to the transfer of surplus value in excess of price of production (where value compositions are below the social average) to departments, sectors, or economies where surplus value is ordinarily less than price of production. This transfer effect is a consequence of competition's yielding prices of production that equalize rates of return upon invested capitals. But in view of this transfer a question may arise – and it arises especially in conjunction with the production of labor power to man the social division of labor – whether the transfer of surplus value does not prove that labor is exploiting labor rather than that capital is exploiting labor. The better-paid labor exploits the poorer-paid, does it not? And labor of the rich countries, for example, exploits labor in the poor countries, does it not?[16]

The brief remarks about to be made on this subject are not intended to exhaust it but only to point in the direction of a definitive and detailed answer. Let us begin with the issue by looking at the international situation of capital. We referred at the beginning of this chapter to the extension of economic interdependencies under capitalism. Growing apace with the network of input-output interdependencies has come a kind of centralization of international capital. The extension of economic interdependencies proceeds through the medium of, and at the same time encourages and promotes, a growing array of international agencies, multinational public and private corporations, and an array of amalgamations among all these units. Charles Bettelheim summarizes the situation:

The tendency of the capitalist mode of production to become worldwide is manifested not only through the constitution of a group of national economies forming a complex and hierarchical structure, including an imperialist pole and a dominated one, and not only through antagonistic relations that develop between the different "national economies" and the different states, but also through the constant "transcending" of "national limits" by big capital (the formation of "international big capital," "world firms," etc., the effect of which is to make the reproduction of the capital thus centralized increasingly "independent" of the "local" conditions of reproduction characteristic of a particular country) and through the tendency for historically formed national markets to merge into a "common market," something that presupposes the "merging" or "alliance" of some big capitalist groups.[17]

In one sense, this is all quite obvious, but in important ways it is not. What is less obvious is that behind the multiplication and consolidations among the agencies described there develops also some increasing degree of unification among national ruling classes. This tendency to class unification proceeds, not only because the proliferation of agencies and their centralization make for international class coordinations on ever higher levels, but because the agencies themselves come to be managed by representatives and delegates who are in fact emissaries of the international capitalist class that is coming into being. Without attempting to spell out with any precision the relationship of these managerial delegates to the class assembly of capitalists, suffice it to say that the managers at the international as at the national level seek to compromise local and national class interests with those of the larger body coming into being. The international managers constitute the executive wing of the international class.

One should not overemphasize the level of development of the international class at this stage in its formation, but it seems true that the principal conveyor of capital in its global missions today is not the bank, the multinational corporation (despite its recent publicity), the development agency, the United Nations, and so on, but that all of these are mere instrumentalities whose popularity and effectiveness may now wax and now wane, taking them individually, but whose constant coordinating component are the managerial strata directly and, over them, the grand bourgeoisie of the various nations whose interests they seek to reconcile and, when necessary, compromise. The development of the international class is thus far from completed, and resurgencies of nationalism may strain from time to time the degree of integration achieved. The present disarray of the European Common Market illustrates the point. However, the tendency is for the international class to become progressively more autonomous of local and national authorities; it becomes, as Bettelheim says, independent of local conditions.

This discussion of the international movement is not at all irrelevant to the question of whether developed labor exploits undeveloped labor at the global level. While an extending network of economic interdependencies among local and national labor forces implies a product that is ever more a cooperatively produced product within a global division of labor, the emerging international class contributes to this unification and to the extension of interdependency in order better to appropriate the surplus generated by the interdependent system of *global* labor.

With the development of the global economy described, and with the accumulation of capital at this level by the international class, the same laws of motion that govern the development of the national govern also the development of the international economy.

The latter exhibits the same features of unevenness and instability as did the formerly predominant national economy. The law of unequal exchange works to promote a differential structure of international wages in which, quite regardless of national boundaries, wages of technical and administratively specialized labor move ahead of the exchange value of this labor power, while wages of simple forms of global labor move behind exchange value, as the law of unequal exchange has shown itself to work at the purely national level. At the international as at the national level, capital moves competitively to establish prices of production for commodities and prices of production for all grades of labor power that equalize returns upon money capitals invested: money capitals invested by capitalists in the production and reproduction of these commodities, including labor power. It is to the capitalists that the gains accrue that follow from the international structure of differential wages, and they all share alike through the reallocation of surplus value from lower to higher departments and economies. This transfer of surplus value from lower to higher departments is merely the way in which capitalism secures its equalization of profit rates for all capitalists everywhere who contribute capital to the common investment pool.

At the level of world economy, too, both the advanced and retarded branches of productive labor contribute to their common exploitation, and although the latter contribute relatively more than the former to the surplus shared out among the capitalists of all countries, the overpayment of the former and the underpayment of the latter are circumstances for which neither is responsible. These are merely the consequence of the extension of capitalist relations of production at the global level. Of course, this system of distorted and differential wage payments does, nationally and internationally, serve also a political purpose quite useful to capital. The fact that the better-skilled and administratively more useful workers are everywhere overpaid, while the less skilled industrial and agricultural workers are everywhere underpaid, helps to keep labor everywhere divided and, hence, conquered. Overpayment distracts the more privileged from the fact that they, too, are exploited along with the less privileged through a mechanism that takes from both of them the surplus value that they mutually and cooperatively produce. The nationalism of the politicians, along with that of the economists, only contributes further to concealing the ever more systematic exploitation of all the productive divisions of global labor. The very language of developed and undeveloped economies that we have ourselves used in the foregoing discussion contributes something to the general confusion. Rey's observations on this are much to the point:

> . . . every day the press speaks of "poles of development," of countries that are "developed," "underdeveloped," "on the road to development." But what is it that is developed, underdeveloped, or on the way to development? The whole world knows, it is the volume of production of material goods, of use values. To be sure. But it is also, and it is above all, relations of capitalist production that are being developed, and among them the relation that determines everything: the extortion of surplus value by the bourgeoisie from the working class.[18]

Capital has, then, a vested interest in unequal exchange and, therefore, in the relations of production that give rise to it. A part of the economic mechanism by whose means the extortion of surplus value is accomplished, unequal exchange at the same time works to develop a network of class alliances (Rey calls them) that consolidates capital's political hegemony. Unequal exchange, and the whole market apparatus that nurtures it, is thus central to capital's economic and political dominion, for it helps to crystallize and strengthen the class relations that are peculiar to the mode. When we come to examining these relations more directly (Chapters 9–11), we shall see in greater detail the actual social significance of the normal functioning of the market order.

But at this juncture it is economic instability that deserves a more careful airing, especially in view of the crisis now riding hard upon us. While the crisis is one in whose generation the market-pricing mechanism of capital has played a considerable part, the latter is, after all, but one of the players in the drama of capitalist collapse.

8

Accumulation in the
advanced capitalism:
the nature of the crisis

The developmental sequence: the first and second phases

Despite an appearance of relative stability in the years immediately following World War II, the unevenness and instability of accumulation remain what they have always been: reflections of contradictions embedded within the apparatus of industrial and circulatory accumulation, contradictions that culminate in economic breakdown and whatever may follow from that. To be sure, in the course of irregular advances the underlying situation gradually alters; times change, and with them come changes in the form of the crisis.[1] As capital accumulates through successive phases, the laws of motion work ever more decisively and powerfully in the promotion of economic exhaustion, of an inability to continue the vital work of developing further the productive forces. In the end, even in periods of activity, the swimmer treads water rather than move against the current. The struggle begins then in earnest for a socialist release from an increasingly intolerable predicament.[2]

But, as always, in order to see a complicated present one must return to the past for understanding. In order to perceive correctly the manner of working of laws of motion in the present phase, one must consider what has previously been. In contemplating the events of the post-World War II period, one must return to the historical setting that throws into proper relief the real character of the phase in which current events are taking place.

Let us go back briefly to the primitive phase of the industrialization process. It has often been said that the base from which industrial accumulation was launched was the wage or consumer goods sectors: "In the initial stage of industrialization, investment is

181

directed mainly to the consumer goods sector."[3] Once the development of these largely agricultural sectors is proceeding, a movement of industrial accumulation can begin when conditions are otherwise ripe. On this situation, Marx expresses what every historian knows: ". . . in short, as the general conditions requisite for production by the modern industrial system have been established, this mode of production acquires an elasticity, a capacity for sudden extensions by leaps and bounds that finds no hindrance except in the supply of raw material and in the disposal of the produce."[4]

In the first stage, limits to development are reached when the value composition of capital reaches a certain level within consumer sectors, and especially when prospects for profit from further investment in those sectors become relatively dim with the advent of better prospects elsewhere. With the freeing of labor for industrial employment, and with the incidence of technical progress in means of production, particularly in sources of power – with the Industrial Revolution – industrial accumulation now accelerates. Then value compositions of capital begin to rise in industrial sectors, and as they rise above the social average, terms of exchange shift in favor of those sectors, confirming and sustaining entrepreneurial expectations of profit. Capital goods sectors now become the leading sectors, and for a time the production of consumers' and wage goods is of secondary importance.

In the second phase, industrial accumulation proceeds by leaps and bounds, but pauses between the jumps are characteristic. At this juncture the economic crises that now and again appear are not primarily the result of intersectoral imbalances, however. Rather, the crises come in the wake of a failure to maintain a rate of growth of profits sufficient to justify continued expansion. Intersectoral balance is not as much of a problem as the tendency for the general rate of profit to fall – but first the intersectoral question.

The requirement for stable exchange between department I (means of production) and department II (wage goods) is that the growth in value of means of production destined for use in II should be equal to the growth of output produced in II but destined for use in I.[5] If we assume what is in fact reasonable in the second phase of industrial accumulation, that department I grows more rapidly than department II, we have:

$$\Delta C_1 + \Delta V_1 > \Delta C_2 + \Delta V_2 \qquad (8.1)$$

while for an exchange equilibrium between the two departments it is only necessary that

$$\Delta C_2 = \Delta V_1 \qquad (8.2)$$

It follows from these that

$$\Delta C_1 > \Delta V_2 \qquad (8.3)$$

that in the second phase an equilibrium expansion *may be* maintained if investment in means of production in department I proceeds more rapidly than investment in wage goods in department II.[6] And *this is precisely what is happening* in the second phase when technical change combines with a favorable movement of terms of exchange to swing to the fore the capitalists' investment in producers' goods sectors. As terms of exchange move in favor of department I and against II, the accumulation of means of production accelerates and investment in wage goods is relatively retarded, as stability requires.

Insofar as intersectoral balance is concerned, phase two is a stable phase and expansion continues until the disposal of the produce becomes troublesome, that is, until the general rate of profit begins to decline; the falling rate of profit, the force to which Marx drew attention in discussing this phase in *Capital*, becomes the primary depressant in the period of industrial accumulation. Profit decline is the result, first, of the slowdown in rise of the rate of surplus value accompanying the rise in productivity; beyond some point the rate of surplus value increases more slowly than productivity as a consequence of the displacement of labor power that goes with technical change (rising value composition of capital).[7] It is the result, second, of the rise in wage rates that follows on the growth of department I's demand for labor power, especially as full employment is reached.[8] Thus as the upswing continues in the second phase, its force gradually weakens, culminating in the classical crisis of industrial capitalism. Corey's reminder is appropriate here:

Up to 1919 these industries (means of production) absorbed an increasingly larger number of workers, relatively more than the industrial producing consumption goods. That meant an upswing of capitalism, an increasing output and absorption of capital goods. It meant also an offset to the displacement of workers by the rising productivity of labor.[9]

But while expansion in the second phase was self-balancing – or the history of capitalist development might have been shorter even than it now promises to be – the tendency for the rate of profit to fall was still powerful even though tracing to relatively limited economic difficulties.

However, over the longer term, the industrial expansion of phase two encounters increasing marketing problems, especially since it is producing an output composed so largely of means of production. Of course, the production of consumption goods provides one vent for department I output, and to this outlet increasing attention begins to be paid. On the other hand, if department II is to absorb an appreciable portion of the output of I, new markets must also be found for consumption goods. This necessity is complicated by the advance in productivity in department II that accompanies its expansion. Nevertheless, an expanded marketing of consumption goods appears as something of a prerequisite to the advance of productivity and of scale that is taking place in department I. Under these circumstances the acquisition of foreign markets, that is, imperialism, appears increasingly as a manifest destiny of capital. Between imperialism with its new market outlets, and the expansion of consumer goods production in II, capital now seeks answers to the dilemmas arising out of the industrial accumulations of the second phase. This brings capital to the threshold of the third phase of development.

The developmental sequence: the third to the fourth phase

Even before the present century opened, and in the then leading countries of capitalism – England, France, Germany, the United States – a new emphasis upon high consumption was in evidence. The drive for markets that came hard on the heels of the industrial accumulation was, as Hobson thought,[10] born of the need to dispose of a growing volume of consumption goods in order to justify and sustain the industrial accumulation and the profits it portended. The growth of department II required to realize and sustain the accumulation pointed to a need for elaborating new marketing instrumentalities at home and abroad. The third period is one, therefore, in which international competitions flourish and intensify, and it is one in which, at home as well as abroad, new circulatory vehicles are rapidly assembled in commercial and financial fields. This is the phase of monopoly capital in which monopoly power is extended to embrace all basic means of production through financial, commercial, and organizational means. Accompanying this movement is a new emphasis also upon personnel, upon the production of the various forms of official and clerical labor that the new administration requires. Not only do the new elements of the working population – engineers, salesmen, accountants and bookkeepers, clerks, and so on – supply more or less sophisticated marketing products and services, but they also comprise new sources of demand for final products, and so number among the new consumers for whom the search is in progress.

Thus we find developing in the third phase a shift from the goal of accumulating means of production to the goal of consumption, so that the latter now appears, although in strikingly new bourgeois forms, as a primary end of capital accumulation rather than what in fact it is, a mere means of sustaining accumulation. From this extravagant epoch come those high-consumption models whose material delights still enliven the bourgeois theoretical and political propaganda.[11]

But now once again, as technical change infects the stream of productive activity, and as value compositions begin to rise in the new sectors of department II, terms of exchange begin to shift. They move now in favor of II and against I. The tendency is, then, for means of consumption to grow more rapidly than means of production ($\Delta C_2 > \Delta C_1$), especially when the scale of ostentatious and militaristic consumptions is taken into account. There now arises, therefore, a new problem of balance in intersectoral exchanges. A new instability appears within the process of capital accumulation, adding its force to that of the declining rate of profit. The latter, of course, as in earlier phases, continues to exert a strong influence in bringing expansions to their close.

The new instability arises from the impossibility of maintaining any longer a balanced exchange between departments I and II. What causes this instability is the fact that the constant capital in department II is expanding in relation to the constant capital in department I:

$$\Delta C_2 > \Delta C_1 \tag{8.4}$$

This reflects the fact that an important part of the new market for means of production is in the production of means of consumption.

With the accumulation of capital proceeding, while on the average the value composition of capital is rising, we have:

$$\Delta C_1 + \Delta V_1 > \Delta C_2 + \Delta V_2 \qquad (8.5)$$

And from (8.4) and (8.5) it follows that

$$\Delta V_1 > \Delta V_2 \qquad (8.6)$$

It further follows from this, in view of the general condition for exchange stability (8.2), that

$$\Delta V_1 > \Delta C_1 \qquad (8.7)$$

Equation (8.7) expresses the new stability requirement when the growth of constant capital in II is proceeding more rapidly than in I. It means simply that the value composition of capital in producing means of production (I) must now decline. If II is to absorb a growing volume of means of production out of I, then in exchange I must absorb a growing volume of means of consumption out of II, that is, if exchange is to be an equal exchange. And this is the condition that cannot be realized in the third phase. In the third phase, then, economic instability follows from *both* the instability of exchange relations between I and II and the usual long-term tendency for the rate of profit to fall, the tendency that results from the decline in the rate of surplus value (or from the decrease in its rate of growth).

When in the course of industrial accumulation the time comes that markets must be found for both the growing industrial *and* the growing wage goods output, an imbalance in exchange is added to the tendency for the rate of profit to fall. Furthermore, the movement of terms of exchange, working always to accelerate the accumulation of capital in whatever realms new profit possibilities are in the offing, works in the third phase to intensify the instability. The shifting terms in favor of C_2 and against C_1 spreads ever wider the gap between the growth of demand for wage goods for department I and the growth of demand for means of production for use in department II. This may all be expressed rather less algebraically and in thoroughly familiar historical terms.

With the acceleration of capital accumulation in department II, an excess of productive capacity and of labor employed in I begins to appear. And the displacement of labor from employment in I makes ever more difficult the sale of wage goods to I on the required scale, that is, on the scale required for an equilibrium exchange between the departments. The new crisis follows from the new consumption. Corey sums up very nicely the special situation of capitalism as it enters its high-consumption phase in the twentieth century:

In the epoch of the upswing of capitalism the number of industrial workers grow constantly. In particular, the capital goods industries *absorbed* more workers than the industries producing consumer goods; but now they *displace* more workers. . . . This complete reversal of previous trends took place when the American economy was still on the upswing, although the rate of expansion was downward; it now becomes the creator of an increasing surplus population of unemployed and unemployable workers. For it not only means that the productivity of labour is rising more than production, but that technological displacement of workers is aggravated by the downward movement of production, particularly in capital goods. [12]

But the worst is yet to come. While the crisis and collapse of 1929 was caused not only by the falling rate of profit but by growing intersectoral exchange instability, more ominous developments were already in view and had been in view for some time. These are developments that come to full bloom in the fourth phase of capitalist development and portend a yet more serious and prolonged interval of stagnation following the crisis. At this point, in addition to exchange instability and the tendency for the rate of profit to fall, there comes a rise in the relative rate of unproductive consumption, a rise in the rate of accumulation of unproductive labor, the leading sector in the phase of capitalist decline.

The developmental sequence: the fourth phase

In the third phase there is a displacement of labor from the production of means of production, whereas stability requires, to the contrary, a relative enlargement of the volume of this labor. The result is what would appear to be a realization crisis, a deficiency of demand for wage or consumer goods, but is in fact only partly a matter of realization. Even more is it a crisis in intersectoral exchange that merely *appears* as a chronic deficiency of effective demand in the aggregate (an appearance on which Keynesians have sought to erect a whole system of political economy). Even more is it caused by a failure of investment in labor power in department I to grow at the pace required for a balanced exchange with department II. Because the crisis does not, at bottom, arise from a failure of effective demand, but from an imbalance tracing to investment failures, the cure for the crisis cannot be confined to the manipulation of effective demand in the Keynesian style.

Actually, well before the collapse in the late twenties, the drive for new markets as vents for the output of consumer or wage goods had led capital far beyond the confines of department I consumers, that is, industrial laborers. It had led already to imperialistic international competitions and to militarism, on the one hand, and, on the other, to a significantly expanding circulatory system. In relation to the circulatory blowup it had contributed to an expanded production of personnel needed to man the extending universe and, hence, to the production of all the material means of circulation that these personnel would require in order to provide their special services for capital. It had led, in sum, to a growing investment in unproductive labor.

Even before World War I, government budgets were increasingly military budgets, reflecting the industrialists' preoccupations with excess capacities, particularly in capital goods industries. Here, too, the unproductive solution to inherent imbalance was being pushed with chauvinistic fervor. Although such developments were neither advocated nor defended as instruments of stabilization through realization, they were seen to help to take up the slack in the industrial order. Particularly in relation to the military expansion, public aversion could only gradually be overcome. Yet the connection between military demands for hard- and software and the seeming deficiency of aggregate demand was sure to be made eventually. The experience of the years of the Great Depression and the recovery from it were most instructive to capitalists and to their administrative assistants. Coontz comments:

> Subsequently, the rise in unproductive government expenditures brought us out of the Great Depression. But the limited welfare expenditures of the New Deal did not suffice . . . it was not until the remilitarization of the economy that Roosevelt became acceptable to the capital goods industry. Some three or four months after Pearl Harbor, full employment was achieved.[13]

Lessons were being learned, and ever since World War II the preference of public managers for unproductive investment – a preference encouraged by their sponsors – has been more easily implemented. As for the liberal solution, even the limited welfare expenditures of the postwar period have invariably included a large and growing complement of administrative overhead, both in personnel and in means of administration, helping to satisfy the demand requirement for goods. But this brings us back again to the laws of motion of the advanced capitalism. How do these laws contribute to the relative rise in unproductive expenditure, to investment on a rising scale in an unproductive circulatory-administrative apparatus?

The general answer to this puzzling question is contained within the *modus operandi* of the earlier movement from one phase to another. Always, the drive to accumulate leads investors within a given phase into realms *outside of those* in which the previous accumulation had centered. With the reduction of rates of profit in sectors where the lead had previously been concentrated, a consequence of the failure of the rate of surplus value to continue its rise, the advance of technique combines with a prospect of more favorable terms of exchange elsewhere – a prospect of surer and better profits in other sectors. Furthermore, this prospect is subsequently confirmed by the favorable movement of terms of exchange that transpires as development of the new sectors proceeds, a movement that gives the competitive edge to those investors who are there "fustest with the mostest." It is essentially this recurring combination of circumstances that leads capital from its third to its fourth stage with its peculiar and misguided solution to the realization problem. The new solution is a highly unproductive one, but it is not brought into being by malefic managerial students of the Great Depression; the capitalist ardor is for profit, not history. It is profit and the prospect of profit brought about by a torsion effect of terms of exchange, favoring new sectors and throwing older sectors into disfavor, that underlies the transition from one phase to the next. In the transition from the third to the fourth phase, the state now appears as a principal vehicle for the investors' conveyance, and total dominance over its functioning is a prerequisite to the unproductive investment of phase four. The new investment targets, technically defined, are broadly in new means of administration, however: in the material means of production with which administrative and managerial personnel must work, and in the production of the new divisions of managerial and administrative personnel themselves, the technicians and professionals whose ad-

ministrative and managerial specialties serve best the new
dynasticism of capital.

Altogether, these comprise the new sectors that are leading sectors in the drive to accumulate, the new highways and byways of
administrative-circulatory operations. To summarize, in the first
phase of capitalist development the drive to accumulate falls upon
means of consumption and in particular wage goods; in the second
phase it is into the accumulation of industrial capitals, means of
production. In the third phase the drive carries into consumption
goods sectors in order to provide outlets for department I and to
provide investment outlets in the expansion of a new consumption.
In the fourth phase the accent is on the accumulation of administrative capitals in circulatory employments (a phase that leads
naturally out of phase three into an expanded output of middle-
class personnel who are the workers of the circulatory sphere). But
in general the mechanism of investment allocation works consistently throughout each and every phase. Always it leads from sectors
and departments where, for whatever reason, the rate of profit is
declining, into sectors and departments where the progress of
technique brings a prospect of a higher rate of turnover on capitals
invested.

In the historical sequence it happens that the fourth and final
phase of capitalist development brings capital into wholly unproductive fields. The tendency to unequal exchange, which on the
one hand provides happy prospects for an extending investment in
administrative capitals employed in circulatory work, on the other
hand causes a rise in the rate of unproductive consumption. The
latter rise combines with the old tendency for the rate of profit to
fall, and together they constitute one profoundly powerful force
making for economic crisis and collapse. As always happened in
previous phases, the drive to accumulate eventually aborts, and
there follow economic stagnation and an effective complete fettering of possibilities for development of the productive forces. This is
the main tendency of capital accumulation in the fourth phase. In
this phase, however, the accumulation of capital, by virtue of circumstances peculiar to this epoch, yields some remarkable and
special symptoms of the economic decline in progress. Among these
are at a certain juncture a strong tendency to inflation, on the one
side, and, on the other, a tendency to secularly rising unemployment. What Samuelson has called "stagflation" is symptomatic of

the laws of motion we have been describing, and we must now look a bit further into this feature of the fourth phase of development.

The nature of stagflation: its relation to the crisis

With accumulation proceeding, the advanced capitalism confronts simultaneously both of the evils that it had previously encountered consecutively: inflation and unemployment. "Compounding the economic problem of inflation," Samuelson writes, "is the fact that, often and in many countries, there persists a simultaneous problem of unemployment and stagnant growth." The problem actually exists with particular force and in a rather special form in the advanced countries. It is summarized, too, in the well-known Phillips-curve construction that shows an inverse correlation between the degree of unemployment and the degree of inflation of prices. Although the phenomenon has been widely discussed in the past few years, the baffled economist still asks in blue and doleful tones: "What did I do to get so black and blue?" While conventional economics simply finds no general simple explanation for the main facts, the mystery yields its secrets quite readily to the Marxian economics. Stagflation is a state whose root cause is an excessive unproductive consumption. The condition worsens rapidly when the rate of unproductive consumption rises.

In proceeding with the analysis, we begin with a state in which unproductive consumption is zero. Assume, first, a rate of accumulation such as $O_{U/S=0}$ (in Figure 8.1). Assume that the rate of growth of aggregate demand suffices to realize the value of the output and that labor power, too, grows at the rate demanded by accumulation. The first observation of importance is that under these conditions the rate of growth of demand that suffices to realize the value of the output ($M_t = O_t$, $M_{t+1} = O_{t+1}$, etc.) suffices also to circulate the productive input of the next period. This is because the entire value of the output of each period is *productively* consumed, so that if the demand is equal to the value of the output, it will also be equal to the value of the subsequent input, since the two are equal. Therefore, with effective demand rising at the required rate, money values are throughout in moving equilibrium with outputs and inputs:

$$M_t = O_t = I_{t+1}, M_{t+1} = O_{t+1} = I_{t+2}, \text{etc.} \tag{8.8}$$

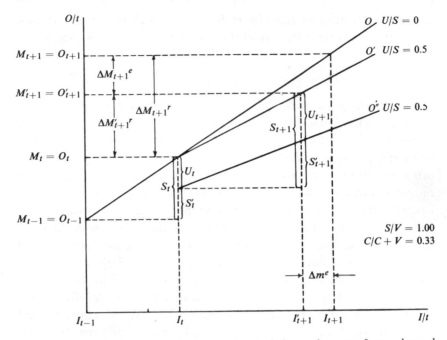

Figure 8.1. Unproductive consumption, economic retardation, and sources of excess demand in stagflation.

As long as the demand in each period rises sufficiently so as to guarantee that the value of the growing output is realized, all money and real values will remain in aggregative balance.

The situation immediatley changes when we assume an increase in the rate of unproductive consumption. This means that a portion of the output – more precisely, a portion of the surplus value – is to be used unproductively; that is, it will not appear as an increment to input in the period following. If under these conditions the effective demand suffices to circulate the value of the output ($M_t = O_t$, $M_{t+1} = O_{t+1}$, etc.), that demand will then be in excess of the exchange value of the productive input of the period following. The realization of what is unproductively consumed ensures that an excess of demand for productive input will be generated. In Figure 8.1, $I_{t+1} > I'_{t+1}$ by the amount of unproductive consumption $U_t(=m_{t+1}{}^e)$. The unproductive consumption generates an excess demand for productive input in the approximate magnitude of the value of the unproductive consumption of the period. For each and every period the same will be true, provided always that demand rises at the rate required to circulate the value of the gross output, and we have the equation:

$$M_t = O_t > I'_{t+1}, M_{t+1} = O_{t+1} > I'_{t+2}, \text{etc.} \qquad (8.9)$$

In each and every period an excess demand for productive input appears: m_t^e, m_{t+1}^e, and so on, as shown in Figure 8.1. With unproductive consumption proceeding at a fixed rate, so that a fixed portion of the surplus of each period is unproductively consumed, the magnitude of the excess demand, like the magnitude of what is unproductively consumed, increases by absolute amounts with each period of reproduction. Demand is thus chronically in excess of the value of the productive input, and as a result it works to drive up the prices of factor inputs, labor power, raw materials, wage goods, machinery, and so on. The underlying fact determines that this should be so. The wage goods and means of production that come to be engaged in unproductive work, that are the means of producing what is to be unproductively consumed, must be drawn from the productive sectors of the economy. They must be brought into unproductive employment through competitive bidding for all means of subsistence that would otherwise be used productively. This is especially the case during intervals of expansion in the fourth phase, when unproductive investment is large and growing rapidly. As a consequence, the prices of means of production and of means of consumption are subject to a continuing inflation from the pressure of a chronic excess demand.[14]

The same rise in the rate of unproductive consumption that pumps an excess demand for productive inputs retards the rate of growth of real output and, at the same stroke, reduces the required rate of growth of labor power and reduces, therefore, the rate of growth of demand for labor power. The rise in the rate of unproductive consumption makes a further addition to the relative surplus population and adds to secular unemployment. If accumulation now proceeds at its new, reduced rate, the demand for labor power rising more slowly than before, secular unemployment will run above its previous level. These effects of the rise in the U/S ratio are not always observable in the short run. In wartime, or during a period of preparation for war, only the inflationary effect is likely to be pronounced, for the growing surplus population is then absorbed into the military. The schizophrenic effect of the two in combination returns on the return of peace. Of course, as emphasized, a rise in the rate of unproductive consumption, and especially its secular increase, is not exclusively associated with the rise of militarism, imperialism, war, etc. With the maturation of capitalism and the relative acceleration in the accumulation of circulatory capitals, and with the elaboration also of a "welfare" system that puts labor on the dole and insures its absence from productive employment, unproductive consumption is subject to a secular increase. This makes inflation and unemployment coexistent and chronic features of a social landscape that is drying up.

There is yet one further source of excess demand in the situation described, and this, under appropriate conditions, makes the inflationary pressure all the greater. It is characteristic of capitalism that it should finance the *increase* in the rate of unproductive consumption in such a fashion that effective demand continues to rise at the rate required *prior* to the increase in unproductive consumption. In Figure 8.1, again, when unproductive consumption rises, the *required* increase in effective demand is reduced from $\Delta M_{t+1}{}^r$, the increase required at the old rate of accumulation, to $M'_{t+1}{}^r$, the increase in demand required at the new, lower rate of accumulation. On the one hand, the increase in the rate of unproductive consumption reduces the real rate of accumulation, and reduces, therefore, the required rate of growth of effective demand. On the other, despite the reduction in the required rate of growth of demand, the actual rate continues to grow at its previous pace, or even at a somewhat higher rate than before, because of the deficit-financing devices on which capital falls when it finds projects to its taste: a military operation, a space race, bread, and circuses. In Figure 8.1 this new bit of excess demand is:

$$\Delta M_{t+1}{}^e = \Delta M_{t+1}{}^r - \Delta M'_{t+1}{}^r \tag{8.10}$$

the further increment to excess demand that results from the circumstances described. This excess, to repeat, is an excess relative to the lowered rate of growth of gross output.

The retardation of the general rate of growth that accompanies a rise in the rate of unproductive consumption is normally accompanied by a growth of money expenditures through deficit financing that exceeds the general rate of growth. This creates an excess demand for gross output, and this excess of demand is over and above the excess demand for factor inputs that is generated whatever the rate of unproductive consumption might be ($\Delta m_t{}^e$, $\Delta m_{t+1}{}^e$, etc.). The normal excess demand for inputs is supplemented by an excess demand for outputs, and the divorce between monetary and real values becomes now perfectly general. For every period in which the growth rate of demand exceeds the requirement, we have instead of equation (8.8):

$$M_{t+1} > O'_{t+1} > I'_{t+2}, M_{t+2} > O'_{t+2} > I'_{t+3}, \text{ etc.} \qquad (8.11)$$

The disequilibrium at the aggregative level is generalized. Accumulation slackens off and becomes more irregular as the crisis threatens a total collapse.

Stagflation is, then, an integral part of the phase of accumulation immediately preceding and blending in with the advanced crisis . It is the observable expression of the law of aggregative disequilibrium attending the secular elevation of the rate of unproductive consumption. This rise, in turn, traces largely to the law of unequal exchange, a law that throws the investment mechanisms of state monopoly capitalism into a wholly eccentric and antisocial role. Investment becomes unproductive because the profit motive combines with shifting terms of exchange to determine this result. The net consequence of the movement of capital into excessive and ever-growing administrative-circulatory extensions is the retardation and repression of economic growth. The advent of the crisis is hastened and its severity intensified as the rise of unproductive consumption reinforces the tendency for the general rate of profit to fall.

The place of stagflation in the advanced crisis

The development of the fourth phase, like earlier stages of accumulation, exhibits the usual tendency for the rate of profit to fall.[15] Among economists, and including among them some Keynesian Marxists, resulting tendencies for unemployment to rise are still traced to deficiencies in aggregate demand even though, as the course of events makes clear, declines in aggregate demand are the consequence of the crisis and not its cause: The drive to bring corporate budgets back into balance, which depresses aggregate demand, reflects the fact that economic decline is already well along. Such facts, however, do not touch the reputedly scientific economist, destroying the theory on which the previous expansion was thought to have been founded. Throughout the advanced capitalism the growth of effective demand has since World War II

been the basic principle of the new economics and its attendant
political economy. The consequences of Keynesian policy we have
already observed at the theoretical level. Not only do its policies
underlie the secular tendency to inflation – a tendency that
strengthens with the rise in the rate of unproductive consumption –
but they underlie the tendency to economic stagnation and regression as well. Throughout the advanced capitalism in its fourth
phase, an extending investment in monetary, commercial,
political, and military promotions has been assiduously practiced
under the banner of Keynesianism. The more systematic the
realization of profits under these auspices, however, the more
powerful and steady the movement into the fourth phase has
become. Capital has taken to heart Malthus' advice and subsidized
unproductive labor on an extending scale, but, as Ricardo feared
and as Marx anticipated, the rise in the rate of unproductive consumption in no way develops Malthus' "powers of production." On
the contrary, that rise retards the real rate of growth, promotes the
inflationary accompaniment to this retardation, and, finally, joins
with the rising value composition of capital to bring down the
general rate of profit.

In the American case the retardation had already become quite
marked with the close of the Korean War in the late fifties. A
decrease in the growth rate and the rising levels of unemployment
then suggest the underlying strength of the tendency for the rate of
profit to fall. Early in the postwar period, the tendency to decline
threatened with the exhaustion of the influence of technical change
upon profits[16] and with the appearance of chronic excess capacity
in means of production and, finally, with a new acceleration of the
accumulation of unproductive labor in managerial and circulatory
employment,[17] including a revitalization of the military establishment from a brief interval of ill fortune following World War II.
Seeds of general disequilibrium are beginning to sprout, but it is
not yet time for the harvest. Consumer demand is still strong, and
with consumer prices rising and money profits growing, accumulation proceeds.[18] The military expansion and an enlarged space race
give continuing fillips to demand, which, in turn, ensure that the
limits of accumulation will soon be reached. By the mid-sixties the
laws of motion were asserting themselves quite forcibly, and their
pressure became most apparent to casual viewers in the social indicators: the antiwar movement, civil rights, women's liberation,
and so on. Nor is evidence lacking in conventional economic series.

It is after 1965, for instance, that the inflation of wholesale as well as retail prices testifies to the dimensions of the growing disparity between monetary and real values and to the reduction in the real rate of growth that underlies it all.[19] Labor productivity rises ever more slowly now, and unit labor costs increase.[20] Corporate profits begin to decline, and this, in particular, forces widespread and strong entrepreneurial reaction. With economic as well as political backs against the wall, monopoly power assumes a more forthright and vigorous stance in order to counter the falling rate of profit. Managerial cadres close ranks, and the administration of a continuing inflation appears as the best way out of the profit squeeze. Corporate and public monopoly power combine yet more intimately in the general administration of price inflation while the rising rate of unproductive consumption creates the monetary conditions that give sanction to the illusion that inflation is an "out." It is at this juncture, too, that the stagflation long implicit in the situation puts in a clear-cut appearance, though some time passes before it is discovered by the economist.

With the retardation in the growth of output resulting from the enlarged war effort in Southeast Asia (that is, in 1965), the accompanying relative decline in demand for productive labor should have resulted in unemployment, according to the theory. But even though the inflationary side of stagflation showed quite clearly, no unemployment was seen for some time. The unemployment was hidden by two circumstances. First of these was the utilization of what would otherwise have been an excess demand for labor power to expand the military output. Secondly, the draft mopped up any remaining excess labor power. These continued operative until the troops came home again. These contributions to the concealment of the underlying difficulty helped also to create the illusion that cost push was the true cause of inflation. This conventional explanation is, of course, highly superficial. It is the dwindling real surplus that underlies the stagflation – the "diminishing S." It is this diminishing surplus that gives rise, too, to the famous liquidity crisis. The latter is but the monetary reflection of a declining margin for realization as profit.[21]

The economists' preoccupation with surface phenomena of price and of quantity prevents them from seeing the real causes of difficulty. The business managers' preoccupation with price and quantity prevents them from dealing effectively with the tendency for profits to fall. In finance the management of higher interest rates is especially revealing of the complicity of the state in the administration of monopoly power. The decline in the general rate of profit forces an increase in the price of money as it forces increased prices of commodities in general. Financial as well as nonfinancial managers struggle to enlarge their relative shares of a dwindling total, to maintain their cash flows. The contrivance of scarcities becomes ubiquitous as desperate managers manufacture crises in oil, sugar, natural gas, electricity, and so on, as part of the energy ploy. The power of the state is enlisted in the cause as the assault mounts against the enemies of monopoly capital, domestic and foreign. At home and abroad, the flailing of administrative arms testifies to the strength of the undertow. The movement toward collapse accelerates.

To recapitulate briefly, then, in the development of retardation and instability, each of the primary laws of motion works its peculiar effects, alone and in combination with each other. With the emphasis upon the accumulation of constant capitals in production of means of consumption and, more recently, in the administrative capitals, excess capacity eventually shows in the means of production. In principle the growing demands of unproductive labor for wage and consumption goods should compensate for the failures of capitalists to invest sufficiently in wage goods; and for a time they do so. However, the accumulation of unproductive labor retards the real rate of accumulation, making it difficult for domestic buyers to absorb the expanding output of means of consumption. The demand for consumption goods grows ever more slowly as expansion proceeds; not, as the Keynesians suppose, because of the decline in the long-run consumption function, but because of the retardation of real growth and of the growth of demand for labor power that is its consequence. Further, the extension of international competition among countries suffering from the same shortage of markets weakens domestic markets everywhere within a system of comparative advantage, particularly in the consumption goods area. The extension of military along with other categories of unproductive consumers serves only for a time to sustain the balance needed. Economic retardation proceeds apace, defeating this solution to the problem. Finally, the rate of surplus value rises more slowly and the general rate of profit begins its fall. The realization of surplus value proceeds on a relatively reduced scale. The liquidity crisis intensifies. The failure of monetary and fiscal stabilizers to reverse the trend only proves the decisiveness of the real-value movement.

Stagflation is thus but the final expression of a set of contradictions that brings to an end an interval of accumulation. It summarizes the imbalances among monetary and real values whose development is intrinsic to the process. The interval of collapse, on the other hand, is no more than a restoration of balance among monetary and real values, a closing of gaps so that accumulation can begin again. This moment is at hand when entrepreneurial expectations are dealt overwhelming blows. Production and investment schedules are then slashed, and unemployment rises as both public and private corporations strive to lower their expenditures in relation to their revenues in one pervasive, internecine contest. As we round the corner at this juncture, the entire scene becomes familiar. We see that we have passed this way before. Whether or not we arrive at the destination of depression depends now more upon the countertendencies to which the main thrust gives rise than upon the direction of the main thrust itself. The strength of the countertendencies, and the forms that they take, vary from country to country according to the historical and cultural experience, the level of economic and political development of the various peoples – for throughout all of the advanced countries the same underlying forces are at work.

The laws of motion and the analysis of development

We have tried to show through an analysis of the advanced capitalism how all of the main laws of motion combine in the course of accumulation in order to undermine the process itself. Within capitalism, as within modes of production preceding it, "reproduction is at the same time necessarily new production and destruction of the old form." What is relatively "new production" in the current phase – new in its extent and in its systematization – is that of unproductive labor, both living, in personnel, and congealed, in the means of administration with which the laborer works. The scale of the circulatory establishment and the force of the energy embedded within it have become so vast that one can almost literally see the entire apparatus of social reproduction sagging under the strains imposed upon it. The strain is especially visible in consequence of the rise in the rate of unproductive consumption, for this is the variable whose operation divorces monetary from real values at the aggregative level and in doing so creates the dichotomous movement of prices and values, that is, stagflation.

But while the effects of the laws of motion are quite visible, they remain hidden from economists who, lacking a labor theory of value, are unable to conceive of the quantitative and qualitative flows of values whose reproduction governs ultimately the entire course of development. Marx, the master theorist, not only defined the main laws but succeeded in predicting the relative rise in unproductive consumption that is the plague of the advanced capitalism:

. . . the extraordinary productiveness of modern industry, accompanied as it is by both a more extensive and a more intense exploitation of labour power in all other spheres of production, allows of the unproductive employment of a larger and larger part of the working class, and the consequent reproduction, on a constantly extending scale, of the ancient domestic slaves under the name of a servant class, including men-servants, women-servants, lackeys, etc.[22]

And he stressed always that relations between prices and labor values were critical for the progress of accumulation. Indeed, the principal relation between price and value that accounts for the phenomenon of stagflation was completely understood by him. The relation referred to is the excess of demand relative to the value of the productive input. This excess traces to any component of the output that, for whatever reason, cannot serve subsequently as a productive input. As a result, the increment of demand is unmatched by an increment of supply. We see this principle at work in the following passage: "Since elements of productive capital are forever being withdrawn from the market, and only an equivalent in money is thrown on the market in their place, the effective demand rises without itself furnishing any element of supply. Hence a rise in the prices of productive materials as well as means of subsistence." The passage continues:

To this must be added that stock-jobbing is a regular practice and capital must be transferred on a large scale. A band of speculators, contractors, engineers, lawyers, etc., enrich themselves. They create a strong demand for articles of consumption on the market, wages rising at the same time. So far as foodstuffs are involved, agriculture, too, is stimulated. But as these foodstuffs cannot be suddenly increased in the course of the year, their import grows, just as that of exotic foods in general . . . and of articles of luxury. Hence excessive imports and speculation in this line of the import business. . . .

And the expansion continues, "until the inevitable crash again releases the industrial reserve army of labour and wages are once more depressed to their minimum and lower."[23] Marx's prescience needs no extolling from this or any other writer; it speaks for itself. What must be emphasized, however, is its dependence upon the labor theory of value, a dependence affecting the quality not only of Marxism but of any and all social science.

The laws of motion that shape the course of capital accumulation in the manner described, shape also the development of the population. The accumulation of capital is the accumulation of population, and we must turn now to consider those qualitative developments within it that accumulation has brought with the successive phases of its evolution. The division of social labor as it now stands, the contemporary structure and alignment of social classes – these are the outgrowth of the drive to accumulate, which, working through the media of specific laws of development, has brought the class struggle to a critical point in the entire history of capitalism. From a consideration of the laws of motion, we turn, therefore, to the relations of production as they now stand vis-à-vis the productive forces.

9

Marx's first and second approximations to the evolution of class structure

To avoid caricature . . .

Relations of production are class relations. They consist of the sum of economic, political, technical, and other interrelations among the social classes participating in the reproduction of the mode of production itself. The reproduction of the mode of production is, at least to the point at which the process undermines the social formation, the objective, so to speak, of class relations of production. In the Marxian theory the reproduction of the relations vital to the mode itself becomes increasingly difficult with the fettering of the productive forces; class struggles – a phrase merely summarizing ever more attenuated relations of production – become sharper and more clearly defined, not only to the outside observer, but even to the participants themselves (class consciousness). This is the thesis of class struggle, a struggle that assumes definite forms in the advanced capitalism, forms that we now proceed to distinguish and explain, beginning with Marx's own analysis.

There is a widely publicized although essentially distorted view of the class struggle that Marx envisioned within final phases of capitalist development. The picture so often tendered is of a world divided into numerically unequal classes, a small body of capitalists confronting a relatively larger industrial proletariat, the latter comprising the active labor army together with its own relatively growing industrial reserve of unemployed. Divided by an irreducible division of interests, these opposing classes are entangled in relations of sharpening tension. Accumulation proceeding, this world moves from crisis to ever deeper crisis, finally dissolving in chaos and revolution.

The element of truth contained in this interpretation of Marx's prognosis is based largely on the general law of capitalist accumulation of *Capital I*.[1] And while parts of it reflect with reasonable accuracy what is said in that important chapter, it contains also an unmistakable element of caricature. This latter element, like all caricature, traces to a subtle point – subtle at least as far as the cartoonists are concerned. Marx's projection in *Capital I* is strictly a first approximation to the development of classes and class relations under capitalism. It is an approximation that Marx had himself qualified elsewhere in important ways, ways that altogether yield important insights into the real character of the developing class struggle. Marx's own qualifications to this first approximation provide us with important clues for helping us to understand our present situation.

In pursuing this thesis, we may best begin with a reconstruction of the first approximation; then it will be easy to see why this is but a first, if quite necessary, approximation to the actual course of social and economic development. For this it is well to have at hand the general law itself:

The greater the social wealth, the functioning capital, the extent and energy of its growth, and, therefore, also the absolute mass of the proletariat and the productiveness of its labour, the greater is the industrial reserve army. The same causes which develop the expansive power of capital, develop also the labour-power at its disposal. The relative mass of the industrial reserve army increases therefore with the potential energy of wealth. But the greater this reserve army in proportion to the active labour-army, the greater is the mass of a consolidated surplus population, whose misery is in inverse ratio to its torment of labour. The more extensive, finally, the Lazarus-layers of the working class, and the industrial reserve army, the greater is official pauperism. *This is the absolute general law of capitalist accumulation.*[2]

And there follows a most significant sentence: "Like all other laws, it is modified in its working by many circumstances, the analysis of which does not concern us here."[3] Here, however, it is precisely the "many circumstances" that do concern us, but we shall begin, nevertheless, with a reproduction of the first approximation on which the modifications to come may be brought to rest.

The essence of our little exercise in Marxology may be economically presented in the form of a diagram showing the developing composition of the population as envisaged in the general law just cited (Figure 9.1). Its main features are these. As long-term tendencies we encounter, first, the *relative* decline in the population of the industrial proletariat, the active labor army of the

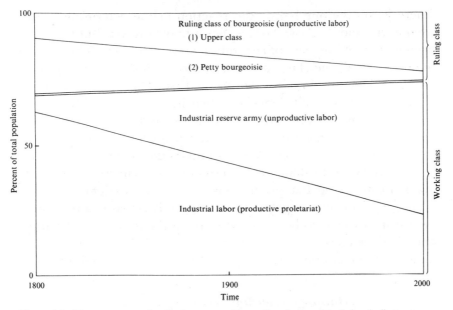

Figure 9.1. Class structure: the absolute general law of capital accumulation (a first approximation). The diagram is largely self-explanatory. The dates indicated on the time axis are meant to suggest the scale of the time relevant to the first approximation. I have settled on this scale because the relative decline of the industrial proletariat, narrowly defined as blue-collar labor, seems to be proceeding at roughly the pace shown.

general law. The accompaniment to this within the working class as a whole is the relative growth of the industrial reserve army of unemployed of various kinds, official paupers and castoffs. So much for the primary features contained in the general law.

To complete this portrait of the composition of the total population as it develops through time we must bring in also the ruling class (above the double line in the figure). It is composed of two main branches, the upper or grand bourgeoisie, and the lower, petty bourgeoisie, the independent farmers, shopkeepers, and assorted entrepreneurs whose decline relative to the grand bourgeoisie is largely a consequence of the centralization of capitals, in particular, of the growing scales of organization that envelop and extinguish the small entrepreneurs. As a first approximation to the changing composition of the population, this portrait abstracts on the one side from any remnants of the previous feudal mode of production, and it abstracts on the other from any portents indicative of a trend to socialism. It abstracts, that is, from all articulations of capitalism with other modes of production.[4]

Two broad reactions are possible to this first approximation:

There is, on the one hand, the reaction of the determinists: But what of the middle class? To this they add the protest: But there has been no relative increase of the industrial reserve army! There is, on the other hand, the classical reaction: What *is* the second approximation? And how does it relate to the first? The latter is the reaction that Marx himself demands when he observes that the law is modified by many circumstances. Somehow and somewhere the second approximation must be built, and it must be simply because this is a requirement of the Marxian methodology of successive approximations, of the dialectical method in its scientific application. Marxism makes no flat predictions, at least as a scientific rather than a speculative enterprise. Marx himself is asserting a tendency, even if it turns out to be, in some sense of the term, an "absolute" one. And we must now look into the matter of the second approximation, especially into the analysis that underlies its construction.

Historical relations between mercantile and industrial capitals: the middle classes

Despite the charge that he ignores their role in the formulation of the general law of capitalist accumulation, Marx is not only aware of the existence of the so-called middle classes but is himself critical of those who, like Ricardo, leave their economic and political role out of account. The passage following is suggestive of his general sociological placement of these classes: "What he [Ricardo] forgets to emphasize is the constantly growing number of the middle classes, those who stand between the workman on the one hand and the capitalist and landlord on the other."[5] He continues with a comment on an economic role of these classes that will prove ultimately to be of great importance in analyzing their composition: "The middle classes maintain themselves to an ever increasing extent directly out of revenue, they are a burden weighing heavily on the working base and increase the social security and power of the upper ten thousand."[6]

There may, it is true, be a level of abstraction here that leaves much to be explained; at the same time, there are undeniably important queries to be posed concerning the political and economic roles of our subject. Is it the case that the middle classes function as a buffer zone,[7] in this sense standing between the workman and the capitalist-landlord class? And what is the economic meaning of stating that they "maintain themselves to an ever increasing extent directly out of revenue . . ."? Finally, precisely how do they manage to "increase the social security and power of the upper ten thousand"? One thing is clear even though much may remain in the air: Marx is imputing quite critical social functions to the classes at issue. It must have been obvious to Marx himself that a second approximation would need to incorporate more explicitly an analysis of the content of these classes. Surely his knowledge of the historical development of these classes would have figured in that approximation.

To reproduce in full detail all of Marx's intricate analysis of the development of what he calls the middle classes in the passage cited would involve us in issues that we need not pursue for our immediate purpose. A sketch of his views will serve to remind us of the kind of function and the kind of work that have been the hallmark of those divisions of labor engaged in commerce, trade, and finance and in the management of these activities so vital to and characteristic of the capitalist mode of production. The capitals that are engaged in supporting those engaged in these activities of circulation have moved into the performance of the work of circulation over an extended period of time. Already by the sixteenth century there was emerging out of the handicraft order a new class of small entrepreneurs and men of commerce who provided aid to, and were subsequently aided by, the new monarchical authority engaged in putting together the nation-state. Their work specialty lay in the vending of handicraft product, and as middlemen grew in numbers, their function also expanded. Their work is work of appropriation of surplus product and value, and this is carried out through realizing the values implicit in the commodities in which they trade; not that they are, at a certain phase of their development, incapable of a more direct appropriation. Perhaps the most famous testimonial of the appropriative function they perform is given by the slave trade, an enterprise spanning two and one-half centuries in the appropriation of labor power, organized, promoted, and conducted by the mercantilists of the seventeenth to the nineteenth centuries. In mythological history these merchant traders are now a defunct class. It would be more accurate to say that the appropriation of surplus value in which the merchant classes are still engaged involves both altered forms of the classes themselves, and, certainly, altered modes of appropriation.

One of these formal alterations occurs with the rise of the industrial capitalists. Under mercantile auspices there was accomplished an appreciable accumulation and centralization of trading and financial capitals, a circumstance propitious for the financing and managing of the industrial accumulation in its formative phases. By the late eighteenth and early nineteenth centuries in England, the classical example, while there was on the one hand an intimate relationship between mercantilists and industrialists, the increase in numbers of industrial entrepreneurs and "undertakers" was so pronounced that it looked to observers at the time that a whole new class was in the making. To the liberals of the day – the physiocrats in France, in England the liberals led by Adam Smith and succeeded by Bentham, Ricardo, and the two Mills among others – the challenge of the new industrial entrepreneur to the mercantile-monarchical coalition brought great expectations. In view of the coalition's bloody record of acquisitive instincts superseding all human values, the liberals viewed with profound suspicion mercantile capital and its agents. Their hope was that the new industrial leaders of the middle class would eradicate what Smith termed the "spirit of monopoly," a hope shortly to be dashed against the rock of capitalist development. With the gradual expansion of industrial accumulation what came about instead was a new blending of industrial and mercantile elements within the ruling class of the industrial phase of development. The error of the liberals lay in confusing a movement of flux within the ruling class, involving the absorption of industrial capitalists, for a movement in fundamental opposition to that class. What was in the making was a merger, a class alliance, of industrial with mercantile capital within an older circulatory system peculiar to the mode of production. The mode was undergoing modification rather than alteration.

These modifications continue, if anything at an increasing rate into the nineteenth century. The industrial accumulation accelerating as technical change is implemented, and a corresponding expansion of the circulatory sphere is both necessary and possible; necessary in that the rapidly growing social product must now be vended on a larger scale; possible in that, the surplus of productive labor rising, the allocation or segmentation (as Marx calls it) of a portion of the surplus into support of circulatory work is more easily carried out. The accumulation of circulatory capitals proceeds apace with the accumulation of industrial capitals: "With the absolute increase of the volume of the annually reproduced virtual money capital its segmentation also becomes easier, so that it is more rapidly invested in any particular business. . . ."[8] Marx is here pointing to the relative enlargement of the annual surplus value, which virtually assures (when realized in monetary form) an expanded investment "in any particular business." A particular business that is favored by investors eager to circulate their expanding values is the business of commerce, finance, and trade and, perhaps above all, the business of managing and coordinating these circulatory operations. Toward the end of the past century the relative enlargement of the circulatory apparatus had reached an astounding scale and the epoch of finance capitalism was in full bloom. Returning for a moment to the longer view, we see this.

The development of industrial out of mercantile capitalism marks only a new phase of evolution, an interlude in the progress of self-expanding capital. Its new captains of industry and captains of finance are but later waves in the rising tide of mercantile and financial overlords. There was never any doubt, after all, that industrial departments of the new economy, no matter what their scale and no matter what the level of technique that they might comprehend, should always be subject to the pecuniary discipline of the circulatory system, to decisive considerations of money profit. To the self-discipline of such decisive considerations the new middle classes, as Marx saw it, are largely given over. The circulatory system is their main abode, their principal source of employment, income, and wealth.

Circulatory labor as unproductive labor

The accumulation of capital proceeds within each of the two spheres peculiar to the mode of production, the sphere of circulation and the sphere of production.[9] The former, the circulatory sphere in which the appropriation of surplus value takes place, grows by segmentation, by a propagation of capitals from the main stem of productive labor, the generator of surplus value. Labor in the former, living upon material means supplied by productive labor, yields up to capital the services of appropriation that capital requires. Labor in the latter produces the surplus value upon whose allocation between the spheres the reproduction of both depends. Thus by segmentation emerge the new middle classes, the sterile offshoots from the surplus of productive labor. This is the allocation to which Marx refers when he describes the middle classes maintaining and advancing themselves out of "revenue," a term that, in pre-Marxian economics, designated the personal consumption of the capitalists, then the main body of capital's unproductive consumers. As a summary statement of the economics underlying this view, Marx's metaphor of the two machines is enlightening:

A certain amount of labour-power and labour-time must be expended in the process of circulation. . . . This advance of capital creates neither product nor value. It reduces *pro tanto* the dimensions in which the advanced capital functions productively. It is as though one part of the product were transformed into a machine which buys and sells the rest of the product. It does not participate in the productive process, although it can diminish the labour-power, etc., spent on circulation.[10]

The phenomenon of the one-way flow is today a dramatic and recognized feature of feedback systems: Home air conditioners derive their power from a primary source to which they do not in turn contribute. When the rate of consumption from the primary source exceeds certain limits, breakdown occurs; economically, too, this is a logical conclusion of an excessive rise of the rate of unproductive consumption, as we have seen. Whether or not the laws of motion cause this rate to rise to the breaking point is not scientifically settled; it seems fair to say hypothetically, however, that it is a tendency that asserts itself under certain conditions and over the long term. Far more certain is the proposition that labor engaged in circulatory work is unproductive. It is labor that is not devoted directly to the reproduction of society's material means of subsistence, yet it consistently draws on those means for sustaining and enlarging its own activities. Because it is, therefore, a labor whose relative rate of growth must reduce the general rate of accumulation or the average rate of profit, this question necessarily arises: Why should capital's investments ever accelerate the accumulation of unproductive labor?

One must begin with the realization that investment in this labor upon some scale must take place, since the mechanisms of circulation are the only devices known to capital for accomplishing this capitalistically necessary work. Nor is there any real doubt that the divisions of labor employed in finance, in wholesaling and retailing, in insurance, advertising and merchandising, in the management of all of these circulatory operations at public and private levels, in the protection and expansion of security agencies, including the judiciary, the police, and the military – that all of these activities, intrinsic to circulatory work, are regarded by capitalists as profitable or potentially profitable in the monetary dimensions with which they are concerned. Although unproductive, these activities, through the medium of the pricing mechanism, bring to investors in these fields – or are preconditions for so bringing – rewards that are proportioned to the amount of their investments. Whatever the aggregate of surplus value generated, the total profit divides among all the individual capitals, no matter what their field of preference, in proportion to their contribution to the total. In circulation, too, each capital profits in proportion to its own magnitude as profit rates are equalized: "The unpaid labour of these clerks, while it does not create surplus value, enables him (the circulatory capitalist) to appropriate surplus value, which, in effect, amounts to the same thing with respect to his capital [that it amounts to with respect to industrial capital]."[11]

But it is the money rate, and not the real rate of profit, that capitalists seek to maximize. By their own criterion, rewards will be as great whether the seed of virtual money capital falls on economically barren or on fertile ground. Indeed, the former may be more attractive if investment in circulation reduces the period of circulation – the period of turnover of investment – thereby increasing the capitalist's profit. The importance of this circumstance in encouraging unproductive investment should not be underestimated.

Especially in the past century, and continuing in intervals of economic expansion into the present century, the segmentation of surplus from industrial into circulatory sectors has raised rates of profit by reducing periods of circulation. Unquestionably, entrepreneurs at the micro plane, both individual and corporate capitalists, have enthusiastically promoted circulation in order to raise their rates of profit. More recently, with the progress of collective capital and its Keynesian economics, the same perception has extended to the macroplane, where, in connection with the realization problem, a prospect of assuredly profitable markets has brought grudging but growing endorsement of monopoly state capitalism with its so-called built-in stabilizers to expand and maintain markets with the aid of the imperial state.

The higher profits that are the direct accompaniment to this enlargement of the circulatory sphere have at the same time further concealed from view what in any event capitalists have never sought to understand: that work of circulation is by its nature unproductive, that surplus value is a direct outcropping of the activity of productive labor alone. Economists have marched in the front ranks in this celebration of economic ignorance, particularly those among them who have spread doctrines of harmony of interests and urged the abandonment of the only theory of value that could give insight into underlying realities. With few exceptions the stultifying effects of the new mercantilism upon the development of the productive forces have been lost from view.[12] Consequently, the possibility of assessing realistically the emergence of the new middle classes, whose economic abode has always been the circulatory establishment, has also been lost.

Whether or not a realistic analysis of the middle classes can be carried out, we conclude, is contingent upon a proper application of the Marxian economics. It should be apparent even at this juncture that the conception of the middle classes as a buffer zone assumes an economic as well as a sociopolitical role on the part of these classes that may be inconsistent with their actual activity. If circulatory labor, comprising perhaps the largest part of the labor of the middle classes, is unproductive labor, then its relative increase portends a decline in the real rate of growth of the system, the advent of economic stagnation or regression, and hence destruction of the economic ground on which the progress of these classes and their buffer function depend. This deterioration would force to a head the problem of doing away with unproductive labor. It would force to a head also, viewing theoretically the possibility of such a development, the question of the class composition of these middle classes. Are they a separate and distinct economic-sociological entity? Or are they composed of separate classes of divergent interests that would in crisis join as opposing forces in a war between the classes?

Clerical labor in circulatory employment

While under certain circumstances the growth of the middle classes may, because of the rise of unproductive labor, foreshadow an undermining of the productive forces, the course of capitalist development scarcely pointed in this direction up to the middle of the past century. Quite to the contrary. The necessity of enlarging the circulatory establishment in order to keep pace with the industrial accumulation provided enlarged employment opportunities for "commercial workers" (as both Marx and Engels called them): "The capitalist increases the number of these labourers whenever he has more value and profits to realize."[13] Now we are not here crediting Marx and Engels with any extraordinary prescience, as one might suppose who takes the appearance of white-collar labor to be a recent phenomenon. The growth of what Engels once called "the commercial proletariat" was in evidence by mid-century, if not earlier;[14] rather, it is the scale of its development by the seventies that is so remarkable. Theoretically, what the growth of clerical labor signifies is the incompleteness of the first approximation. To put it more precisely, Marx's first approximation in *Capital I* is a matter of dialectical methodology, made in full cognizance of the need to modify it. What had become apparent, in view of the ascent of the commercial worker, on the one side, and the general law of capitalist accumulation on the other, is the essential connection between these. The connection is simply this. The relative growth of the industrial reserve army is countermanded and held in check by expanding employment opportunities within a growing circulatory establishment. The displacement of industrial labor that does take place under a complex accumulation does not result in a rising relative volume of secular unemployment as long as there is a sufficiently rapid absorption of a growing portion of the working population into the circulatory system, a mopping up of *what otherwise would have been* surplus labor in the form of industrially unemployed.

From the standpoint of class analysis all of this only underscores the importance of unravling the skein of the middle classes, and it is the extent of Marx's contribution to this work that we are for the moment concerned with. Certain characteristics of clerical labor Marx drew attention to, and one sees readily enough why so many have, following Engels, looked upon it as a part of the proletariat. While presently of the category of better-paid labor, for instance, the prospect of clerical labor is for a decline in its wage and in its employment as a consequence of its education and training.[15] Although a labor that does not produce surplus value, it must be paid at its own costs of reproduction while its employer profits like any other, on the average at the average rate. In this respect, it is exploited like productive labor.[16] It is exploited, further, in its subjection to a one-sided development, due in part to the narrow commercialization of its education and training, in part to its employment within an ever-narrowing division of labor.[17] In all of this it resembles industrial labor while remaining, nevertheless, unproductive. If clerical labor is unproductive, can it be said to have an interest in opposition to that of the capitalist? Or are capitalists and clerks natural allies in their mutual exploitation of the productive labor whose surplus supports them both?

Theoretically, there is a simple answer that Marxists can give to these questions, an answer more consistent with proletarian tendencies of clerical labor than with the flirtations of some clerks with their exploiters. Clerical labor is a branch of social labor that is potentially productive but is de facto wasted within the circulatory superstructure. Indeed, this appears to be Marx's own view, as is seen in his ridicule of those political economists who confuse work of capitalist administration, purely circulatory work geared to the realization of profit rather than to the creation of value, with the work of coordination that economic reproduction requires: ". . . he [the political economist] . . . treats the work of control made necessary by the cooperative character of the labor process as identical with the different work of control, necessitated by the capitalistic character of that process and the antagonism of interests between capital and labor."[18]

Capitalist administration by no means coincides with social administration, and under capitalism the use values of clerical labor are employed for the realization of profit and for the coordination of activities to that end. This is in the first place. In the second, wastage of clerical labor follows from bureaucratization with its relative overproduction of clerical labor, overproduction relative to the needs of a social administration of economic coordination. Clerical labor is thus seen as a form of administrative labor that awaits a social utilization of its capacities on an economical scale. This view, underlying Marx's own explicit analysis, is an inference consistent with much of the observed history of clerical labor.

Finally, we must point to the interesting prediction on the molding for commercial service of educational curricula.[19] It is not the statement per se as much as its reminder of the subsequent enormous growth in educational facilities, and in the personnel involved both as producers and as administrators within those facilities, that again raises the question of the composition of the middle classes. While a quota of clerical labor is employed in administrative work throughout formal education as elsewhere, the great bulk of the labor in this field is pedagogical in terms of the use values it generates. Moreover, this is labor power that is itself engaged in the production of labor power, functioning as producer labor even though this labor is itself unproductive in some undetermined portion. But while the extent to which the teacher is unproductive is problematical at this point, it is surely doubtful that all this labor can be put into the clerical category. Where do the teachers belong along with all those other portions of the middle classes serving educational and training functions? Somehow, this important body must be fit into a second approximation. Marx's own discussion of the subject is incomplete, although, in comparison with much of the indecisiveness of current discussion of educational producers, it is powerfully suggestive.

Concentration and centralization: official labor

In identifying clerical labor as a segment of the middle classes we distinguish it from the labor of the industrial proletariat that, as productive labor, falls within the social division of labor that is industrial, broadly defined. Clerical labor, also a branch of the general division of labor in society, is formed more as a consequence of circulatory needs than of the requirements of an advancing industrial technique. A similar distinction may be made with respect to yet another branch of the social division of labor, a branch shaped by essentially the same forces that reflect circulatory requirements. This is the branch composed of the officials and managers whose task is one of supervision, first of the circulatory apparatus itself and, second, beyond that and through the medium of circulatory mechanisms and agencies, of the whole of the economic order, including the industrial workmen, the productive labor of the base: "An industrial army of workmen, under the command of a capitalist, requires, like a real army, officers (managers), and sergeants (foremen, overlookers), who, while the work is being done, command in the name of the capitalist. The work of supervision becomes their established and exclusive function."[20]

And again, while economists may regard their labor of superintendence as *faux frais* of production, these costs are peculiarly capitalistic, Marx tells us. The development of all of this labor of capitalistic supervision and control, with its origins in circulatory needs, is in proportion to the growing scale of circulatory operations and is intimately bound up, therefore, with the concentration and centralization of social capitals, notions that need some elaboration.

Concentration and centralization denote the two essential dimensions of the thrust of capital toward an ever broader and more consolidated control of the social economy. "Concentration" is simply the extended reproduction of a capital; it is "only another name for reproduction on an extended scale."[21] The term's familiar connotation is appropriate, for it suggests an ever-growing volume of exchange values falling within the organizational precincts of an enterprise or of an administratively coordinated group of enterprises. Historically, the concentration movement has been intimately connected with what economists call the concentration of economic power; still it denotes only one aspect of the power phenomenon. The other dimension of capitalist hegemony is denoted by centralization. This refers to an amalgamation under a progressively unified administrative authority of what were previously independent capitals: firms, enterprises, corporations, and, in more recent times, even nations (as through common-market or other administrative arrangements). Centralization, like concentration, also involves an enlargement in the scale of organization, but the enlargement is in this instance the result of a combination among formerly autonomous units, and this may or may not be accompanied by a simultaneous *concentration* of capitals. In the Marxian vocabulary, "centralization" is practically synonymous with "concentration" as the latter is used in conventional economics; that is, it refers to combinations among previously autonomous entities. The principal objection to the restricted conventional usage, which fails to perceive the progress of concentration in extended accumulation, is that centralized control in fact develops along two routes rather than simply the one. A highly concentrated system of political and economic control could, and actually has developed under capitalism, while a considerable and even large number of competing corporations still exist. It is more difficult to entertain illusions that monopoly capital is appreciably "competitive" – as the economist uses the term – when concentration is seen in a full light.

The rate of concentration (accumulation) of an enterprise is on the average limited to the average rate of accumulation of the economy as a whole. This is tautology, certainly, but there is a point to be made here, namely, that there *are* limits to the average rate of growth in the scale of units of organization. On the other hand, these same limits may always be transcended through centralization. In centralization the limit in the growth of administrative power is the control of all social capital by a single administrative unit. It is because centralization transcends the limits of economic and political power that concentration allows that it becomes, under certain circumstances, capital's preferred device for consolidating its power and authority. In periods of boom and prosperity, centralization breaks out in a familiar panoply of instruments: trusts, gentlemen's agreements, mergers, conglomerations, common-marketing arrangements – moving always to higher and higher levels of administrative accomplishment, moving centralization in the direction of its logical limit. In time of crisis the tendency is to approach that limit forthwith through the devices of bourgeois authoritarianism: coup d'état, dictatorship, and others.

What Marx perceived are the interconnections between the administrative ways of the old mercantilism and the circulatory departments of the developed capitalism – in commerce, finance, trade, and, most importantly, the state – which radiate political forces tending to centralize the system. In the evolution of capitalism the centralization movement proceeds toward ever more elevated and generalized arrangements of administrative control, and already toward the end of the past century, with the rise of finance capital, the logical climax was in view so far as the nation-state was concerned. Monopoly capitalism had arrived, as Lenin noted. Marx anticipated this movement with great precision and recorded his anticipations in *Capital I*: ". . . in its first stage [merchant's capital] furtively creeps in as the humble assistant of accumulation, drawing into the hands of the individual or associated capitalists, by invisible threads, the money resources which lie scattered over the surface of society, in larger or smaller amounts. . . ." So much for the situation before industrial accumulation gives fresh impetus to the movement through an expanding circulatory system. Then comes a second phase: ". . . it soon becomes a new and terrible weapon in the battle of competition, and is finally transformed into an enormous social mechanism for the centralization of capitals."[22] At the moment these words were being written the transformation was taking place. New forms of circulatory agency appropriate to industrial capital were advancing rapidly: a multiplication of banks and in their degree of specialization; the erection and consolidation of central banks; expanding money and credit markets; new administrative subsidiaries for the firm; the state moving in to order and to systematize centralization, all under the aegis of captains of industry and finance. All of this is familiar enough to historians and, most certainly, to students of Marx. But familiarity must not be permitted to breed contempt for the sociological accompaniments to the movement. And what were these?

In relation to the administration of centralization a form of social labor emerges more significant by far than that of the clerks. The movement requires its directors, and directors are called forth. Monies and credits must be amassed for effecting new combinations, new liaisons; and new men are needed for this work. New legal, commercial, and financial arrangements, preliminaries to and sequels of centralization, must be made, and they need their makers. Who are the new administrators? The answer to the question depends upon the phase of development in view, but in general once economic interdependence has reached a certain point, the forementioned functions of supervision and management become sufficiently specialized that they must be carried out by specialized personnel operating in the name of the capitalist. The work of circulatory administration, formerly done by the handicraft producer himself, later by the merchant and his various factors, is now performed by the soldiers of a new division, the division of hired managers:

The labor of supervision and management, arising as it does out of an antithesis, out of the supremacy of capital over labor, and being therefore common to all modes of production based on class contradictions like the capitalist mode, is directly and inseparably connected, also under the capitalist system, with productive functions which all combined social labor assigns to individuals as their special tasks.[23]

As members of the middle classes, standing between the capitalists and industrial labor, we must insert above the clerical contingent the supervisors and superintendents of a mode becoming ever more centralized. The addition of new strata of specialized managers, reflecting the level of centralization already attained, further accelerates and advances the process – but accelerates it how and in what direction?

In his projection of the prospective development of the

manager, Marx may appear to suggest a more rapid and perhaps frictionless evolution of the mode than subsequent history reveals. This "numerous class of industrial and commercial managers" becomes essentially a salariat, divorced from the ownership of capital.[24] This divorce, coupled with an advancing social character of money and credit, seen in the systematization of money and credit supplies within a managed banking network, undermines the position of the capitalist, who becomes as thoroughly redundant to financial as he has become to economic proceedings. Finally, with centralization approaching its limit, "only the functionary remains and the capitalist disappears as superfluous from the production process."[25] While it is far from inconceivable that something like this is transpiring, the divorce of the manager from the ownership interest is not yet completed. On the other side of the managerial coin it is doubtful that he has become the skilled technician, blending into the ranks of skilled labor as one capable of representing in administrative proceedings the best interests of the working class and of society at large. While this disappearance of the capitalist through his obsolescence does not appear in *Capital III* as a specific prediction, it is unmistakably one eventuality that Marx contemplates. Certainly it is a kind of a development that many capitalists and their apologists would for obvious reasons have us believe has already taken place: "The modern corporate or joint venture capitalism has largely replaced tycoon capitalism. The one-man-band owner-manager is fast being replaced by a new class of professional managers, dedicated more to the advancement of the company than to the enrichment of a few owners."[26] What in fact is the object of managerial dedication and what it has to do with the manager's class position are quite arguable issues to the present day. Yet there is no doubt that these determinations must be made if the prospects of the managed capitalism are to be realistically assessed.

The rise of the middle classes

It is not our main intention to rediscover what so many have for so long declared not to be present in Marx's work:[27] an explanation of the rise of the middle classes. There can be no question that while, on the one hand, he distinguishes important components of what must figure into any responsible analysis of those classes and into any reasonable assessment of their social function, his analysis remains incomplete. Of course, we are here commenting on Marx's analysis of the capitalist mode in its pure or ideal form, untrammeled with vestiges of its historic passage through feudal and other modes. Were we to take these into account, the portrait Marx offers of class actuality even to the present day would be far more comprehensive than has been indicated here. But what we have been concerned to present is his analysis of class structure as a peculiarly capitalistic phenomenon, and it is in this dimension that one encounters a lack of relevant detail and a certain equivocation on one side, while on the other there are vital clues to be found as to where to go in order to unravel the remaining portions of the puzzle. The clues he provides are of two kinds. First are the direct suggestions, certainly invaluable for anyone wishing to pursue further the issue, as in his analysis of the making of the commercial worker and of the manager. Second are the clues contained in his own economic methodology, which we shall not specify at this point but shall reserve for exploration and for use in the following chapters.

What Marx is charged with having failed to see – the rise of middle classes and their merger into a buffer zone that gradually encompasses the whole population – there is no question that he failed to see. What he does see is a growing body of white-collar labor tending itself to proletarianization over the long term, merging gradually into the working class, taking over gradually all of the economic and circulatory functions required by the mode of production, thereby making superfluous the capitalist and, presumably, the institution of property on which the latter reclines. However sketchy his outline of this development, it is there. Had he been able to fill out his analysis, would his conclusions have indicated this same tendency? It is difficult to say, and, of course, the question is not really very pertinent. What is pertinent is whether or not contemporary Marxists can fill out the analysis required, required not merely for the satisfaction of idle curiosity, but for political utilization in the struggle of our time.[28] In this endeavor the clues that Marx provides are handy and helpful, but even they are probably dispensable. What is absolutely necessary in order to get to the bottom of the issue, however, is the Marxian methodology. This is absolutely basic to formulating an analysis of social class embracing the situation of advanced capitalism.

Nor should clues be ignored. Marx underlines the role of the educational system, its growing quantitative and qualitative importance with the maturation of the mode. While he does not probe into the make-up of the producer population as it develops within educational departments, the present scale of those departments, if nothing else, points up the priority that must be given to this inquiry. There are, further, some matters to be looked into concerning the managers: their property interest and the orientation this occasions in their work of command and supervision should be considered; the education of the managers and the competence they acquire and what comes of it must be examined. It is further evident that the problem of the managers is complicated in certain historical dimensions. From whence have the managers come, and who were their predecessors? Has not capitalism always featured its managerial personnel: the military, the ministers, the lawyers and judges, the teachers (even)? Have these not served as members of the capitalist directorate? Where do they stand in relation to the technicians and professionals of the present day? These and many other questions must be answered in putting together a second approximation that will be sociologically sound and politically useful. In the approximation that follows, we extend Marx's views in order to test their adequacy by determining more fully their implications.

PART FOUR
The development of class
structure and relationships

10

Class structure and conflict
in the managerial phase I

Approaches to the study of power

Since Marx, and despite – or perhaps because? – his insistence that the truth is to be found elsewhere, the study of social power, its sources and its vagaries, has centered on what might be termed the "agencies" of power.[1] In an effort to solve the riddle, scholars have identified and examined with care the trusts, gentlemen's agreements, combines, vertical and horizontal and mixed integrations, conglomerations, infrastructures and technostructures, national and international corporation alliances, governmental departments and bureaus, and combinatory arrangements among these. The more or less explicit aim has been to clarify the functioning of the whole by providing an answer to the old question, *"Cui bono?"*

In practice, however, agency studies have shied away from politically hazardous answers to the old query, often concluding with the intimation that we would all be better off were economic organization a bit more competitive. The study of agencies meanwhile continues, and while it has yielded much that it is important to know, it has had one unwonted effect. It has distracted investigators from certain other fundamental questions. By whom are the devices of power utilized? For whom? Are the agencies class agencies? If so, what is the nature of the class whose agencies these are? On the other side, who are the ruled? How do the agencies figure in the class struggle? While sharpening social tensions have recently given rise to fresh studies of class structure and function,[2] relations between these two lines of research are not really intimate.

225

Yet they belong together in roughly the following kind of relationship.

The centralization of capitals that has brought us to, and even beyond, the phase of state monopoly capitalism exhibits two basic aspects. Centralization appears, first, as a set of shifting consolidations among organizational units. The agencies and their working liaisons vary as competition waxes and wanes in accord with the needs of capital and the pressures of profit rates; in accord also with the level of development of administrative technique, we shall see. The tendency may or may not be toward the logical limit of centralization: administration through the agency of a single unit.

There is a second aspect of the centralization movement. Whatever the number and intensity of clashes among agencies, there is a secular trend to a class coordination of activity, a centralized coordination that proceeds through the medium of agencies but by virtue of a homogeneous interest among those seeking to drive home that interest. It is class and class interest that the agencies serve.

The continuation of competition here and monopoly there is thus quite consistent with a progressive and simultaneous interlocking of ruling-class activities, their planning and execution. The state of affairs may be described this way. There is a real state of monopoly power whose development is in the short run independent of the organizational units through which power is exercised. This real state is, at the present time, at an extraordinary pitch of development. The level of real power achieved by the ruling class is now testified to by the advent of a mangerial "class," a body of specialists in directing affairs. This body is but the bottom layer of the ruling class, which is itself a hierarchical order. In relation to these managerial decision makers, agencies of organization, public and private alike, are no more than convenient habitat, temporary perches from which and through which authority is exercised in the class interest.

The managers themselves do not constitute a class, nor are they on their way to becoming such.[3] To be sure, they have achieved a certain financial and political economy within the limits of profit parameters to which they are and must be subservient. The prospect of a managerial economy under their hegemony is an illusion, however. What is the actuality here, of course, we can determine only by looking and seeing; and if the continuing volume of discussion of the managers is any indication, there is ample need to explain the technocratic directorate in terms of its social origins. In explaining this fourth, managerial phase of capitalist development we shall try to show that its expression of centralized power may be traced to: (1) interrelations among strata within the managerial body itself and (2) interrelations between the upper arm of the ruling class, the "guardians" of capitalism, and its lower arm of managerial "auxiliaries" (to use Plato's terms). When the structure of the ruling class is considered in all its relations to agencies of power, there is in fact very little of the riddle of power left to be resolved. This is the first pole about which the study of the modern power structure must revolve.

A note on methodology

The failure of agency studies to dissolve the mysteries of class rule traces partly to their methodological limitations.[4] We refer to their failure to utilize definite and simple principles that would throw into sharp relief the social significance of the agencies by making clear their instrumental character. By way of contrast, the first principle here utilized is simple. Technical change leads to changes in the division of labor. These changes in the forces of production lead in turn to shifting relations of production. To be a bit more specific, with a development of the productive forces taking place, new divisions of labor appear within the working class while still others may become obsolete. Further, we generally observe analogous developments taking place within the ruling class, and its composition also undergoes alteration. A familar instance or two may help to make clear the meaning of the principles.

The long career of capitalism has spanned more than one series of changes between the forces and the relations of production. There is the familiar instance of the rise of the industrial capitalists relative to their mercantile predecessors. We saw earlier that the liberals saw the new industrialists as natural enemies of the mercantilists, failing to understand that the struggle between them was purely intramural. The conflict within the ruling class was accompanied, of course, by changes in the forces of production outside its precincts, and the emergence of an industrial working class was the most significant of these. The changing forces of production brought changes in relations of production within ruling and producing classes both, as was shown in unforgettable detail in

Capital I. Again, even before the advent of industrial capital, the mercantile expansion contained similar features. It, too, rested in part upon changing technical foundations, especially in transportation and communications, but also in handicraft as the latter blended into manufacture. Reflecting these changes in the productive forces is, on the upper side, a mercantile bourgeoisie rising in relation to a gentry whose political and economic role it tends to supersede. On the underside was a growing artisan, handicraft, and manufacturing workman, a nuclear working class.[5] Again we see changes in class composition, relations of production changing as a consequence of changes in the forces of production. Given that change is continuing, and at an accelerated pace within the capitalist mode, a further principle may be worth keeping in mind. One looks for that phase within the process when the mode of production no longer contains within itself a possibility for further adjustment to and mediation of the changing productive forces. When that juncture arrives, the conflict between ruling and working classes enters its revolutionary phase.[6] Taking such principles as tools of inquiry, we can undertake the analysis of contemporary society.

For further clues as to how to proceed the method of *Capital* is instructive. In *Capital I* we are given a first approximation to the explanation of the developing composition of the population under capitalism (see Figure 9.1). Accumulation proceeding, there is a gradual widening and deepening (rising value composition) of the constant and variable industrial capitals. The industrial accumulation proceeds ever more systematically (if erratically), multiplying divisions of industrial labor caught up in work processes in which they utilize absolutely and relatively growing volumes of congealed labor, the whole expanding in an irregular and a pulsating rhythm. Above the producer class sits the owning, ruling class. Through its command over circulatory media, this class subjects the producers to a continuing and increasing exploitation. Under the general law of capitalist accumulation there comes a relative growth of the consolidated surplus population, a relative decline in the active worker army, while the ruling class undergoes a progressive compression with the concentration and centralization of capitals. Between the primary classes the conflict of interests intensifies. Appropriation by the rulers and creation by the producers define the ultimate conflict between them. It is not merely the originality but the continuing relevance of this first approximation to capitalist class structure that demonstrates the efficiency of the underlying methodology. Of course, this is not to say that the sketch of *Capital I* is a finished portrait, particularly for the advanced capitalism. But it is a sketch that can readily be filled out through the medium of a consistent application of the methodology, as we shall soon see.

It is a matter of putting the Marxian methodology to work once more, to test directly with its assistance the realities of contemporary society in order to see whether their secrets can be wrested from them. With the model of *Capital I* in mind, three sets of questions must be asked of contemporary evidences. First, what is materially and technically distinctive within the whole field of social capital today? Is it the industrial, or is it some other form of capital? A second question follows: What are the divisions of labor accompanying the presently dominant capitals? What are the presently dominant techniques and technologies? Finally, the forces of production identified, the new relations of production must be considered. On the upper side, the side of the ruling class, we must keep in view the principle of dichotomous development; the ruling class, too, will contain new divisions somehow related to the advance of technique. On the under side, the working class will be modified as well. Proceeding along this route, we approach a final approximation to the structure and content of class society today.

The administrative capitals and the circulatory system

The need for a reapplication and testing of the principles is apparent when the very first of its questions is posed: What is nowadays materially and technically distinctive within the whole field of social capital? For all of the fuss about industrial society, the fact is that it is no longer within industrial sectors that what is strikingly new is most readily seen. The leading technique of our era, while industrially applicable, does not have its principal emplacements in sectors of heavy and of light industry. Rather, the leading technique is administrative more than industrial in character, and it finds its main applications even outside industrial management. In terms of its characteristic use values, the leading technique is primarily suitable for coordination of activity, and under capitalism coordination is a byproduct of something else.

Since the acceleration of industrial accumulation, capital has as a matter of fact found itself increasingly pressed administratively. From time to time it has struggled – futilely, to be sure – to deal with inherent unevenness and instability. And it comes to look upon the new technique as a blessing that opens the way to administrative salvation. With the enthusiasm of desperation, it has taken the new technique to its bosom, moving it steadily – or as steadily as it can – into the circulatory sphere in which are performed the operations of realization so vital to profit making. While science and invention have produced a new form of material wealth, of use values applicable to work of economic and social coordination, capital has directed it into the work of appropriating surplus value and of converting it into profit.

While analysis reveals that there is far more to realization than an equilibrating of aggregate supply and aggregate demand, that is, far more than the Keynesians allow, capital has pressed into the monetary service all technique applicable to appropriation through the realization of aggregate values.[7] This is why the circulatory facade is today stuccoed with a startling array of scientific instruments, tools, and divisions of labor, in principle applicable to the coordination of activity, in practice dedicated to appropriation through realization. From the file to data processing, from the account book to the memory bank, from the cable to the telephone and television, from arithmetic to cybernetics, from abacus to computer, from wagon to jet aircraft – in the interval of a century there have been enormous advances in the hard- and softwares useful for work of social coordination. It is, however, an advance rather than a work of primary originality. The original mercantile expansion also rested in considerable part upon foundations in administrative technique: in transport and communications, the arts of navigation, printing, accounting, and so on. The latest upsurge in administrative technique is but a repetition on a grander and higher scale of a phenomenon before experienced at a lower level of development. What has taken place is a technical renaissance within a sphere of use values administratively specialized, and, as usual, capital has taken these and sought to turn them to profitable account.[8]

Marx himself was well aware of capital's technical aspirations in this realm of invention; the corporation itself is an administrative improvement. He emphasized that the enlargement and refinement of circulatory specialties were necessary for vending the rapidly growing product. And this is essentially what has happened. While the scale of circulatory activities has extended from an also extending industrial base, the circulatory accumulation has become steadily more complex. By virtue of technical progress within fields relevant to administrative work – communications, record keeping, transportation, even scientific research itself – a qualitative improvement has taken place within both the living and the congealed capitals moving into circulatory employment. One is not used to thinking of work of coordination as a field that, like industry or agriculture, is subject to technical advance; yet it is. Even in the managerial parlance, in which improved garbling is often the main result of generations of scientific progress, the scientific application of technique to administrative work is dignified with a special name, that is, "operations research."

There is no wish to belabor the obvious. The need, rather, is to assess the economic and social impact of the circulatory-administrative accumulation that has come in the wake of the industrial accumulation. Insofar as the composition of the population is concerned, there are some obvious changes to be seen. On the one hand, the accumulation of circulatory capitals features new contingents of administratively specialized labor power, divisions of labor engaged in producing and manning the administrative technique and technology. This is an inescapable feature of the new circulatory accumulation. On the other hand, the circulatory expansion contains, as usual, a dichotomous feature. Above the new divisions of administrative labor extend whole new cadres of technocratic managers, the newest and latest auxiliaries of big capital. Once again we see the historical tendency of capital to bisect with the knife of property the structure of social class, here slicing off managerial echelons for the consumption of capital, there cutting off new ranks of administrative workers whose techniques become subject to managerial dictates.

In the fourth, managerial phase of capitalist development there is the managerial capitalist juxtaposed in the office to the administrative laborer just as, within the factory, we once found the industrialist opposed to the worker. "Silas Snobden's Office Boy" has been rejuvenated and promoted to the rank of managerial scientist.[9] Along with this goes the repression and decline of the technician and professional to the ranks of the subjugated and exploited. Within the circulatory sphere of social economy, and extending into every nook and corner of its bureaucratic agencies, capital repeats the breaking of social labor that it has already carried out in other spheres. The historical successor to the captain of industry and to the captain of finance is the captain of administration. The successor to the industrial worker– successor within as yet undetermined limits – is the technician and professional, who, by virtue of his attributes as a use value, falls along with industrial labor into the producer class.

Thus the accumulation of administrative capitals for circulatory employment (circulatory capitals) occasions yet another schism within class society. To the separation of industrial labor from capital must now be added the separation of administrative labor from capital. This separation is effected with the assistance of the managers, as the mode of production requires. While administrative labor mans the tools and instruments of administrative utility, the managerial labor appropriates the products and services rendered by the former. It turns those use values to capitalistic ends, and especially and immediately those of realization. While the argument outlined cannot be substantiated by referring to erroneous interpretations of the phenomena at issue, certain familiar accounts may be referred to in order to make clearer the salient features of the Marxian theory. Two interpretations among the many available should perhaps be mentioned, that of James Burnham (*The Managerial Revolution,* and so on), and that of Thorstein Veblen (*The Engineers and the Price System*).[10]

Administrative labor and the managers

The managerial class that Burnham has so widely and uncritically publicized is composed of essentially the same categories of managers and officials that we put within the managerial strata. These are the executive inhabitants of corporate offices, national and international, private and public. As Burnham sees it, this class has revolutionized, or is in the process of revolutionizing, social economy by means of an imminent application of wisdom and technical skill to production, distribution, and whatever other social functions may be subject to its ministrations. There are two main difficulties with his thesis.

First, by the criteria of revolutionary change that Burnham himself enunciates, it is apparent that no revolution has taken or is about to take place.[11] That the managers do bring us something from the top down, the direction from which this author sees hope coming, is doubtless correct. In his uncritical devotion to the managers, Burnham confuses revolution with counterrevolution, however. Secondly, Burnham's catalog of managerial attributes is far wide of the mark. The virtues that he attributes to the managers, especially the virtue of technical skill, are a property of administrative labor rather than of the manager. Technical prowess belongs to administrative labor rather than to the executives. Again Burnham founders in confusion, this time between the managers and the technicians and professionals of administrative labor.[12] Playing alternately upon two of his strings, Burnham produces a noise that has distracted many from seeing that he is caught in his own net.

Veblen's earlier, more penetrating analysis of the dichotomy between the engineers and the captains of industry is much closer to the truth. Seeing the historical role of technique more clearly than Burnham, Veblen understands full well the economic need for a technically sophisticated captain – which the captain of industry was not. The rise of the engineer (broadly defined) is thus placed upon a sound technical foundation. On the other hand, his prediction of rule by a "soviet of technicians" is unsound. Something is missing from his analysis.

Veblen is well aware of the existence of a pecuniary or circulatory sphere of activity within capitalism, and he contrasts this with the industrial substructure. His difficulty is his inability to carry out the implications of this distinction into an analysis of class structure and relations. The real deficiency of his analysis is methodological. The hypothesis of a dichotomous class division is missing. Consequently, he fails to see that the very same necessities giving birth to the technicians as such, give birth also to their subjugation by a managerial cadre of nontechnicians. Instead of rule by a soviet of technicians, we are faced with rule by a soviet of managers. These are by no means the same thing.

There is an alternative to the views of either Veblen or Burnham, one that conforms appreciably better to the main facts. We are faced neither with a technical nor with a managerial elite but with direct rule by an emerging managerial class (loosely defined) over new divisions of administrative labor and from thence over the whole of socially necessary labor. There is no Veblenian prospect of technicians and professionals acting in isolation from the main body of productive labor, seizing power from the managers and putting the economy upon a rational footing. There is no prospect of rational rule until administrative labor learns to participate in the class struggle. Before turning directly to this thesis in order to assess it reasonably, we turn back once more to the motive forces behind the accumulation of industrial and of administrative capitals. We wish to show how certain organic changes in capital have come to affect the balance between the forces and the relations of production.

Organic changes and accumulation: the general law

Over the past century a great concentration of industrial and of administrative capitals has occurred. However remarkable the quantitative extension of these capitals, however, the organic changes taking place both within and between the two basic forms of social capital are of still greater significance. The laws governing these changes govern the evolution of social classes and their interrelations.

Let us look first within each of the two spheres, of production and of circulation. With respect to the organic composition of industrial capital, no one seriously doubts – apart from those wallowing in theoretical confusions[13] – that the value composition has on the average risen considerably. The reason for the rise in the production ratio, C_p/V_p, is that technical improvements have been labor saving. This, coupled with the capitalists' Faustian love of science and the drive for profit, has brought high rates of innovation and the relative displacement of labor. At the moment, it is perhaps true, one sees that innovation lags far behind invention, and a failure to realize the technical potential for automation is in full view. Even so, the rise of the ratio has sufficed to produce the main effects described in Marx's first approximation. From that point the development of a second approximation is relatively simple.

While out of the surplus of productive labor have come the material means of extending the circulatory accumulation, capitals within the circulatory sphere also divide into their constant and their variable components, into their congealed and their living members. Like industrial work, administrative work with its means of production, its work processes, becomes more or less automated as the value composition of the administrative capitals rises. (This is the ratio C_u/V_w, since this is unproductive labor.) This tendency is apparent within the circulatory sectors even though the high rate of accumulation of these capitals has brought a bureaucratization accompanying the administrative-managerial concentration that to some extent conceals the full measure of administrative mechanization.

Now the increase in the rate of the unproductive accumulation retards the general rate of growth of the system, and this reacts back upon the former, which must ultimately proceed at a reduced pace. Therefore, while a rise in the value composition of the circulatory input capitals occurs, and this tends to displace a certain amount of labor, as in industrial sectors, *the reabsorption of this labor through an extension of accumulation can only proceed to a certain point.* We observe the blowup of unproductive labor to be most striking during great expansionist upsurges; otherwise, stagnation afflicts also the circulatory activity. Given these tendencies, administrative and to some extent managerial personnel must encounter diminishing career and employment opportunities. White-collar unemployment and the reactions to which it gives rise are thus integral to the political-economic situation of the advanced capitalism. The contradiction shows itself partly as a preference for public investments that absorb administrative-managerial personnel at high rates: bureaucratic welfare programs are preferred, for instance. It shows in the political phenomenon of fascism when the managerial class is thoroughly activated.

One can very easily see that, *even with* the expansion of the middle classes proceeding under the drive to accumulate, technical progress in administration and in industry, in combination with the reduced overall rate of growth, bring forth a relative surplus population as the general law predicts. In this respect the general law may be said to be absolute. Its operation is at first forestalled by the acceleration of the administrative-managerial accumulation and the emergence of new divisions of social labor into which those can be fed who would otherwise be unfed. Eventually, however, the acceleration of the circulatory accumulation and the rise in the organic composition of capital in this sphere yield once again a consolidated surplus population that hangs like the sword of Damocles over the head of society. Just as capital compounds interest, it compounds the growth of unproductive labor, and compounds thereby all the problems of a population that is surplus relative to the requirements of economic reproduction.[14]

These effects may be summarized by saying that there is a tendency for the value composition of the *social* capitals to rise.[15] The total value of social capitals is partly invested in circulatory, partly in industrial sectors. A portion of this total creates no additional value: the labor, living and congealed, employed in circulatory work plus the labor unproductively utilized in the industrial sphere. All of this value relative to the productive power of living labor constitutes the *social* organic or value composition of capital. Casting the general tendency in these terms will help to make understandable a point to be developed subsequently. The rise in the social value composition of capital signifies a rise in the ratio of unproductive to productive labor, which is now at a considerable pitch of development. We shall return in the following chapter to fill in quantitatively the portions of the total population that fall into the numerator and into the denominator of this ratio.

The realization problem and the rise of the social value composition of capital

The productive labor of the social economy reproduces not only itself, but a vast aggregate of social capitals consisting of both congealed and living labor that is in one way or another unproductive labor. As we proceed to distinguish the forms of productive and of unproductive labor as they show themselves within the advanced capitalism, it will become quite apparent that the accumulation of capital has caused the ratio of unproductive to productive labor to rise to an extraordinary level. But before proceeding with the empirical delineation of these forms of modern labor, the forces making for the rise of the social organic composition of capital, the ratio of unproductive to productive labor, should be more precisely indicated. While the requisites of vending the social product have contributed most to the rise in this ratio, this explanation is too general to reveal all that needs to be seen. The realization problem, too, contains its dialectical aspects. These aspects have only recently come to light.

In point of fact, the Great Depression contributed not only to the Keynesian analysis of the deficiency of aggregate demand but to the rediscovery by the Marxians of what Marx had said about the problem of realization. With Gillman's discovery (1956) that the general rate of profit fails to decline when calculated on its traditional industrial basis (leaving out of account all other sectors of the economy), a new appreciation was born of the force of the capitalistic compulsion to invest in its vending establishment.[16] As Gillman saw it, the law of the falling rate of profit having forcefully asserted itself in the 1870s and again in the depression of 1884–1886, a countertendency arose to exorcise the evil. This tendency is seen in the array of counterformations accompanying the rise of monopoly capital and of state monopoly capitalism. This array includes the expanded instrumentalities of the vending apparatus of commerce and finance; it includes the allocation of capitals into the blowup of state agencies, departments, and bureaus; it includes the construction of a military establishment that breaks the way for adventures of commercial imperialism. All of these combine into one chronic enlargement of unproductive expenses, pushing up from below the falling rate of profit, countervailing against the long-term tendency of the rate of profit to decline. In this way Gillman explains the alleged failure of the law of the falling rate of profit since the time of World War I.

On the whole, the theorists of monopoly capital[17] have accepted and elaborated on this theme. Confronted with what seemed at the time (1950s and 1960s) to be a new capitalist stability, these theorists sought to explain a society of affluence with its "colossal capacity to generate private and public waste."[18] To this end, Baran and Sweezy have gone as far as to formulate a new law, a "law of rising surplus," to substitute for the presumably defunct law of the falling rate of profit. As they see it, the drive now is to find outlets for the rising surplus, and the grotesque sales effort, military and imperial probings, and so on, are all born of the need to utilize profitably the rising surplus. Apart from some theoretical difficulties in connection with their conception of the surplus, they do not really explain why the exotic and dangerous forms of investment grow relative to "capitalists' consumption and accumulation." The scale of unproductive consumption does rise, and it rises relatively; but the law of rising surplus is logically inconsistent with this phenomenon.

As it now stands, the realization theory of circulatory expansion runs into serious difficulties. Gillman himself – although his lead was not taken up by others – recognized the basic fact that contradicts the rising surplus explanation: The expanding circulatory system is composed of unproductive labor, living and congealed, and the relative growth of this labor *diminishes rather than augments* the surplus. As previously explained, a given rate of unproductive consumption pulls the real rate of accumulation below its feasible maximum; an increase in that rate further reduces that rate of accumulation. To be sure, the accumulation of circulatory capitals may stimulate a rise in aggregate demand, in this way helping to reduce the "deflationary gap," as the Keynesians refer to it. But the accumulation of unproductive labor, and the growth of unproductive consumption, helps to solve the realization problem from *two* directions, and not merely by the stimulus it gives to aggregate demand. At the same time that unproductive investment raises aggregate demand in proportion to its own growth, it *lowers* the real rate of growth of the system. It reduces thereby the increase of demand required to close the deflationary gap and solves the realization problem. In other words, the problem of the deficiency in aggregate demand tends to disappear with the capitalist solution of the realization problem, with the accumulation of unproductive labor, that is, the allocation of social capitals into circulatory activity on an extending scale. The solution of this problem, however, gives rise to others at least as serious. First of all, it tends to economic stagnation, and this *reinforces* the tendency of the general rate of profit to fall. Secondly, by retarding the growth rate, it gives rise to a higher rate of secular unemployment as the population and the labor force continue to grow. Finally, it occasions the plague of inflation.[19] All of these are best seen, not as a response to a new law of rising surplus, but as *a new response to the old tendency* of the general rate of profit to fall.

The tendency for the general rate of profit to fall still is the primary affliction of contemporary capitalism. The prosperity of the post–World War II period was in large part illusory; the growth of gross national product always exaggerated considerably the real rate of accumulation and especially of the productive capitals.[20] Gillman's observation of a failure of the tendency to the falling rate of profit after World War I was probably inaccurate, and improved estimates show almost precisely what the Marxian law predicts.[21] Furthermore, since World War I we have had a major depression and are now wading in the shallows of another into which capitalism has been pushed by the law in question. It is thus the force of the law that produces the characteristic capitalist response to economic crisis: to paper the cracks with money capital in order to avoid any deep-probing move to reconstruct the faltering social economy. The building up of guaranteed markets for social product, the solution to the realization problem that Keynesian economists propose, does nothing whatsoever to forestall the onset of economic crisis. In promoting the development of the circulatory mechanism, it undermines the vitality of productive labor and contributes directly to the crisis that it is designed to avoid by lowering the real rate of accumulation and, in time, the money rate of profit that makes the system go.

The mystery of capitalist affluence in the advanced managerial phase is that anyone ever regarded it as affluent. Capital nowadays promotes economic retardation and regression quite as vigorously as it once promoted industrial accumulation. In days of yore, when the complex accumulation of industrial capitals was running strongly, the system could sustain a rapid circulatory accumulation. Those days are gone. Capital accumulates with its old fervor, but its pace is more staid and its destination more problematical. There are yet other circumstances contributing to the rise in the social organic composition of capital and to all of the difficulties of capitalism in the managerial phase of its development.

Terms of exchange and the rise of unproductive labor

Realization difficulties that trace to the law of the falling rate of profit have brought forth as a response to these difficulties an expanding population of administrative and managerial workers within circulatory employments. The movement of terms of exchange in various ways also contributes to a relative growth in demand for capitals to be utilized in circulatory rather than in industrial activity.[22]

The modern corporation, the dominant organizational unit of our day, is a bureaucratic as well as productive assemblage of capitals, and in some instances the former altogether predominates the latter, which reduces to zero. There are many reasons why the ratio of the corporation's administrative to its industrial capitals is high. Circulatory capital has proved useful in servicing the profit and pricing calculations of management; the corporation holds circulatory capitals as its pro rata share in capitals required for the realization of profits throughout the system. It retains and enlarges administrative capital holdings because of their usefulness in competitive struggles, in disciplining and bargaining with labor, in besieging the state and holding its place in the sun, and so on. Whatever the proportion of circulatory or administrative to industrial capitals within the enterprise, however, terms of exchange will turn in favor of the enterprise to the degree that the ratio of the administrative to the industrial capitals is *above* the social average. This is particularly true of those large-scale corporations whose production is diversified and whose markets are not "competitive" in the narrow sense of the term; it is true of those 2000 or 3000 corporations that control the bulk of the social product.

The pricing mechanism of real-world competition gives automatically to the giant corporation an advantage in terms of exchange that, in turn, intensifies the effort of all to be giants. This is not to say that the entrepreneur in the corporate bureaucracy understands why these terms move in his favor; whether capitals are productive or unproductive is of no interest to the entrepreneur, corporate or otherwise. He merely supposes virtue to be rewarded. The investment in the circulatory capitals pays its way, however, and the reason this is so we may review briefly, the economics having already been dealt with. Economically, the circulatory capitals of the administrative superstructure function like the constant capitals of industry. They do not *create* surplus value. Economically, the circulatory capitals function like constant capital. Their accumulation relative to productive labor causes the organic composition of capital to rise. When the organic composition of the firm's capitals is above the average value composition of firms with which it deals, terms of exchange tend to move in its favor. The capitalist pricing mechanism, assigning prices in excess of exchange values to all whose value compositions are above the social average, rewards disproportionately the firms that bureaucratize, that invest in a relative growth of their administrative or circulatory capitals.

The modern corporate entrepreneur is now, and has long been, convinced of the economic virtues of bigness per se. The investment agenda of the corporation reflects this preference for the administrative capitals, and this preference yields in time the bureaucratic and top-heavy organization that is the managerial playground. From the social standpoint the relative accumulation of administrative capitals, the systematic production of bureaucracy, is wholly irrational. Perhaps for this reason its predominance is presumed by the economist to be the consequence of laws of sociology, social psychology – anything, as long as they are not economic laws. But economic laws they are. Bureaucracy pays; it is but another irrational institution of an irrational mode of production.

Terms of exchange have their influence also on the supplies of inputs suitable for circulatory employment. In the production of generous supplies of administrative and managerial labor powers, and in the production of the machinery, tools, raw materials, and so on, with which this labor works, above-average value compositions of capitals are generally required. The pricing mechanism responds to these high value compositions needed in the production of machines, computers, managers, engineers, and others by setting wage and salary scales above the exchange values of the products and services rquired. (At the other extreme, it sets wages for labor-intensive services at levels below exchange value of the labor power.) Through this torsion effect on the structure of wages the pricing system succeeds in overpaying – at least for a time, until supplies become excessive – the managers along with numerous categories of technicians and professionals. The ultimate over-production of these grades of labor is perhaps most noticeable in the oversupply of managers, and this is politically as well as economically troublesome. The long-term tendency for all of this labor is for its rates of pay to decline as supplies become excessive, and this tendency shows itself also for those grades outside of the managerial categories.

The triumph of the middle classes

The economics of the circulatory accumulation may at times be boring, but its consequences are profound. There are evidently built into the capitalist order very powerful forces that swing the composition of the total population in quite definite directions. The division of social labor in time shifts in favor of white- and against blue-collar personnel. The proportion of salaried managers and officials tends to rise. The proportion of technicians and professionals rises within the total working population (see Table 10.1). The general movement may be summarized by saying that eccentric investment mechanisms promote the enlargement of a circulatory apparatus that houses the so-called middle classes of contemporary society. These classes do not constitute a homogeneous political or economic entity, however. Suffice it to say that the "great middle class" has arisen on a technical foundation underlying the administrative labor, on this side, and on a pecuniary, property foundation underlying the managerial and official population, on that side.

There is a dualism in the very foundations of middle-class ex-

Table 10.1. *The proletarianization of the U.S. labor force (in percent)*

Year	Wage and salaried employees[a]	Self-employed entrepreneurs[b]	Salaried managers and officials	Total[c]
1780[d]	20.0	80.0	—	100.0
1880	62.0	36.9	1.1	100.0
1890	65.0	33.8	1.2	100.0
1900	67.9	30.8	1.3	100.0
1910	71.9	26.3	1.8	100.0
1920	73.9	23.5	2.6	100.0
1930	76.8	20.3	2.9	100.0
1939	78.2	18.8	3.0	100.0
1950	77.7	17.9	4.4	100.0
1960	80.6	14.1	5.3	100.0
1969	83.6	9.2	7.2	100.0

[a] Excluding salaried managers and officials.
[b] Business entrepreneurs, professional practicioners, farmers and other property owners.
[c] Defined as all income recipients who participate directly in economic activity; unpaid family workers have been excluded.
[d] Figures for 1780 are rough estimates. Slaves, who comprised one-fifth of the population, are excluded; white indentured servants are included in the wage and salaried employees category.
Sources: From Michael Reich, "The Evolution of the United States Labor Force," in Edwards, Reich, and Weisskopf, op. cit., p. 175. Data for 1780 from Jackson T. Main, *The Social Structure of Revolutionary America* (Princeton, N.J.: Princeton University Press, 1965), pp. 270–77. Data for 1880–1939 from Spurgeon Bell, *Productivity, Wages and National Income* (Washington, D.C.: Brookings Institution, 1940), p. 10. Data for 1950–1969 computed from U.S. Dept. of Labor, *Manpower Report of the President,* various years; and U.S. Dept. of Commerce, Bureau of the Census, *Census of Population,* 1950 and 1960, and *Current Population Reports*, Series P-60, various years.

istence such that, taking into view all those who might advance a political, sociological, psychological, or economic claim to membership in this class, the class itself does not exist as a homogeneous body in any of these dimensions. It is in actuality not a social class per se but a pastiche of fragments of the totality of social labor. The middle class is but the appearance of which the reality is a division between administrative labor and the managers. This division, we shall see, is a reflection of a still more fundamental division between productive and unproductive labor, or between producing class and ruling class.

This means, too, that the familiar white-collar–blue-collar dichotomy has only rhetorical significance. The more profound distinction is between those technicians and professionals employed productively in coordinating social activity (or at least trying to do so), or in producing socially useful product (industrial labor), and, on the other hand, the unproductive managerial workers and their ruling-class superiors. Within the white-collar portion of the population the interests of administrative labor are diametrically opposed to the interests of the managers, and we shall shortly investigate in some detail the nature of this conflict within the middle class. Administrative labor, it turns out, is *not* a part of the managerial labor with which it is often confused; it is part of the working class, emerging as a distinct and important segment of that class in the managerial phase.

What is the significance of the managed capitalism? With the appearance of the managers on the scene, the class structure reaches the very outer and final limits of its economic, its sociological, and, hence, its political development. All of the productive forces of any society are comprehended within activities of production and its coordination. Administrative and industrial laborers now account for all that is technically necessary to the productive work required. The present order contains a full-blown embodiment of these activities within an expanded, well-articulated, and technically sophisticated collective laborer. While the chrysalis now envelops a full set of the productive forces, however, the chrysalis itself prevents the emergence of these forces. The political assignment of the managers is to prevent the emergence of the productive forces to an administrative and industrial predominance and to ensure that the play of these forces is confined within profit parameters. But the rise of the managers is symptomatic of the existence of the whole consolidated surplus population for which no socially useful employment exists, or can be made to exist, within the confines of an obsolete mode of production. The managerial phase marks the final integration in the centralization of power. On the right stands a well-filled-out and integrated decision-making class, owing its power and function to the defunct principles of an expiring mode. On the left stand the still divided but inescapably interrelated branches of productive labor, administrative and industrial.

11

Class structure and conflict
in the managerial phase II

The dual accumulation and breakup of the middle class

Within the countries of the advanced capitalism - elsewhere the vitality may be greater - the mode of production is reaching the outer limits of its development. Industrial accumulation is slackened, weighed down by the burdens of circulation. Within the dual accumulation of unproductive and of productive labor, of circulatory and of industrial capitals, the productive forces are seriously weakened. The struggle between capital and labor intensifies, and this is seen not only in relations between capital and the industrial working class but within the so-called middle classes, where there is a sharpened tension between the managers, as executives of the ruling class, and the branch of the working class over which it rules directly, administrative labor.

The split between the managers and administrative labor divides white-collar labor into economically and politically opposed divisions in an ineradicable and growing schism whose depths we have yet to plumb.[1] While we come immediately to this task, let us say first that this conflict between administrative labor and the managers is merely a part of the broad struggle between capital and labor. It, too, traces to the accumulation of capital, to old drives that are still powerful but working in an ever more eccentric manner. With the incidence of science and invention upon techniques of administrative utility - use values inherently serviceable for the coordination of social activities - the great accumulators have promoted the administrative capitals with mounting enthusiasm at the outset and with mounting desperation with the passage of time.

The technical basis having been laid for this accumulation in a host of fields ranging from communications and transportation to operations analysis, from accounting to the mathematical and statistical sciences, from social psychology to the science of chemistry, new divisions of technicians and professionals have appeared to produce and to work with the new technique. But with the accumulation of administrative labor in both its living and congealed forms have also come new cadres of overseers, the new technocratic managers of the property interest. When the full extent of this dichotomy is seen, the full fragmentation of the middle classes becomes apparent. What one finds instead of a middle class is an enlarged working class with its administrative workers, on the one side, and, on the other, an enlarged ruling class with its managerial population.

This bifurcation of what might be termed the "administrative classes" in general may be traced historically into the Middle Ages and probably beyond.[2] Yet the distinction between these bodies becomes sharper, and the rift widens in the managerial phase of capitalist development. The great wedge of accumulation drives ever deeper into the population. Just as technical change under capitalism brought forth the industrial worker while placing the industrialist within the ruling class, so now the administrative accumulation brings a further division between the administrative and the managerial worker. New forces bring new relations of production. What is the nature of the resulting class struggle, and what is its prospective resolution? What is happening to the composition of the total population in the present phase of the proceedings?

Managerial traits

With the value composition of social capital rising, the social division of labor proceeding, the new executive appears as a quite necessary appendage of big capital. The manager's origins are twofold. Like the administrative worker, he is delivered of an advancing technique. But his conception is in financial and commercial exigency.[3] As the merchant's capital grows and its functions become more specialized, the managerial function breaks away as a distinct branch of the entrepreneurial function, but the main political and psychological features of the new executive reflect the proprietary father rather than the scientific mother. The responsibilities of managers and officials revolve around the custody of property, its valuation and extension. In these undertakings the manager is a hireling; yet he is and must be an overseer of administrative and of industrial labor.

The gubernatorial personality is split by circumstance. In its technical aspect the manager's proximity to the functioning technician proscribes his education and training. In order to make use of the technician's services he should be trained always in the latest administrative crafts: engineering, cost accounting, science, economics, business administration, operations research, and so on.[4] There is a definite historical progression in the sequence of specialties that make the manager. The specialty makes the manager in that it provides him with needed qualifications. In his work career he has little opportunity and less need to practice regularly the craft that launched him. The work is supervisory, where craft and craftiness overlap. The tendency in his education and training is to conceal technical deficiencies beyond what is needed to secure his employment. The deficiencies are solved by education in "generalist" fields, so that a smattering of information will cover all the eventualities with which he may later need to contend.

The divorce of the manager from the work of the administrative craftsman is implicit in his role as aide-de-camp of capital. It helps to set the stage for his psychic instabilities. He must also contemplate the needs of those above him in the hierarchy, for they provide him with work and reward; his comportment becomes imitative of their ambience. Even at low levels of management, within industrial or even educational corporations, attitudes and values often resemble in miniature those working in the highest echelons, say, as money managers. At the uppermost levels where financial and psychological security is maximized, the arrogance is more consistent, yet more subtle and profound. There one finds the totemic figurations that testify to the office-boy origins of the class as such.

The technocratic manager ranges sociologically from the upper ranks of administrative labor to the lower strata of the upper ruling class. He inhabits the directorial echelons of industry and is almost the exclusive resident of many circulatory agencies. From the directorates of the great financial groups he approaches, hat in hand, the threshold of the great dynastic families.[5] As happy executor of the imperial drive, he runs national and multinational corporations, public and private, and neither humane nor patriotic constraints impede his exercise of authority in the ruling-class interest.

Contrary to the myth that "the separation of ownership and control" has left him shoeless, he is heavily vested financially.[6] What is true is that, his own portfolio being diversified, he does not own the corporation from which he draws his pay. This very diversification, however, attenuates as it suffuses the managerial interest. It socializes the manager in that what he does not own he would yet like to own. Like his forebears in the manorial household, he identifies his interest with that of his master. The master's interest he confuses with the social interest; this is flattering and it pays well. The vacuity and duplicity of his loyalty he conceals from himself – and would like to conceal from others – with the "plate and livery" of a typically bourgeois consumption.[7]

But the main clue to his political and social-psychological peculiarities lies in his removal from productive labor. For the majority the degree of this removal is absolute (there are individual exceptions to the unproductive rule). This removal ensures a futility of existence driven home by a furious practice of make-believe. This accounts for the cultivated aura of romanticism, blended more or less carefully with crude empiricism, surrounding so many members of the team. The collective laborer of this species spans a range of philosophical belief from a pragmatic marriage of natural law and technological scientism (law and order plus salvation through gadgets) to a vulgar Social Darwinism or political Hegelianism so useful to apologists for tyranny. Such stultifying philosophies aid greatly the troubled mind when, as Brecht expressed it, "the bitch is in heat again" and political reaction goes hot on the trail.

Like his petty bourgeois antecedents, the new entrepreneur desires to be master builder but finds that the road hence demands a consistent servility. Since the most obedient are the best rewarded, he listens always for the whistle that others cannot hear, thus preserving his vertical mobility and dreams for a better life. On the other hand, conceits endemic to command become personal as well as class features; Byzantium is his heavenly city. One sees everywhere the desiccated imaginations and calloused moralities that managed capitalism brings proudly forward in its overtly fascistic interludes.[8] For those close to the technician and professional, the advanced echelons of administrative labor, the strain is great. The manager at these levels blends almost indistinguishably into the ranks of working technicians. There is a managerial branch of the intellectual elite, and within it all of the traits we have mentioned coalesce into a thoroughly familiar compound. Marx's famous description of Proudhon describes precisely the intellectual spokesman for the managerial club:

> ... as he never grasped really scientific dialectics he never got further than sophistry . . . the petty bourgeois is composed of On the One Hand and On the Other Hand. This is so in his economic interests and therefore in his politics, in his scientific, religious and artistic views. It is so in his morals, in everything. He is a living contradiction. If, like Proudhon, he is in addition a gifted man, he will soon learn to play with his own contradictions and develop them according to circumstance into striking, ostentatious, now scandalous or now brilliant paradoxes. Charlatanism in science and accommodation in politics are inseparable from such a point of view. There only remains one governing motive, the vanity of the subject, and the only question for him, as for all vain people, is the success of the moment, the attention of the day.[9]

Administrative labor proper

We approach now another segment of the modern population that Marx did not clearly separate out of the middle classes, a body that is more easily identified with the aid of the general managerial traits before us. Not that administrative labor shares these traits; on the whole it does not. True, in the advanced divisions of administrative labor, in the phalanx of technical progress, intimacy of the laborer with the manager is great, and this is a realm in which movement either way is easy. Yet they are conceptually and practically quite different. At bottom, it is their differing relationships in production that condition their special responses.

It is above all the fact that administrative labor, viewed in its technical aspect as use value, provides a product or service that could contribute to social coordination that distinguishes it from the labor of the managers. Not that the worker is in actuality contributing either directly or indirectly to this socially useful function. He may be wasted labor sofar as this is concerned. Yet the difference remains. The managerial function derives from the circulatory imperatives of capital; the administrative worker exercises a craft skill (which may be, to be sure, quite serviceable in the managerial interest). As with other forms of socially necessary labor, administrative labor is valuable to the capitalist and is an object of accumulation because of the profitability of its employment. Its accumulation takes place because, whatever its technical capacities may be, these can be pressed into profitable service. Nevertheless, even though demands and supplies of administrative labor are governed by pecuniary considerations – like everything else within the mode – and the technical coefficients of coordination on production are not at all decisive in determining how much of it is employed, the utility of this labor for work of coordination inheres in its sinews.[10] At present, the great bulk of administrative labor finds employment within two intimately related lines of activity, both of which are overwhelmingly directed to the extended and complex reproduction of the circulatory establishment. First, it is employed within circulation proper, providing commodities – goods and services, as they say – directly useful to decision-making managers, themselves directing the appropriation of surplus value. The work here is essentially clerical in that the worker's product or service, from that of the clerk to the scientific adviser, is given over to realization chores under the direction of superiors preoccupied with one or another administrative aspect of this realization. The political and psychological subjugation of the worker in proximity to the manager has powerful effects upon the former, we know; it corrodes his moral and intellectual capacities while it strengthens his superiors' conceits.[11]

A second field of employment for administrative labor is of at least equal political and economic significance. It is an area in which, even under capitalism, the laborer has been somewhat better able to realize his potentials. This is in the production of labor power itself. The branch may be designated educating labor. (The term "educators" has long since been appropriated by the managers.) Educational workers are engaged, though in varying degree, in producing all of the grades of social labor, and this product, the commodity labor power itself, moves into three main fields of endeavor. The most highly trained divisions emerging from the schools are either themselves administrative craftworkers (for instance, teachers); or they move into the managerial population; or (in lesser numbers) they move into the industrial population. The largest part of the output from upper levels of education moves into the middle classes, and it is to the production of this main body that the greatest portion of educating energies is given. We are speaking now of the historical drift from northwest to southeast in the labor power flow matrix (Chapter 5).

With, in other words, the rise of the social value composition of capital, the powers of educating labor are increasingly spent in the reproduction of managerial and of administrative labor. To a lessening degree, administrative labor of the educating branch contributes to the production of industrial labor whose own energies are similarly wrenched away from economic reproduction in the managerial phase. Both of the basic varieties of productive and potentially productive labor, administrative and industrial, contribute a relatively growing value to reproducing the material and administrative means of their own subjugation. They generate on an extending scale the managers who tyrannize them in a larger interest.

Both administrative and industrial labor reproduce their own labor powers in a more or less cooperative if an unbalanced relationship, and in the course of this reproduction they produce also the new forms of the consolidated surplus population. Not only their cooperative interrelations but their productivity, however, distinguish them from the managers and from all those unproductively employed. The managers do not return to their own producers a reciprocal service of reproduction; they do not contribute to the production of surplus value; rather, they are themselves a form of surplus labor. The managers merely appropriate this value, with the aid of their own retainers, ensuring that a portion is regularly utilized in their own reproduction.

Formal education by no means absorbs the whole energies of educating labor. While perhaps the largest portion of its powers is spent in formal education, much goes into other essentials of reproduction of labor power in fields distinct from but closely connected with formal education. We must define educating labor to include teachers, yes; but also to include scientists and social scientists, men and women of arts and letters, medical and psychiatric workers, journeymen journalists and producers within the mass media and in cultural affairs. Above all, it must be defined to include those women who are economic *as well as* biological producers. Their work of educational and cultural production, in view of the still limited role of formal education in the production of social labor, is still absolutely vital. It produces and sustains the technical and cultural heritage even though a tendency to their supersession is in one sense far advanced. As producers, women have moved out of the home and into the schools, out of the bourgeois family and into systematic production.[12] To the extent to which they make their productive role secure in new dimensions they secure their central position in the working class.

All of this labor, clerical and educating (broadly defined), is in *principle* productive, and this holds even though de facto much of this labor power is wastefully and therefore unproductively utilized, both in clerical work within the state and within corporations, and in educating activities. All of it exercises a technique in order to yield a service that would be administratively useful outside the framework of the capitalist mode. This is not to say that administrative labor constitutes a new working class of new proletarians. It is only to argue, first, that it is definitely not a part of the managerial population with which much of it is confused and into which, to be sure, it tends to run at certain levels of circulatory operations. It is to argue, second, that administrative labor is a part of the working class, emerging definitively as a portion of that class at a certain phase of capitalist development.

Administrative labor works directly with means of administration that, like industrial labor's means of production, it does not own. It produces products and services useful for social coordination by virtue of the technique it embodies, a technique that is reproductively useful. Fragmented, dispersed, torn by the overall contest between capital and labor, administrative labor is nevertheless quantitatively large and qualitatively well developed as a technical entity. This last point is important. With the appearance of the managerial branch of the ruling class, and with that of its antithesis, administrative labor, the class structure of modern capitalism reaches the final limit of its economic and, hence, of its political development. All of the productive forces of society are comprehended within activities of reproduction and its coordination. The main body of these forces is fully developed with the emergence of a social class embracing fully articulated divisions of labor within production and its coordination, for this is a social class whose technical self-sufficiency renders wholly superfluous the existence of other classes and other forms of social labor. In relation to this class, all other divisions belong to the consolidated surplus population.[13] Capitalism completes the construction of the modern working class, and this presages the working out of the class struggle to a possibly favorable terminus.

The wastage of productive labor

The consciousness of administrative labor as a branch of productive labor is probably less developed than that of industrial labor, but the appearance of self-consciousness has been notable of late and may move to a par with that of the industrial portion of the working class. The administrative worker is aware, for example, of the chronic distortions of work taking place daily in the office, within processes of production and of administration both. This cognition underlies new attitudes in education (the new teacher militancy); in medicine and public health (the technician's challenge to the doctor); in the mass media (the fight against censorship and for interpretive reporting); in the theater and the other arts (the battle against dilution of standards); in labor unions (revolt against the manager); and so on. Within each and every department in which administrative labor works an aberration is seen. In addition to the teacher, scientist, artist, writer, factory worker, economist, there is the *managerial* teacher, scientist, artist, and so on. There is everywhere the false Ivan. Everywhere self-serving managers sow salty seed within the potentially fertile grounds of social labor, negating its productivity. Indeed, the phenomenon of the counter-producer is recognized by managers themselves who see the world inverted in order to avoid self-recognition. The infiltration of the manager into forbidden territory traces to a larger impulse than that of the bureaucrat making his way.[14] While ambition is the occupational hazard of management, the real cause of its expansion is to be found in relations of production in a definite phase of development. The root cause is, as S. Menshikov says, "that the separation of functioning capital from capital as property, which reaches its apex in the age of monopoly capitalism, leads to the emergence of a numerous category of managers."[15]

Far from being a simple and ineradicable expression of human nature – a theme that is part of the managerial apologia – the managerial bureaucratizing is connected with the mode of production. It is an expression of the contradiction between the appropriation and the production of surplus value, between capital as property and functioning capital, between unproductive and productive labor. From this contradiction arise the great circulatory factories within which profits are made under the auspices of managerial authority. This involves an enormous accumulation of wasted administrative labor that earns its living within mercantile establishments, within education, within the executive and policing agencies of the state juridical network, the latter holding together, by force when need be, the entire unwieldy amalgam of productive and of unproductive labor.

In addition to the wastage of talent in finance, commerce, law, the military, the corporation, and in government, there is all the administrative labor power spent in the production of wasted and unproductive labor. All of this growing wastage cannot help but affect profoundly those employed within formal education and within the educational branches of communications, arts and letters, and the other cultural and informative pursuits in which pap must be made to flow. The total of labor so aborted is enormous, and much of the unrest of this labor traces to its sharpening awareness that its energies are going down the drain. The very scale of the wastage guarantees that the craftsman should be increasingly sensitive to his exploitation, just as he is sensitive to the petty despotism of the office boy looking to be a major tyrant. True, the capitalistic source of the malaise is to some extent still hidden. True, too, the problem of the alternative remains to be resolved to the satisfaction of the laborer, who does not, after all, want things to worsen when they are bad enough already. Under these circumstances the impoverishment of their arts and crafts arouses relatively little resistance from the labor so depreciated.[16] No doubt, also, the continuing censorship by managers in the schools, in the mass media, in government, in the police and the military, plays some part in concealing the fact that the trouble lies in the accumulation of capital.

With a plethora of confusion more or less systematically engendered, the managers are able to maintain and even to enlarge historic antagonisms between administrative and industrial labor, antagonisms always exaggerated and made out of whole cloth where nonexistent. Yet it is also the case that, because of the excessive demands on his services for reproduction of circulatory capitals, the worker in education is unable to return to industrial labor a value proportioned to reciprocal exchange. Sandwiched between the managers above and his brothers below, his energy is claimed by those of highest social priority. A disproportionate energy is wastefully consumed and cannot be recovered for more worthwhile purposes. This distortion of exchange relations between branches of socially necessary labor affects adversely political relations between them and is part of the mechanism of divide and conquer, since neither branch as yet realizes that its own emancipation must be a joint production.

And yet, the rise of the surplus population continuing, the administrative laborer is forced to contemplate its paradoxes. He sees and is dismayed by the organization man who rules over him. He knows that the manager is unable to compose a harmonious score and is unable to direct it effectively in any case. He knows that the directorate lacks the moral qualities that leadership demands. He sees the constant shirking of social responsibilities and knows who benefits. He regards with deep misgiving the now pusillanimous, now aggressive bourgeois gentleman and sees in him the very personification of a system of values threatening his own.

The managerial *Weltanschauung* is a world apart from that of administrative labor. The latter's business is to create scores, though they are never performed. It is to extend communications and to enlarge understanding although his efforts are constantly nullified. It is to propagate the moral and aesthetic values in an operational social setting, and the opposite of this is expressed by the marching band of managers. The ultimate paradox is that the main body of administrative labor possesses the entire complement of those values that the real work of social management requires. Yet the collective administrative laborer finds his skill, his art uselessly dissipated among the *faux frais* of capitalist production. The energy of the administrative worker is thus lost: "If the thing is useless, so is the labor contained in it: the labor does not count as labor, and therefore creates no value." This principle applies de facto to administrative labor, but it applies de jure to the managerial body. This is what makes inevitable the conflict between them.

The disproportions still extend and with them the polarization that brings to light the true situation. The awareness is unmistakably growing that the skills of the educating laborers are futilely employed; the clerical worker is increasingly proletarianized, and especially the women who are sorely misused in economic as in other dimensions. The greater the scale of the wastage, the more surely the effort will be made to recover what is being lost. For both administrative and industrial labor, means of production must be returned to their creator's hands.

The second approximation and the value conflict

A century after Marx's seminal analysis, his main thesis is very much intact. The primary elements of social class are still twofold (see Figure 11.1). There is at the top the owning-managing class,

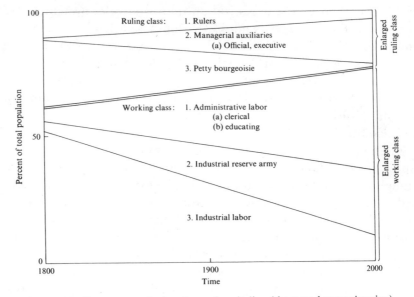

Figure 11.1. Class structure in the advanced capitalism (the second approximation)

the guardians and auxiliaries in a pecuniary-technocratic coalition held together in an admixture of values aesthetically bizarre, economically obsolete, politically dangerous. There is at the bottom (below the double line) the working class. Within each of the primary groupings major subdivisions are seen. Just as the ruling class contains an upper branch together with a lower, working executive division, so does the producing class contain two major departments, the industrial and the administrative; below the better-paid stratum of white-collar labor is the traditional working class. Both branches contain subdivisions of more or less interest, for example, the clerical-educating division referred to. Both feed into the industrial reserve army in slack times and feed out of it in periods of expansion. Allowing also for class remnants of previous modes of production (French *rentiers* or petty bourgeois shopkeepers everywhere), whose traces are still to be found in the present phase, the class composition of the total population is thus accounted for in the second approximation.

Since this filling out of the second approximation has been carried out in strict conformity with the principles of dialectical materialism, it is of course important that the structure revealed not be illusory. The fact that we have accounted for the total population so easily confirms the analysis, but the analysis is still further confirmed if we proceed to examine the ideological, political, and psychological aspects of the terrain mapped out. Again a principle is needed, and again one lies at hand. In principle the closer a given branch to the processes of economic reproduction – and that branch is closest that engages directly in reproducing either the administrative or industrial capitals (especially in their productive forms) – the more certainly does the labor power fall into the productive category and the more certainly will it reflect the frustrations arising out of an order that militates against the fulfillment of the reproductive function. On the contrary, the further removed from economic reproduction the branch or division of social labor, the more surely will that labor reflect the reproductive needs of capital alone, the structure of values that governs the mode of production rather than reproduction itself. (Reproducing the circulatory superstructure is not the same as economic reproduction; it is economic reproduction once removed.)

In the case of educating labor, for example, it is not at all surprising that teachers and women should adhere to functional values of economic reproduction, those of workmanship and craftsmanship as against the distorting values peculiar to the mode. The root interest of this labor power is in direct opposition to the class interest furthest removed from productive activity. It is hostile to the surplus labor embodied in the managers and at the level of values, if not yet in practice, to all that lies beyond this insulating stratum. Conversely, the further the branch or division from productive employment, as among those employed in circulatory work within entrepreneurial stratospheres – and whether male or female is of no consequence at these levels – the more decisively are values bourgeois and pseudo-aristocratic. That is, even within the administrative branch of socially useful labor, a range of values and attitudes is discernible that accords almost precisely with the occupational plane in the overall hierarchy. In other words, a fairly precise ideological grading is to be seen when correlated with economic interests as defined by the labor theory of value and especially as that theory defines productive and unproductive labor. Even within the administrative branch of social labor a certain structure of values, attitudes, loyalties, emerges *parri passu* with the labor hierarchy. At its upper limits, administrative labor blends into the managerial stratum and assumes its politically reactionary system of values. At lower levels, it blends into the industrial work force and is proletarianized.

Putting aside for the moment the "Lazarus layers of the reserve army," and observing the main body of active social labor, productive and unproductive together, stretching between the upper limit of idle wealth and the lower depths, the distribution of values between these limits is not at all random. Attitudes and values correlate with the division between productive and unproductive labor. At the upper side of the managerial stratum, in the vicinity of the inactive and upper-class elite, there is an undeviating dedication to the capitalistic interest, to the preservation of the whole cocoon of values enclosing the ruling class as a whole. (Within the leisure class above this, the pecuniary values of the system are given a religious expression through ritual dancings.)[17] At intermediate and lower levels within the managerial ranks, ideological cant is less reverential and placatory, the conservatism of the gamesters reflected in homely pragmatism and in the opportunism of daily verbiage and other conduct. Consumptions are here ostentatiously bourgeois.

Within the active divisions of productive labor, whether wasted or not, one finds on the whole a different hierarchy of values. This holds even for the higher ranks of administrative labor so often interlarded with managerial aspirants, but differences become decisive as one descends to educating labor and the traditional proletariat. On the whole, the clerical branch is more conservative than the educating branch of administrative labor, but industrial and administrative labor contain between them the bulk of what ideological and other forms of resistance there may be to the rule of capital (apart from the anarchy of the Lazarus layers). Even in the top ranks of clerical labor, for instance, sufficient insubordination obtains to provide the screening principles needed by management in its work of occupational segregation.

Within the industrial proletariat, heavy infiltrations of managerial delegates have taken place. It would be going too far to say that all labor managers have been bought off by capital, but clearly the pressures have been great, and the fact that they have been so is a testimonial to the importance of the work that managers perform in holding down the claims of workmen. The separation of the managers from the workers is again a reflection of the broader and deeper schism between ruling and working class and, more narrowly, between managerial and working-class labor.

The response to this entrapment of industrial labor by managerial delegations is varied and well known: wildcat strikes, aversion to unionization, political unreliability of rank-and-file labor, and so on. With the passage of time, administrative labor faces a predicament that more and more resembles that of the oppressed industrial worker.

It is true of both industrial and administrative labor that their economic interest lies in the further development of their productive forces and that this interest is frustrated and countered by the development of unproductive labor and of unproductive consumption of which private bourgeois consumption is the least significant and interesting part. The degree of exploitation of administrative labor may at present be less in one dimension than that of industrial labor, but in other dimensions its exploitation is equally noxious.[18] There is its extensive wastage; but this happens to industrial labor, too, a significant portion of whose employment opportunities hinge upon military production. Politically, administrative labor is sometimes handled gently, sometimes threateningly as in the recurrent witch hunts, imprisonments, assassinations, threats, and cajoleries to which it is sporadically subjected. Yet strikes are broken by scabs, and industrial labor often has faced the military and the police in direct confrontation. Both branches of productive labor are subject to a wide variety of ideological gambits to calm the restless, to conceal the fraudulence of managerial claims and the perfidy of managerial conduct. In this connection administrative labor is subject to special lures designed to keep it from seeing that it and not the manager is the natural decision-making authority.

So the polarization of attitudes and values extends apace with economic stagnation and regression. On the one side are the mounting if uncoordinated insubordinations of productive labor, forced by economic repression to contemplate its actual situation and its possible destiny. On the other is the sullen authoritarianism of the managers, reined in from natural inclinations by the old leaders of the capitalist mode of production, unleashed to do their work when tensions become too great and there is a clear need for that so-called middle-class authoritarianism known as fascism.

The fetters placed

Under capitalism the accumulation of the administrative capitals is governed far less by the technical coefficients of coordination on production than by monetary requirements of circulation. The result of this peculiarity of the mode which, like Narcissus, prefers its own distinctive features, is yet another differentiation within the structure of social classes. As the efficiency of administrative labor advances and its accumulation accelerates, there is installed on a correspondingly increasing scale, for the sake of profit, the unproductive counterpart to that labor. The basic difference between owning and working classes is complicated by a higher degree of specialization within relations of production. Supported by the segmentation of capitals out of surplus value, the new division rests upon technical progress in the administrative capitals but draws upon property for its antithesis. While accumulation of the circulatory capitals – the administrative plus those required for direct support of the managers – enlarges steadily the volume of unproductive labor, it impairs the generation of surplus value in proportion to its own expansion. To the familiar, chronic instabilities of the mode is thereby added stagnation tending to regression.

In this manner, capital places the fetters of unproductive consumption upon the productive forces and contributes to a heightening of class tensions. Tension grows because the obscene enlargement of circulatory sectors involves a dwindling capacity to meliorate tension. The wastage and excessive depreciation of labor power leave no means for replacing vital energies. The struggles of labor provoked by these deprivations give rise, in turn, to political repressions. There is absurdity in these proceedings even though their termination is vital. Between them, industrial and administrative labor provide whatever powers fuel the engine of accumulation; they feed the surplus from which profits derive. But because of their inability to control the disposition of the surplus, the engine of production turns against them like a boomerang. The counting house continues to supplant the factory, and the superstructure prospers while the substructure decays – until both together threaten to topple. In the crisis that ensues, the welfare poorhouse is resuscitated to keep the bottom from falling out, and meanwhile the prospect for learning dwindles as vocation replaces education. Must all of this go on so that the smashing of the productive forces may continue?

The drive to accumulate continues its erratic and destructive course. As the value composition of social capital rises, the managerial ascendancy rigidifies the class structure and militarizes the hierarchical mode. The numbers and grades of men are needlessly multiplied, and in their alienation they are held together by force and chicanery. In order to continue exploitation at home and abroad, hierarchy is exhalted and subordination glorified. The contradictions of capitalism are suppressed in the name of freedom and of democracy. These hypocrisies are compounded with cries for law and order. As profits lag, repressions intensify. For its own subversions, capital must find scapegoats.

These assaults upon the social integrity, upon the main body of productive labor, can only be countered by those whose vitality is at issue. There is no one else. The operational agencies of social change that socialists have long sought can only consist of the devices that productive labor may employ in seeking its own emancipation. The only instrument for social change is politicized labor, and this transformation is in process.

Along with a heightening of consciousness, the greater heterogeneity of the modern working class may be a hopeful omen. The multiplicity of its divisions and the variety of its skills suggest ever more numerous and varied possibilities for promotion of the common interest. A more systematic utilization and coordinate employment of these devices must be a primary objective of the leaders of the movement. These leaders, meanwhile, come from among those who are least likely to be integrated within the managed order: blacks, the young, the technicians and professionals of the new administrative mode, the labor rank and file, the official paupers, the women of the enlarged working class. The resourcefulness and versatility of such as these can hardly be overrated. All together, they may foster a higher level of class consciousness and a more coordinate and vigorous promotion of social change.

The problem still is to wrest control of the means of production and, in view of the level of administrative technique, the means of administration, from the hands of unproductive labor. Because of the sophistication of administrative technique, important responsibilities for the capture of social control and for its subsequent political and economic exercise must fall to administrative labor and especially to its educating divisions. To effect a socialist control over reproductive processes, there must be a replacement of the ruling class, including its managerial auxiliaries, by administrative in cooperation with industrial labor. A decisive and competent control over modern means of administration is to socialism today what control over the means of production has long been: the immediate and imperative need of productive labor for the realization of social goals.

Control, however, for whom? For what? And by what means? These are questions to which socialism must give its own distinctive responses, for it is its differentiated response that sets socialism apart from other claimants to the social directorship. To these we turn, therefore, in our final comments on the passage from the advanced capitalism.

12

Rotational employment and the transition to socialism

Socialist theory and the advanced capitalism

From what we have seen of the evolutionary tendencies of the advanced capitalism, it is only reasonable to suppose that at some juncture, and probably in more than one country, a socialist administration will assume control of economic and other affairs. When that time comes, it will become possible to modify capitalist relations of production more or less radically; more or less depending upon many circumstances, among them the ability of the socialists to proceed systematically and methodically with methods appropriate to the work to be done. Whether or not, in the wake of the revolution, there is again a reversion to capitalist relations of production will then very much depend upon what is done during the early period of the socialist tenure. What must be done in order to promote a continuing movement toward socialist society must now be considered. What special problems of transition are sure to be encountered? How are they to be dealt with?

It will be understood, of course, that what is said in response to these questions in theoretical investigations such as the present one can only apply with more or less qualification in practice. In actual revolutionary situations, circumstances peculiar to countries and peoples will be decisive. Nevertheless, Marxists have always prided themselves – if not always with full justification – on their reliance on theory for formulating and implementing programs. In this tradition we propose some elements of a socialist political economy built up directly from the principle of economy in the use of labor and applied to certain features of the advanced capitalism that will require direct and effective attention by socialist administrators in the period of transition.

The ideas to be discussed are socialist in that, first, they contain an ideological potential useful to the working class and those who speak in its name. They are socialist, second, in that, while deriving from the labor theory of value and an analysis of socialist experience, they can only be implemented through an administration functioning under the auspices of the working class. Within such a political economic context the mechanisms of rotational employment that concern us will be seen to contribute in definite ways to the dissolution of capitalist relations of production, although that dissolution will require a calculated and persistent practice before those relations can be annulled. Before we deal with specifics, one further remark on the transition is in order.

One may expect that the departure from the advanced capitalism and the transition to a new mode of production will follow – or perhaps may be made to follow – the route suggested by Marx in examining precapitalist transitions:

> The aim of all these [precapitalist] communities is survival, i.e., reproduction of the individuals who compose it as proprietors, i.e., in the same objective mode of existence as forms the relation among the members and at the same time therefore the commune itself. This reproduction, however, is at the same time necessarily new production and destruction of the old form.[1]

Especially for capitalism with its advancing technique, "reproduction . . . is at the same time necessarily new production. . . ." Of interest in the analysis of transition is, however, the precise manner in which the "destruction of the old form" takes place. Insofar as socialists are concerned, the key question is the conditions under which that destruction will culminate in a transition to socialism rather than in that other ominous possibility, "the common ruin of the contending classes."[2] And this defines fairly well one of the main tasks of socialist theory today: to specify the conditions whose realization will meliorate class conflict and help in the avoidance of "common ruin." A system of rotational employment appears to be one of those conditions. To begin with the main issue, we first make clear what we mean by the phrase.

The meaning of rotational employment

While definition for the purpose of theorizing is itself a theoretical undertaking, the common-sense meaning of rotational employment is readily seen in the postrevolutionary experience of many peoples in recent times: the Chinese, the Cubans, the Cambodians, among others.[3] Their experience has in many ways been illuminating, but in no way more than in relation to rotational employment. The sharing of administrative work within work brigades, communes, factories, as in China; the sharing of agricultural tasks at planting and at the harvest by urban with rural workers, as in Cuba and elsewhere; the decentralization of production decisions within workers' councils, and so on. All of these contain some common denominator within and among labor processes to which the term "sharing" applies. These practices reveal the importance to workers and peasants of many things, especially the importance of an equitable and cooperative sharing of necessary labors. The term "necessary" is here most suggestive of the Marxian economics, as are its opposites, "unnecessary" or "disposable," the latter a term that Marx often utilizes analytically, as when he says, for example, that "Capital creates a great deal of disposable time. . . ."[4] And this brings us again to the advanced capitalism.

This phrase "disposable time" may itself take on two meanings, each of which is of theoretical importance and needs to be distinguished from the other. First of all, it may refer only to what Marx calls "free time," the difference between the total day (week, month, year, and so on) and the portion of the day in which necessary work is proceeding. Unquestionably capital has created a great deal of disposable time in its sense of free time although, to be sure, its inequitable and bizarre allocations of that time are familiar to all. The reduction in the average length of the workday is perhaps the best indicator of what capital has over the long haul accomplished in the generation of free time. But this difference between the total day and the portion of the day that is necessary labor time is by no means an indicator of the total of disposable time available. This brings us to the second meaning of the term.

Capital has also created vast quantities of disposable time in the sense of labor time that is not necessary for the reproduction of productive labor, that is, labor time that is economically redundant. Suppose we call the labor time necessary for productive laborers to reproduce their own means of subsistence "socially necessary" time. This time is socially necessary in that without the reproduction of productive labor no society can long endure, but the total workday is longer than this because it is necessary, in order to reproduce the mode of production, to reproduce also the means of subsistence of labor's dominant partner, the capitalist. Under capitalism the laborer works a surplus time in which the capitalist's means of subsistence are reproduced in the form of surplus value. (Suppose the total workday is ten hours; five hours are socially necessary for reproduction of the laborer's means of subsistence, and the other five hours are necessary to provide subsistence for unproductive labor. The remainder of the day is free time.)

The time that the worker is required to spend above socially necessary time is also in a sense disposable time. It is disposable in that were the worker not required to provide subsistence for others – in this case the capitalist – that necessary time would appear as free time or, more precisely, as a gain in free time. Now in modern capitalist society the total of this surplus time is very sizable. Its rough magnitude is in fact indicated, not by the reduced length of the workday, for this shows only the historical gain in free time, but by the magnitude of the unproductive ratio, the ratio of the value of unproductive to the value of productive labor. In other words, the actual total of disposable time available to productive labor under certain conditions consists not only of free time but of the necessary labor time that would be available for its disposal were productive labor not required to provide material support for unproductive labor.

The total of labor time required to be performed in capitalist society consists of the labor time that is socially necessary plus the time required to be spent by productive labor in providing material means of subsistence for unproductive labor. Alternatively, the labor time expended by unproductive labor is time that may be socially disposable under certain conditions. As a rule, this latter variety of necessary time, the time expended by unproductive labor, can become free time for productive labor only insofar as the dissolution of capitalist relations of production is accomplished.

Behind the historical rise of the unproductive ratio lies capital's insistent conversion of surplus into necessary time unproductively expended. This tendency is not evident to casual view, and for this reason some of the most significant events attending it are improperly interpreted. Almost everyone sees that the advance of technique, by virtue of its reduction of socially along with other necessary time, makes it possible to enlarge the volume of free time. But it is hardly understood at all that the course of accumulation has actually prevented the realization of the gain in free time that the advance of productivity creates. On the one hand, capital enlarges (within limits) free time. Simultaneously, in keeping with its laws of motion, it converts surplus labor into unproductive labor, putting surplus time into forms that make that time inaccessible as free time to the worker, whether or not that worker be productively employed. Viewed from this angle, the rise of the unproductive ratio signifies an enormous rise in *potential* free time, or in net disposable or nonworking time. And no doubt it is possible somehow to recapture this time, to reconvert into free time this time that comes to be spent in unproductive activity. The devices of rotational employment are best seen as instruments for recapturing for social labor its potential free time, releasing that time from its imprisonment in the camp of unproductive labor.

The meaning of rotational employment may be brought out with the aid of one of those theoretical models of an excessive simplicity so often used by standard economists, a model of a type implicit in apologetic presentation of capitalism's alleged tendency to provide ever more free time for the entire population. Suppose – to think the unthinkable – that the productivity of labor were to advance under capitalism to the point where but one man-year were annually required for reproduction of the mode. With capitalist relations of production this work would be performed by one man, the working class of this theoretical utopia. The remainder of the population would enjoy free time. Of course, the enslavement of the last man would be an absurdity, as absurd as the assumption that the reduction of necessary time can go on indefinitely under capitalist auspices. The burdens of our Atlas could be lifted were the necessary time of one man-year to be rotated or shared among all members of the population. This is what rotational employment means: an equal sharing of necessary time *and* of free time among all members of the population. In this hypothetical case were the performance of necessary time put upon a full rotational basis, the last man would be virtually free from required time – along with everyone else. Free time for each individual would be at its maximum and equal for each; time required for work would be equal for each individual and at its minimum. It must be repeated, however, that rotational employment of this type is unattainable within capitalist relations of production.

The reason this is so is worth further comment. Under capitalism the relation of production that is determining – that is decisive for the reproduction of the mode itself – is that relation that permits the ruling class to reproduce itself and to reproduce the conditions of its dominance; to reproduce itself and the social and economic activities necessary to the mode. Under capitalism this reproduction of the mode depends upon the control by capital of mechanisms and personnel of the circulatory system, of market mechanisms and their juridical supports, devices that convey to the ruling class its material means of reproduction.[5] To the extent, therefore, to which a ruling class gives up, or is made to yield up, some portion of the means of subsistence that it is accustomed to appropriate from surplus value, it acquiesces in its own destruction. This is why rotational employment cannot proceed under capitalism. It is a means of reappropriating from the ruling class what is now taken from the producers through the medium of the circulatory system. This is why the rotational employment that the working class now enjoys is enjoyed *within* that class, why it runs along horizontal lines primarily and never cuts through class lines vertically. The sharing of necessary work is among workers at the factory or production level and never comes to a systematic sharing of all necessary tasks by working people belonging to different classes of the population.

This is why the model of the capitalist utopia is false when used to suggest a developmental tendency of capitalism, a development of relative free time. In actuality the accumulation of capital expands the scale of reproduction of unproductive labor, the bulk of which is employed in precisely those circulatory occupations on whose functioning the appropriation of surplus value depends. As Olsen's study shows, this long-term tendency to enlarge the circulatory system, causing the unproductive ratio to rise, has asserted itself with an irregular but persistent force over the past 70 years (and more). While in 1900 for every ten productively employed only two were unproductively employed, by 1970 the situation had reversed itself and for every ten productively employed almost eight were unproductively employed, and the ratio continues to rise. Still more significantly, measured in terms of the *value* of unproductive relative to productive labor, the ratio already stands well above 1 to 1 and may even approach 4 or 5 to 1.[6] Our calculations following, assuming the working population to consist of half-unproductive and half-productive labor, underestimate the potential gains at issue.

Under the 50–50 assumption, suppose it were possible to eliminate altogether unproductive time, with unproductive workers sharing equally with productive workers the socially necessary time annually required. The per capita or average labor time required of each individual would be reduced by 50 percent for the entire working population and free time increased by the same amount. Were such a rotation to be accomplished, an enormous gain in free time would follow from the conversion of necessary or net disposable time, and an equal sharing of socially necessary time would yield an enormous gain in free time per capita. These truly sizable gains, moreover, are not contingent upon the reduction of socially necessary time to its vanishing point but only upon the elimination of unproductive labor, upon the elimination of unnecessary labor time *and* the sharing of remaining time required to be performed. The contingencies, of course, are not easily realizable, and not realizable at all within the context of capitalist production relations.

Difficulties of realization, however great, in no way negate the magnitude of the potential gain even though, as matters stand, both the size of the gain and, above all, of course, the essential means for realizing it, are effectively hidden from view, including the view of the bourgeois theorists who would prefer that they stay that way. They are hidden, among other things, by the harried existence of the unproductive laborer and by his publicizing of his frenetic endeavors.[7]

We see how true it is that capital has already created enormous amounts of disposable time, the larger portion of which is only *potential* free time, a net disposable time that can only be tapped by altering capitalist relations of production, for these relations work constantly, especially in capital's expansionary phases, to convert surplus into unproductive labor.[8] This means that a primary problem of socialist political economy is to devise specific means of capturing this potential by dissolving capitalist relations of production. This dissolution cannot be accomplished through utopian speculation on the magnitude of the potential gain[9] but only by specifying and then implementing the means of seizing it. In general, these means revolve around the maintenance of a socialist full employment, a full employment in whose realization rotational employment must play a significant role.

Toward a socialist full employment

A socialist program for realizing potential free time must not only be informed by the labor theory of value, implemented by appropriate methods of calculation, it must also harmonize with other primary socialist objectives. Most importantly, it must be consistent with the goal of full employment. This consistency of full with rotational employment will ensure that socialist full employment should differ from the conventional variety.

The occasional and crude approximations to full employment that capitalism provides are necessarily based upon an acceleration of the rate of accumulation that brings into employment some portion of the industrial reserve and of the growing labor force. This method of solving the problem of employment is no longer tolerable. Even many supporters of capitalism are troubled by an acceleration of growth that so threatens the social and physical environment that the benefits of accumulation seem hardly worth the candle.[10] This difficulty had become apparent even before the advent of an energy crisis whose origins lie in high rates of unproductive consumption. The energy dilemma also has two horns. First of these is the exorbitant scale of unproductive consumption driving deeply into social energy, always taking, never giving. Second, is the weakening of the productive forces, always giving, never taking. Since whatever expansion can be forced under advanced conditions entails a renewed outburst of unproductive accumulation, the old drive to expand must be followed by economic stagnation, by stagflation and exhaustion of the productive forces. The rise of the unproductive ratio is merely the empirical sign of the fettering of the productive forces which is capital's final hitch.

On any reasonable view of the matter, Marx's perception of the growth of a "consolidated surplus population" – the observational basis of the absolute general law of capitalist accumulation – was perfectly accurate. The absolute expression of the law is reserved, however, for periods of acute crisis; otherwise, the relative growth of unproductive labor has been and continues to be the principal response or countertendency for the reserve army to grow. With the productivity of labor rising, surplus labor engendered by the rising organic composition of capital has simply been absorbed into circulatory employment. This solution to unemployment through the beefing up of circulatory operations is one that society can no longer afford, and not merely because of the sporadic lapses into which the absolute law drives us. Indeed, where socialism has failed to avoid similar bureaucratic solutions, we observe the same damages to physical and social environment, the same cost burdens

falling upon the working class, as are found everywhere in the advanced capitalism.

The present scale of the consolidated surplus population is such that, apart from postwar reconstruction and recovery from depression, when a normal restoration of previously destroyed values is taking place, capital has no regular use for the total of labor power seeking employment. Despite the absolute surplus of population capital surely will "forcibly restore" if possible (as Marx appropriately puts it) the conditions for economic revival. The very effort is absurd. The point is that the reflex of accumulation makes the chicken jump when the head is gone. This is the pitiful condition of the advanced capitalism today. A recovery of the old drive to industrial-circulatory accumulation only renews and further intensifies underlying contradictions.

This means, further, that the old time vertical mobility is largely a thing of the past. In the present century the so-called vertical mobility has in fact been nothing other than the capitalist mopping up of superfluous labor power, the kicking upstairs of surplus population engendered by the advance of technique and the rising organic composition of capital. This same conversion of surplus into unproductive labor that destroys economic growth makes it appear that vertical mobility is still inherent in capitalism. The misnomer that the name connotes is seen, however, in the peculiar two-way mobility in the working class: some go up into privileged occupations during expansions, but down they go again in periods of contraction. What little real mobility there is is entirely for the managerial retainers of capital. In truth vertical mobility is no more than a myth resting upon a misinterpretation of a recent experience. It is doubtful, however, that even this experience can be sustained for much longer. In England, Italy, France, and elsewhere the fettering of the productive forces is well advanced. Indeed, it is in this unproductive dimension that capitalism is most advanced.

No doubt economists will continue for the most part to see no alternative to the traditional acceleration of accumulation in providing for what they call "full employment." Some socialists may drift along in this same canoe. But a true political economy must run counter to primary contradictions. Therefore, while the old accumulation is clearly unserviceable, what is to be put in its place is yet to be determined. It does not suffice to reply to the question –

what of unemployment? – to say that socialists can better solve the problem. No doubt they can. But how? And in what way better?

Both theory and experience reveal that the investment agenda of capital is obsolete, and they prove by the same token the need for a new agenda. We do not call here, however, for a new agenda composed of semantic eels and fishy clichés, an optimal allocation of resources, reassigning production priorities, maximizing net benefits, or the like. It is perfectly obvious that the main haven of unproductive labor is the circulatory establishment. This means that the reduction of that superstructure is a necessary part of the business of capturing potential and converting it to actual free time. Further, it is equally evident that the organizational agencies of that establishment comprise the great bulk of the bureaucracy of modern society. The reduction of this bureaucracy can proceed as bureaucratic workers, and especially their managers, are transferred gradually but permanently out of unproductive employment within corporate superstructures, public and private. This transfer, proceeding apace with the centralizing and streamlining (rationalizing) of organization and with the automation of circulatory tasks as the advance of administrative technique allows, must put those workers in free time and in necessary occupations on an equal sharing basis with others. Thus socialist full employment may be realized as a necessary accompaniment to the dissolution of bureaucracy. What capitalism has created through accumulation must in part be undone, but the undoing must proceed through a systematic sharing throughout the total working population of necessary time remaining after labor-displacing techniques are utilized administratively and industrially in the highest possible degree.

Socialist full employment must be accomplished through methods that realize three basic conditions for converting surplus labor or potential time into free time. First of all, all must be employed. This is essential to the restoration of productivity to the individual through a continuing – although not constant – exercise of work capacities so as to extend and enlarge those capacities. Secondly, all technically useful industrial and administrative labor, presently employed in unessential or wasteful lines, and especially in circulatory occupations, must be returned to productive employment. The activities in which potentially useful labor is now caught up frustrate and complicate its conversion into useful labor, in part

by reinforcing its own illusions concerning the productivity of its capitalistic way of life, in part through the drag upon productive labor that its consumptions entail. Thirdly, is the elimination of hard-core unproductive labor, labor unproductive by virtue of its very lack of socially useful skills. "Elimination" is not here used in an underworld context but merely denotes the conversion of what are mainly managerial divisions into functioning workers within a socially necessary division of labor.

The fulfillment of these conditions for capturing the productive potential of the whole of the working population is the hub around which the wheel of socialist planning in transition should revolve. Only Marxian theory is capable of yielding a relatively simple program that will move us toward a simultaneous realization of all of the conditions for releasing the productive forces from their capitalistic fetters. Only the labor theory of value is capable of identifying with necessary precision the unproductive and productive divisions at issue together with the programmatic means for modifying obsolete relations of production.

What this program comes to, putting it at a fair level of generality, is the supplanting of the market as the primary agency of circulation, which is no more and no less than supplanting those activities of circulation that go to make up the market. Just as capitalism multiplies the numbers and divisions of laborers engaged in activities of commerce, finance, and trade, and above all their management, so socialism must withdraw wherever possible the material support and the personnel that animate these activities. The scale of unproductive investment must be methodically reduced, while at the same time a full employment of surplus personnel is maintained through a shared rotation among productive and free-time occupations. How is the principle of economy in the use of labor to be implemented at the same time that a reduction in the scale of capitalistically necessary labor power inputs is being engineered? There is one key device that will avoid contradictions as a matter of principle. This is rotational employment.

A note on the economics

The role of the socialist planner in the period of transition can only be to assist in satisfying the needs of the modern enlarged working class. Many of these needs may be served through a system of rotational employment, and the early period of transition is ideal for its implementation.

As the mode of production enters its transitional phase under socialist administration, rationalization and automation will reduce the total of necessary time (socially plus capitalistically necessary) and thus enlarge free time beyond its present limits. Within a planning period if the total of annually required time is known together with the total size of the working population, the average required time per capita will be known and this will serve to fix the average length of the workday. Similarly, the average gain in free time (the average reduction in necessary time) can be estimated in relation to its level in the previous period. In principle these gains and reductions should be shared equally by all members of the working population, since maximizing free time for the individual requires an equal sharing among all of required labor times.

While in practice all those employed within the necessary division of social labor must come to enjoy equally their free time, vacations, sabbaticals, and so on, deviations from the main rule of equality will need to be made in order to correct inequities hanging over from the advanced capitalism. Where the stress of routine labor is above the average, there is need for above-average compensation in free-time allocations. Where the converse is true and work conditions are less arduous, something less than an equal share in gains in free time may be desirable. The allocation of required labor times throughout the total working population – an operational objective of rotation – needs both forethought and a sensitive as well as calculated administration. Marx's observation on the character of the transition period is to the point: "What we have to deal with here is a communist society, not as if it had *developed on a basis of its own,* but on the contrary *as it emerges from capitalist society,* which is thus in every respect tainted economically, morally, and intellectually with the hereditary diseases of the old society from whose womb it is emerging."[11]

These are the circumstances under which a socialist regime, whose powers in the transition period can only be tenuous, will confront an entire structure of occupational divisions of socially and capitalistically necessary labor, the great bulk of which *cannot* be eliminated at one stroke but only reduced within narrow limits in the short run. Within the hierarchy of all necessary occupations those at the upper end in terms of technique and pay tend to be unproductive, not so much with respect to the technical usefulness of the various divisions as with the tainting of the workers themselves in consequence of their having been locked into unproductive assignments within the old regime. Within the subordinate and lower occupations of the social division of labor, on the other hand, labor is predominantly productive.[12] The administrative problem of a planning period, insofar as rotation is concerned, is to see that as large a circulation of workers takes place as the maintenance of productivity and the costs of rotation allow. Within these constraints, workers may be moved as much as possible out of the lower productive and into the higher unproductive (but still necessary) occupations, and vice versa.

The devices of rotation should perhaps be viewed as a system of social apprenticeship pointed to broadening the skills and attitudes of the working population through vertical rotation, a socialist alternative to vertical mobility. As much of this as may be realizable within any given period must of course be limited by the condition that the total of required labor times, in the aggregate and within each technical division of labor, be fully met by inputs allocated. Economic reproduction must be secured.

To meet this condition requires a great deal of information and calculation as bases for assignments. This is not surprising in view of all that is known about economic planning in general. For instance, the entire agenda of socially necessary occupations will need periodic revision in order to admit new specialties and eliminate old ones as the level of technique advances, in order to facilitate the matching of available and required labor skills and times for each division of labor within the planning period. In instituting rotation, the required agenda must be supplemented with estimates of required and available *values* of the different labor power inputs; that is, quantitative estimates must be value units in values reduced to units of simple, socially necessary labor time so that all balance equations can be properly satisfied and target allocations calculated in standard labor value units (simple, socially necessary labor time). Value coefficients of production, for example, will be needed in calculating required labor times for each grade of labor to be put into motion. All of this means, in turn, the construction and utilization of labor value accounting as an aid to socialist planning in the transition period. It would be well to recall a familiar remark:

Book-keeping, as the control and ideal synthesis of the process, becomes the more necessary the more the process assumes a social scale and loses its purely individual character. It is therefore more necessary in capitalist production than in the scattered production of handicraft and peasant economy, more necessary in collective production than in capitalist production.[13]

The system of social accounting will require elaboration and refinement beyond its present state, but this does not mean that required calculations are infinite in number or complexity as old-school critics of socialism are fond of maintaining. In moving practically to rotate the working population, socialist planners will find that some starting points provide larger and more accessible toeholds than do others. It is obviously undesirable in many lines where techniques are far advanced to uproot the practitioner in order to broaden his experience whether in a simpler or in an equally refined occupation. A periodically revised agenda of necessary occupations will always show what occupations can be reduced in scale (the total of required time) or eliminated altogether in a given period. It must show also what new quantities and divisions of labor power may be required. For the former, retirements from the labor force or enlarged assignments of free time will go far toward balancing required reductions in labor time with the reduced availability of labor powers, while, for the latter, the flow of new recruits from apprenticeship and educational programs will serve growing needs. In early stages of transition the main burdens (and pleasures) of rotational employment should probably impinge primarily on younger sections of the work force and in early years of the individual's work career.

In the broadening of individual work careers, open education and open employment join hands in a common project. Vocational and educational institutions must produce not merely the required increments of graded labor powers, but they must press simultaneously to broaden the intellectual and work capacities of all individuals through experience. Especially in early years of the work career, the exercise of a variety of manual and intellectual work capacities should be systematically cultivated so that each person's lifetime work career spans a more extended gamut of necessary *and* free-time occupations than is possible in the class system of one-sided specialties. As work careers are widened through open education and open employment, and as free time is enlarged and filled with cultural and recreational opportunities, the realization of traditional socialist goals becomes less difficult. The reduction of alienation follows upon "the development of a totality of capacities in the individuals themselves."[14]

The discussion of rotational employment has thus far put priority on necessary work and its performance, setting aside the utilization of free time in pursuit of the arts and sciences and in culture and recreation generally. However, since free time cannot be wasted time, its utilization is also to be considered. To the effective utilization of this time capital has contributed much; it has created "the *means* of social disposable time."[15] To all of the problems this utilization raises, only a preliminary consideration can be given, and this consists of the observation that the effective use of this time is more easily realized in the long run if in the short run there is an equal sharing of free time in combination with an equal sharing of required time. The latter requirement is of special importance for two reasons.

In the first place, only if required time is equally shared can average free time for the individual be maximized. In the second, while the totality of capacities will and must grow gradually, it may not grow as rapidly or as fully as when the means of free time are not only made available but used efficiently by all. In this connection, too, one sees the significance both of open education and open, rotational employment. The rotation of necessary occupations must be topped off with an expanded cultural and recreational experience for whose common access the equal sharing of free time is a prerequisite. Rotational employment is a necessary but not sufficient condition for appropriating the totality of instruments of production.

The need for the kind of full employment we have been discussing and for an equal sharing of free time has its origins not only in the need to eliminate unemployment and all forms of dependency originating in that criminal condition, but in Marxian individualism as an object of socialist administration. It is impossible that the exploration of the natural and of the social universe should for much longer be preserved as the private playground of the offspring of the bourgeoisie. The specifying of all of the means needed to break this monopoly is what the theory of rotational employment is all about, and, just as the economics of social reproduction is more complicated within the advanced than within the less developed context, so the work of the theorist is more necessary in the former than in the latter. Otherwise, it is possible that, lacking detailed guidance, socialist planning may revert to cruder and simpler measures for solving problems of employment and unemployment, ignoring the real elements that will mark its affairs as distinct from and more advanced than those of capitalism. These requisites include first of all open and full employment. For with education alone, no matter how open, the fruits of education and training can only decay from disuse. On the other hand, given employment without open education, the individual remains bound in his alienation. There he stays until oppression brings him to his feet.

The theory as ideology

Turning in conclusion to the ideological or political usefulness of the theory, its significance for the revolutionary epoch and afterward is not difficult to see, especially for workers. This is because, as experience of revolution in the less developed world has amply shown, rotational employment coincides with profound and virtually universal conceptions of social justice. This holds for the workers of the advanced capitalism, too. To the extent, for instance, that a functioning program succeeds in broadening lifetime careers by exposing one to occupations of differential skill and pay, it will succeed also in promoting economic equality *even though* differential rates of pay attach to different occupations. If wage rates for all tasks are proportioned to the values of labor power to which they attach, the rotation of individuals through an extending variety of differential occupations will tend to equalize lifetime earnings. In this way, the equalization of incomes becomes a byproduct of the socialist mode of production, even in the period of transition. Redistribution is a subject on which Marxian socialism has much to say, but there is never a need for it to descend to utopian proposals that bypass the problem of reordering production relations. The reordering of production relations is in fact a prerequisite to income redistribution. The utopians put the cart before the horse, as usual. But in the period of transition a powerful movement toward economic equality can and must develop, re-creating in the setting of an advanced technique the equalization that we have hitherto observed only in the wake of peasant revolutions.

At the same time, the redistribution of income that follows from revising relations of production enhances the individual's access to a growing cultural life. Individual choice, whose existence is now limited to old-fashioned textbooks and board-room propaganda, becomes concrete reality. The enlarged work and social experience breaks down alienation as the universality of the individual develops. Rotational employment takes all individuals in their given condition, regardless of race, creed, color, sex, and whatever, attacks directly all forms of social discrimination by making the need for individual development the principal criterion for work experience; the principal criterion, not for deciding whether or not one is to be able to work, but for deciding what line or lines of work one is to pursue, and in what sequence. Social discrimination is struck at its vital center as the diversification of work and the experience of free time undercuts principles of segregation, and especially the disease attaching to the capitalist division of labor, the "one-sided development of the labour capacity."[16] In time the circulation of workers will promote the reduction of class tensions, broadening the experience of the bourgeoisie while at the same time breaking down occupational monopolies built up by workers under capitalism for their own self-defense. All of this can be accomplished, not by destroying the division of labor, a division needed until all production is fully automated, but by breaking open that division so as to allow growing numbers to benefit from challenges contained within it. Meeting these challenges strengthens the individual just as, within the system of capitalist specialization, the individual is weakened and destroyed. The problem of socialism is to produce, systematically and consciously, "an ungraded and masterless race of men" (Veblen).

Such benefits will be apparent to all those whose present confinements are oppressive, and this means that they will be more or less apparent to most workers, using the term in its larger meaning. Of course, one should not expect that a rotational program should please all those predestined to higher things within the old scheme of things. For the young, including many belonging to the bourgeoisie, however, it may be received with some enthusiasm, and certainly it invites all to participate directly in socialist reconstruction. But one need not expect in general a happy response to the R.S.V.P. issued by the working class. For this reason a firm and sure socialist administration will be needed in the wake of what Althusser calls the "condensation."

What has been proposed, then, is merely a sketch of a kind of program that one may fully expect to be instituted wherever in the advanced capitalism a genuine socialist administration comes to power. With the aid of the labor theory of value, it should be possible to go much further than we have gone in this chapter in detailing the workings of a plan applicable to the transitional state. The labor theory lays bare the full extent of the potential gains in free time, identifies the obstacles to be overcome in realizing that potential, and suggests means of overcoming them, means that can be made as specific as the planning principles of socialism itself. It enables us to plan the economic foundations of socialist society.

It has long been understood that economic foundations are basic to class society and to the means necessary for a movement beyond that type of undemocratic and otherwise noxious social order. The connection between the development of the productive forces and emancipation from exploitation has been seen, if only partially and sporadically, since the time of Aristotle. Aristotle perceived emancipation as a poetic rather than as a political-economic possibility, however:

> For if every instrument could accomplish its own work, obeying or anticipating the will of others, like the statues of Daedalus, or the tripods of Hephaestus, which, says the poet, "of their own accord entered the assembly of the Gods"; if, in like manner, the shuttle would weave and the plectrum touch the lyre without a hand to guide them, chief workmen would not want servants nor masters slaves.[17]

To the realization of the age-old dream, capitalism has contributed much. Its statues, its tripods are before us, in some instances as functioning instruments, in others as actors waiting to be summoned from the wings. The disposable time is there, although much of the potential is concealed in the circulatory activity of the administrative establishment. The means of free time exist on a large scale, if still short of what is needed.

In modern times, Marx first saw the meaning of all of this. He saw that the growth of the consolidated surplus population had its dialectical aspect. That growth was at once the essence of the accumulation of capital and the means of escaping from it. He saw how capitalism would forge the fetters of productive labor with the chains of unproductive labor. He saw simultaneously the other side of this repression, the promise of the stroke that would break those fetters.

Notes

INTRODUCTION

1   Engels to J. Bloch, September 21, 22, 1890, *Selected Correspondence,*
    Moscow, 1955, p. 417. Emphasis is mine.
2   *Capital III,* Moscow, Foreign Languages Publishing House, 1959, p. 233. On
    p. 229 Marx also refers to the working of this law as "a tendency, i.e., as a law
    whose absolute action is checked, retarded, and weakened, by counteracting
    circumstances." We adhere strictly to this methodological principle and shall
    encounter it again. All references to *Capital I, II,* and *III* are to the Moscow
    edition. The reader will find the same edition available from International
    Publishers, New York.
3   Engels to F. A. Lange, March 29, 1865, op cit., p. 172.
4   The by now famous *Grundrisse der Kritik der Politischen Okonomie* (Berlin,
    Dietz Verlag, 1953), published for the first time only in 1939, consists of
    papers written as preliminary studies for *Capital* in the period 1850-1858. An
    English edition has recently been published: Karl Marx, *Grundrisse,* Martin
    Nicolaus, trans., Middlesex, Penguin Books, 1973, to which all references
    hereafter will be made. This book is important not merely because it reveals
    Marx's methods of work as a theorist but because important theoretical
    materials only implicit in *Capital* are here made explicit, for example, in con-
    nection with the tendency of the rate of profit to fall, the role of the rate of un-
    productive consumption, and other matters taken up subsequently.
5   Marx to Kugelmann, July 11, 1868, op. cit., p. 208.
6   Ibid., p. 210.
7   A good, popular description of input-output as seen by Leontief is his
    "Input-Output Economics," *Scientific American,* October, 1951. For further
    discussion see his *Input-Output Economics,* New York, Oxford University
    Press, 1966, and Goldman, Marimont, and Vaccara, "The Interindustry
    Structure of the United States," *Survey of Current Business,* November 1964.
    For a presentation of the Marxian economics see Oskar Lange, *Introduction
    to Econometrics,* London, New York, Pergamon, 1959; and by the same
    author, "Some Observations on Input-Output Analysis," *Sankhya,* 17, pt. 4.

8 "Marxism: Religion and Science," *Monthly Review*, December 1962, p. 427.

9 *For Marx*, New York, Vintage, 1970, p. 22.

10 But see Althusser's discussion in *For Marx*.

11 Robinson, op cit., p. 425.

12 Althusser, op. cit.

13 A good example of this is Piero Sraffa's *Production of Commodities by Means of Commodities*, Cambridge University Press, 1960, along with other "neo-Ricardian" works of the Cambridge school. A survey and criticism of some of these works, especially Sraffa's, appears in E. K. Hunt and J. G. Schwartz, *A Critique of Economic Theory: Selected Readings*, Middlesex, England, 1972. For further indication of the antilabor, anti-Marxian tendencies of the school, see M. Lebowitz, "The Current Crisis of Economic Theory," *Science and Society*, Winter 1973–1974; and "On the Monopoly Theory of Monopoly Capitalism," *Science and Society*, Winter 1971, "The By-Pass to Ricardo." S. Coontz's characterization of the neo-Ricardian theories as "anti-classical" is apt, and he spells out their reactionary heritage in *Productive Labour and Effective Demand*, New York, Augustus Kelley, 1966, esp. ch. 4, "Anti-Classical Theories in the Twentieth Century," "A, The Fascist Solution." I am grateful to Doug Dowd for drawing this work to my attention.

14 In particular, this emphasis has been taken up by the Frankfurt school, whose well-known members include H. Marcuse (*One Dimensional Man*), T. W. Adorno (*Negative Dialectics*), Albrecht Wellmer (*Critical Theory of Society*), J. Habermas (*Theory and Practice*), Max Herkheimer (*Eclipse of Reason*), and others. The writings of the school are notable for their lack of economic analyses, and all are more or less reminiscent of what Marx and Engels called "the German ideology," with its traditional idealism.

15 A look at one or two of the leading texts will confirm the inability of the writers to embark on causal analysis of social problems, for example, P. A. Samuelson, *Economics*, 8th ed., New York, McGraw-Hill, 1970, or C. R. McConnell, *Economics*, 3rd ed., New York, McGraw-Hill, 1966, or L. G. Reynolds, *Economics*, 4th ed., Homewood, Ill., R. D. Irwin, 1973.

16 The classical Marxian statement is that of N. Bukharin, *Economic Theory of the Leisure Class (1914)*, New York, Modern Reader, 1972.

17 The term "models," used extensively by economists to refer to all simulations of historical processes, is not a very happy one. The simulations of standard economics are generally mechanistic, rather than dialectical, and are often purely normative, for instance, the popular models of pure or perfect competition. For these reasons the terms "schemes" and "schema" are preferable for Marxian simulations of historical processes.

18 *Capital I*, ch. 25, "The General Law of Capitalist Accumulation."

19 See Althusser's *Avertissement* to *Le Capital*, Paris, Garnier, Flammarion, 1969. In reading *Capital I* the reader should begin with Part III ("The Production of Absolute Surplus Value") and finish the volume straight through. Then return to Parts I ("Commodities and Money") and II ("The Transformation of Money into Capital").

20 The form of classical scientific explanation to which Marx adheres has been widely influential in the natural and in the social sciences. See, for example,

Albert Einstein: Philosopher-Scientist, P. A. Schlipp, ed., Evanston, Ill., Library of Living Philosophers, 1949, "Autobiographical Notes," pp. 2–95.

21 Adam Smith, *An Inquiry into the Nature and Causes of the Wealth of Nations*, Canaan ed., V, II, p. 314.

1. METHODOLOGICAL GLASSES FOR THE LONGER VIEW

1 For a simple yet comprehensive discussion of dialectical hypotheses, see Maurice Cornforth, *Dialectical Materialism: An Introduction*, 3 vols., London, Lawrence and Wishart, 1955.

2 Marx's own application of his principles to precapitalist formations is admirably discussed and relevant excerpts offered in Eric Hobsbawm, ed., *Precapitalist Economic Formations*, New York, International Publishers, 1965. The revival of Marxian anthropology now underway promises new advances into the analysis of modes of production and their interrelations. Compare Georges Dupre and Pierre-Philippe Rey, "Reflections on the Pertinence of a Theory of the History of Exchange," *Economy and Society*, 2 (May 1973). Rey's works, *Les Alliances de Classes* (1973) and *Colonialisme, Neo-Colonialisme et Transition au Capitalisme*, Paris, Maspero, 1971, well illustrate the utility of Marxian economics in anthropological inquiry.

3 The study of Paleolithic cave paintings suggests to many scholars a preoccupation of early man with both biological and economic reproduction, with fertility magic and hunting magic. The form and content of signs and symbols apparently relating to these suggest an "embeddedness" in ceremonial and other institutions of practices pointed to sustaining and regulating these reproductive activities. An excellent critical summary of theories indicating the economic function of the symbols is contained in P. J. Ucko and Andree Rosenfeld, *Paleolithic Cave Art*, New York, World University Library, 1967, especially chs. 3 and 4.

4 The first discussion of the social impact of reproductive necessities is that of Marx and Engels in *The German Ideology*, Moscow, Pt. I, *passim*.

5 In current anthropological inquiry the need to recognize separate spheres of economic and of appropriative-regulative activity has become clear. The historical material itself forces scholars to develop theoretical categories long functional within the Marxian economics. See, for example, the interesting essay by Fredrik Barth, "Economic Spheres in Darfur," *Themes in Economic Anthropology*, R. Firth, ed., London, Tavistock Press, 1967. Barth identifies two spheres of activity in Mountain Fur society: (1) the "cash" sphere, "associated with market place facilities," and (2) a sphere in which work proceeds that is "communal and reciprocal [in] character," and which he designates the "labour-beer sphere." The latter would correspond approximately to activity of economic reproduction, and the former to the unproductive consumption of the sphere of circulation (in Marxian terminology) in which appropriation takes place and a regulatory influence is exerted over the whole of the process of social reproduction. Rey analyzes well these spheres

in a clearer and more decisive theoretical presentation in *Colonialisme, Neo-colonialisme,* op. cit.

6   The essay in which Karl Polanyi advances this thesis, so popular among non-Marxians, is "The Economy as Instituted Process," in *Trade and Market in the Early Empires,* Glencoe, Ill., The Free Press, 1957. There is no doubt that the primitive economy is embedded, but it is a *non sequitur* to argue that therefore its influence is not decisive in shaping other social institutions. The fact that reproductive activity at the base is embedded in ritual, ceremony, and so on, by no means demonstrates the secondary importance of economic life. On the contrary, the economy is embedded because its functioning *must* be ensured whether by the gods or by whatever arrangements a secular intelligence can bring to bear.

7   For this suggestion see *The German Ideology,* op. cit. Proceeding from the assumption of an evolving social division of labor, both Marx and Veblen have suggested that the subjugation of women was an early manifestation of the tendency to class society. In Neolithic society, women were primary producers, both the domestication of plants and animals tracing to their manual work, thus freeing men for the mental military and governmental preoccupations. Compare Veblen, *The Instinct of Workmanship and the State of the Industrial Arts,* New York, Viking, 1914.

8   Marx's analyses and applications to capitalism will be found in *Capital I.,* ch. 23, "Simple Reproduction," and *Capital II,* ch. 20, "Simple Reproduction." Our presentation adds to Marx's only in that we stress the applicability of the general theory to precapitalist formations, an applicability of which Marx himself was well aware. Compare *Precapitalist Economic Formations,* op. cit.

9   *Capital I,* p. 566.

10 Ibid.

11 The student of history should not find it surprising that, under certain circumstances, a community should ceremonially endorse a periodic destruction of surplus product, as in the famous Kwakiutl potlatch. Destruction may be viewed as a primitive device for stabilizing and revitalizing productive activity by pressing labor back to a renewal of productive work. In modern times we observe in the wake of war or popular revolution an analogous outpouring of energy even though the destruction is less certainly ceremonial and within the capitalist mode of production traces usually to more dubious, less socially serviceable circumstances.

12 The rejection of this evolutionary standpoint by economists, a rejection evident in their politics and economic theories alike, traces in good measure to an unwillingness to treat systematically the problem of transition *out of* modern capitalism, that is, the problem of the transition to socialism. For a still valid analysis of the failure of the economists at the theoretical level see Veblen's "Why Is Economics Not an Evolutionary Science?" in *The Place of Science in Modern Civilization,* New York, Russell and Russell, 1961. Of course, the unwillingness of the economists to move into a useful and valid framework of "evolutionism" has its origins in their conservative social function, to be examined at a later juncture.

13 The "Asiatic" mode designates a surplus-supported bureaucracy with a way of

life to a considerable degree divorced economically and culturally from the underlying communal and reciprocal system of economic reproduction from which it extracts its material means of support. The degree of divorce between superstructure and substructure may, in turn, help to explain the durability of this mode of production. Compare Eric Hobsbawm, ed., *Precapitalist Economic Formations,* op. cit. Some Marxists feel that where this mode is still dominant in modern times, as in Turkey, Russia, and elsewhere, socialism may assume a special form, the problems of transition being quite different than elsewhere.

14 On the transition to socialism the work of Charles Bettelheim is of first importance. See his *Calcul Economique et Formes de Propriete,* Paris, Maspero, 1970. On the phenomenon of regression in the transition, Bettelheim's study of the Soviet Union is of special significance and interest: *Les Luttes de Classes en URSS l'ere période 1917–1923),* Paris, Seuil-Maspero, 1974. Both of these volumes are now available in English translation from New York, Modern Reader, 1976.

2. SIMPLE AND COMPLEX ACCUMULATION

1 For Marx's discussion see *Capital I,* pt. VIII, "The So-Called Primitive Accumulation," *passim.* Also see Maurice Dobb, *Studies in the Development of Capitalism,* New York, International Publishers, 1963, ch. 2, "The Decline of Feudalism and the Growth of Towns"; ch. 3, "The Beginnings of the Bourgeoisie"; also, the discussion by Paul Sweezy, Dobb, and others, "The Transition from Feudalism to Capitalism," *Science and Society,* New York, 1967.

2 Marx and Engels, *The Manifesto of the Communist Party,* Moscow, Progress Publishers, 1971, pp. 33, 34.

3 *Capital I,* p. 35.

4 Ibid., p. 209.

5 Ibid.

6 Harry Pearson, "The Economy Has No Surplus," in *Trade and the Market in Early Empires,* op. cit.

7 Letting ΔC and ΔV designate the additional means of production and wage goods of which the surplus product is composed, we assume that $\Delta C/\Delta C + \Delta V = C/C + V$. The marginal organic composition of capital is equal to the average organic composition. If the accumulation of capital at the margin features capital of above-average composition, then the average composition of social capital will rise. Since the effect of technical advance at various economic margins within the economy is to raise the marginal organic composition, the *complex* accumulation of capital raises the average composition. For the moment, however, we deal only with the simple accumulation in which marginal and average compositions are equal to each other.

8 *Capital I,* p. 581.

9 *Capital II,* p. 77.

10   Increases in the rate of surplus value brought about by an intensification of the work effort - lengthening the workday or stepping up the pace of work - Marx refers to as "absolute" increases in order to distinguish them from the "relative" increases that occur when, technical change proceeding, the productivity of labor is rising. To illustrate the absolute increase: If the workday is eight hours, of which four are needed for labor to produce a value equivalent to its costs of reproduction, then the other four hours are surplus labor. The ratio of the surplus labor to the necessary portion of the workday, also four hours in this example, is then 4/4, and the rate of surplus value is 100 percent. If the workday is lengthened to ten hours, the ratio of surplus to necessary labor rises to 6/4 and the rate of surplus value increases from 100 percent to 150 percent - hence the profitability of sweating the labor force and hence the contribution to economic growth of an intensification of work effort in the wake of popular revolutions in the less developed countries. Theoretically, whether the intensified effort is voluntary, as in the latter case, or involuntary, as in sweating operations, the result is an increase in the rate of growth or the rate of profit, and extended accumulation may follow.

11   As the reader is by now aware, our discussion for the most part runs in terms of value *flows* of the inputs and outputs, rather than in terms of their *stocks*. This emphasis above all helps us to keep in sight the vital role of material flows in supporting all types of social activity and so facilitates our discussion later on (Chapters 9, 10, and 11) of the importance of these flows in contributing to the changing class structure and class relations of capitalist society. However, in the measurement of the rate of profit what belongs in the denominator of the profit equation $p' = S/V \div \overline{C}/V + 1$ is the *stock* of constant capital net of depreciation (call it $\overline{C}$) rather than the depreciated portion of the total capital stock, the flow of constant capital. The flow variable tends to exaggerate the rate of profit, since it is only the depreciated portion of the total capital stock. No harm is done to our reasoning provided this is born in mind. Further, the organic composition of capital Marx also considers as the ratio of the capital stock to productive labor and should be symbolized $\overline{C}/V$ to indicate that it is the capital per worker whose rise is economically and socially so significant. For discussion of these matters see Shane Mage, *The "Law of the Falling Tendency of the Rate of Profit": Its Place in the Marxian Theoretical System and Relevance to the U.S. Economy,* unpublished dissertation, Columbia University, New York, 1963.

12   For a table of comparative growth rates providing some interesting data for application of the theorems described, see Wilcox, Weatherford, and Hunter, *Economies of the World Today,* New York, Harcourt, Brace, 1962, p. 20. Following a common convention, the list is broken down into mature and developing countries, but the criteria for their segregation are not at all clear. In terms of Marxian theory countries whose value compositions are above the average of all countries might be viewed as relatively developed economically while those of below-average composition would be undeveloped, at least in the economic dimension. In view of the diversity of such categorizations by conventional economics, it seems only fair to say that the economics contains no significant and unambiguous criteria.

13 In a curious essay the Englishman J. Enoch Powell suggests something to this effect: Hennessy, Lutz, and Simone, *Economic "Miracles,"* London, Institute of Economic Affairs, 1954.

14 The removal of the bureaucracy releases like a spring the energies of productive labor, as will be explained in some detail in Chapter 3. This phenomenon is sometimes noted by conventional economists (for example, J. K. Galbraith, *The Affluent Society,* Boston, Houghton Mifflin Co., 1958, pp. 161–163, in connection with the reduction of German bureaucracy brought about by the Hamburg bombings of World War II). However, the lesson is usually not extended to an endorsement of popular revolutions whose economic effect may be similar as a consequence of the removal of a sizable volume of unproductive labor from the backs of workers and peasants, for example, by its conversion to productive labor.

15 See note 11.

16 The economist John von Neumann is well known for having provided a proof of equality between the rate of interest and the rate of growth in a model strikingly simliar to the Marxian model of simple accumulation. See "A Model of General Economic Equilibrium," *Review of Economic Studies,* V, 13, no. 33, 1945–1946. The similarity may not be evident to all. Basic assumptions are: (1) Labor and land are available in unlimited quantities. This is the equivalent of the more realistic Marxian assumption of a labor productivity high enough to permit a surplus to be produced while labor power is growing at the technically required rate ($\Delta V/V$). (2) Each process uses some quantity of each product previously produced in producing current output. This is to assume that the production of wage goods requires wage and capital goods, while the production of capital goods requires capital and wage goods. (3) Labor is held at the subsistence level of wages, with the capitalist class investing all the proceeds from a period of production. This assumes the productive consumption of the whole of the surplus, that unproductive consumption is zero. It treats both capitalists' personal consumption and capitals invested in work of circulation as productive capitals. Marx's comments on the contributions of the capitalists to production and to its growth through abstinence, what von Neumann and conventional economists call "savings," are still quite relevant. See *Capital I,* pp. 596–598. The savings theory of growth on which von Neumann relies leads logically to the conclusion that it is the rate of interest, rather than the gross profit rate, that is equal to the rate of growth. The surplus value hypothesis leads to the conclusion that profits, interest, and rent derive from the surplus value, and that the *gross* rate of profit divides into those forms of property income, thus explaining the categories of income that the von Neumann theory must provide special premises to account for.

17 Marx's theory of the role of wage rate changes in influencing the cyclical movement has become a central part of standard economics. Compare *Capital I,* p. 620.

18 *Grundrisse* (Nicolaus trans.), op. cit., p. 340.

19 We are emphasizing not only the failure of technical change to sustain the growth of profitability of production but its very contribution to the tendency

for the rate of profit to fall. The failures of the critics of the "law of the falling tendency of the rate of profit" are thoroughly analyzed and the law itself defended both on logical and empirical (statistical) grounds in the work of Mage, op. cit., especially ch. 5, "Theoretical Criticisms of the Law." There Mage stresses the crucial point that "the rising organic composition of capital is 'but another expression for the increased productivity of labor' " (p. 151). The quotation referred to is from Marx, *Capital III,* p. 253 (Kerr, ed.). See Marx's discussion pp. 208–209 of the Moscow, International Publishers, edition.

20   *Grundrisse,* p. 340.

21   *Capital III,* p. 245.

22   The most striking statistical confirmations of this are offered by Mage in the work already referred to. Mage tests these propositions among others: (1) The rate of profit over the nonfarm economy will decline over the period of 1900–1960. The rate of profit tended to decline at a rate of 1.62 percent a year, with precipitous collapses and recoveries on the occasion of the Great Depression and afterward. (2) The value composition of capital will rise. This was confirmed by its measurement at business cycle peak years: 1910, 1920, 1923, 1926, 1929, 1937; and for all years after World War II except for the recession years 1949, 1954, 1958. For the pre–World War II period the value composition of capital rose at the rate of .75 percent; for the postwar period it rose at the higher rate of 2.4 percent. For the period 1900–1960 the value composition of capital rose some 31 percent. Data are calculated in units of socially necessary labor time (*not* as will be explained in Chapters 4 and 5, in units of *simple* socially necessary labor time, a factor that probably leads to an understatement rather than overstatement of actual trends). See Mage, op. cit., in particular ch. 7.

23   *Capital I,* p. 622.

24   Ibid., p. 644.

3. UNPRODUCTIVE CONSUMPTION

1   *Capital II,* ch. 6, "The Costs of Circulation"; *Capital III,* Pt. IV, "The Conversion of Commodity-Capital and Money-Capital into Commercial Capital and Money-Dealing Capital (Merchant's Capital); in the *Grundrisse,* op. cit., "The Chapter on Capital," Notebook V, especially pp. 537–555; *Theories of Surplus Value,* Pt. I, ch. 4, "Theories of Productive and Unproductive Labour," and Addenda, no. 12; and scattered passages elsewhere. Among Marx's theoretical disciples in this century the analysis of unproductive labor and consumption has until recently been conspicuously absent. Exceptions to this rule have not been numerous, but in addition to Gillman's *Law of the Falling Rate of Profit,* London, Dennis Dobson, 1957, his *Prosperity in Crisis,* London, Marzani and Munsell, 1966, has a chapter on the theory (ch. 3). A more extended historical and theoretical treatment of the subject will be found in Sydney Coontz, *Productive Labor and Effective Demand,* op. cit.

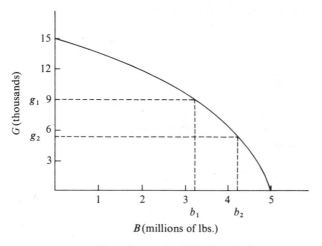

"A production possibility function"

2   The assumption that all commodities are productively consumed is not only
     pervasive within but is theoretically necessary to the conventional theory of
     production. A more realistic assumption vitiates the entire analysis. Thus the
     conventional analysis of production begins with the production possibility
     function as shown in the diagram above. Compare Paul A. Samuelson,
     Economics, 9th ed., New York, McGraw-Hill, 1973, ch. 2, "Central Problems
     of Every Economic Society," p. 22. The production possibility function
     defines society's menu of choices of production possibilities, given the state of
     technique and assuming the "law" of diminishing marginal productivity
     (which makes the function concave with respect to the origin). It provides
     what Samuelson calls a "rigorous definition" of scarcity, a notion central to
     conventional economics. Given the production function for each product, G
     and B, an increase in the output of one will necessitate a definite decrease in
     the output of the other, and vice versa, as may be seen by comparing any two
     production possibility points on the curve G–B. For instance, a given increase
     in the output of guns from g_1 to g_2 will necessitate a definite decrease in the
     amount of butter produced, from b_2 to b_1.
         If, however, the menu of choices is between commodities unproductively
     and commodities productively consumed, it is no longer possible to assume
     fixed production functions (productivity functions) for each commodity and it
     is no longer possible to conclude from that assumption that an increase in out-
     put of the one will, at the production frontier, necessitate a definite decrease
     in the production of the other, or vice versa. If, for instance, G (guns) is the
     un-productive line, then as the production of guns is increased the entire
     production function of B (butter) is lowered , as we explain in relation to
     Figure 3.1: a rise in the rate of unproductive consumption *lowers* the produc-
     tion function of products productively consumed. On the other hand, a reduc-
     tion in the rate of production of the commodity unproductively consumed will
     raise the production functions of commodities productively consumed. This
     makes nonsense of the scarcity postulate on which conventional economics

hangs much of its wearisome argument. But whether we consider an increase in the production of what is unproductively consumed, or whether we consider its decrease, the production possibilities function connecting the two production functions becomes theoretically indeterminate and the analysis falls apart. It is not possible to construct a menu of choices on realistic assumptions, and the standard analysis of production is wholly inapplicable. As a general theory of production it is definitely inadequate. We see, then, that economics has something of a vested interest in setting up moral prohibitions against the theory of unproductive consumption.

3 James H. Breasted, *A History of Egypt,* New York, Charles Scribner's Sons, 1912.
4 Ibid., p. 7.
5 Ibid., p. 15
6 Ibid., p. 107.
7 Ibid., p. 207.
8 Ibid., p. 403.
9 Ibid.
10 Ibid., p. 492.
11 Maurice Dobb, *Studies in the Development of Capitalism,* New York, International Publishers, 1946.
12 Ibid., p. 36.
13 Ibid., p. 40.
14 This pressure threatens the productive forces with overexploitation, or, as we express it theoretically, a rate of unproductive consumption in excess of the rate of surplus value.
15 Coontz, op. cit.
16 *Grundrisse,* op. cit., p. 493.
17 *Capital I,* p. 530.
18 See *Capital II,* Pt. I. In the formula the circuit $M - C$ signifies the conversion of money capitals into real capitals and placing the latter within their production unit; $C \ldots P \ldots C'$ spans the conversion of inputs into outputs; $C'-M'$ represents the realization processes, the converting of the real forms of output into their monetary equivalents.
19 Under capitalism, circulation processes utilize the market and all its ancillary instrumentalities, public and private, state and corporate, and these activities of circulation are *necessary* within this mode of production. Marx's comment may be helpful: "This advance of capital (into circulation) creates neither product nor value. It reduces *pro tanto* the dimensions in which the advanced capital functions productively. *It is as though one part of the product were transformed into a machine which buys and sells the rest of the product. It does not participate in the productive process, although it can diminish the labor power, etc., spent on circulation*" (*Capital II,* p. 133). My emphasis. The circulatory system of capitalist marketing functions like the air conditioners in apartment houses: They draw down power from the main generators without returning anything significant to them.
20 We shall see shortly that when the rate of unproductive consumption is zero, the rate of expansion of the system may be at its technically feasible maximum.

21 For historical details see Dobb, op. cit., ch. 5, "Capital Accumulation and Mercantilism."

22 It has meant, in brief, a heavy expenditure increasingly oriented to *unproductive* purposes.

23 The revival of the theory of unproductive consumption in Marxism begins with Gillman's influential book, *The Falling Rate of Profit*, op. cit., in which the "diminished S" is seen to follow from unproductive consumption. This is followed by an interesting discussion of the history of the theory in *Prosperity in Crisis*, op. cit., ch. 3, "The Social Surplus, 'Excess Savings,' and Unproductive Expenditures." These works contributed also to revival of the realization thesis, the proposition that modern capitalism is increasingly shaped by the growing difficulties of vending an expanding surplus, and that this leads to enlargement of the state, the corporation, mass consumption, to militarism and imperialism. The thesis is further developed in P. Baran and P. Sweezy, *Monopoly Capital*, op. cit., and in its ascendancy was dominated more by the Keynesian (in the style of John Hobson) than by the Marxian economics. In seeking to protect this thesis, rather than inquire into its limitations, the Keynesian Marxists have, indeed, quite consistently opposed a reconstruction of the labor theory of value, proposing instead, like many East European Marxists, to scrap the theory entirely. Compare Paul Sweezy, *Monthly Review*, "Some Problems in the Theory of Capital Accumulation," May 1974; and the interesting review by the bourgeois economist W. Baumol, of M. Morishima's *Marx's Economics: A Dual Theory of Value and Growth*, in *Monthly Review*, February 1975, in which the case for discarding the value theory is advanced by all parties. Morishima's work illustrates the not at all unusual aesthetics of the logician who, perceiving an inequality between prices and values within the dual theory, concludes that the problem is within the theory rather than within the real world that the theory explains. Perceiving the differences between prices and values, he fails to understand how in reality these differences are eradicated and the gaps closed, that is, in economic collapse.

24 By pulling down the rate of (real) accumulation, unproductive consumption makes it easier for capitalists to realize the gross value of the product. With the lower growth rate, aggregate demand need not rise as rapidly in order to maintain a given rate of unemployment. The effect of unproductive consumption in reducing the real rate of profit is, however, not understood by capitalists - nor would their understanding lead in any way to an improved investment allocation. Given its relations of production, capitalism "solves" its realization problem, first by raising the rate of growth of the effective demand for unproductive labor, and, second, by repressing the real rate of growth, the latter being the unperceived effect of the former. As we shall see later, the accumulation of capital in unproductive realms contributes also to the growing instability of the system.

25 The elimination of the old ruling class as former rulers and their retainers, as idlers, vagabonds, unemployed, and so on, are all put to work, may lead to a considerable enlargement of the input of productive labor. Thus for the less developed countries as well as for the developed countries (as discussed in Chapter 12, on the transition to socialism), a successful termination of the

class struggle allows the famous poverty-breeds-poverty cycle to be broken.

26　Among others, the discussion of Simon Kuznets is interesting (*Six Lectures on Economic Growth*, Glencoe, Ill., Free Press, 1959, Lecture II). While he perceives already in 1959 the postwar tendency for the rate of profit to fall, he attributes retardation to failures of demand rather than of supply, in the fashion of the Keynesian economics of the time. Bereft of a theory of unproductive consumption and, as a consequence, equipped with statistical data only partly processed, Kuznets declared that "there are no inherently compelling reasons for the rate of growth of per capita product to decline . . . technological and other limitations *on the supply side* can hardly be viewed as an important factor" (ibid., p. 38). In a manner characteristic of standard economics, the whole of Marxian and other unconventional theorizing (for example, Veblen) is thrust aside.

27　The extent of the depletion has become more evident with the rise of the energy crisis. But see the work of Seymour Melman, *Our Depleted Society*, New York, Holt, Rinehart and Winston, 1965, among others on the theme.

28　Critics of national income statistics have in fact been numerous, although they have had no success in stemming the tide of huckstering that has swept through economics. Among the critics, Oskar Morgenstern has been particularly persistent despite his political and theoretical conservatism. He quite aptly refers to economics as a "one digit science." See *On the Accuracy of Economic Observations*, rev. ed., Princeton, 1970.

29　The historian Henry Adams and the political economist Thorstein Veblen are probably best known. Adams' scientifically unacceptable suggestion (*Degradation of the Democratic Dogma*, Macmillan, New York, 1920) that the second law of thermodynamics applies to American development was an attempt to account for the expansion of unproductive consumption in his time. Veblen, too, sees the tendency, but ascribes it correctly to forces endogenous to capitalism. His explanation in detail is not altogether adequate, however. Compare Veblen, *Absentee Ownership*, New York, Huebsch, 1923. Among artists, observers of the tendency have been too numerous to list, but one would need to include *inter alia* Samuel Beckett, George Gross, Robert Musil, Thomas Mann, Bertolt Brecht, a host of poets, painters, musicians, playwrights, and so on.

4. THE MEANING AND MEASUREMENT OF VALUE

1　This summarization of the limitations of the labor theory pervades much of the writing of the revisionist groups. Compare Oskar Lange, "Marxian Economics and Modern Economic Theory" (1935), in *Marx and Modern Economics*, New York, Modern Reader, 1968. The following statement is rather typical: "The labour theory of value, as a theory of the relative prices of commodities, operates on two levels. On one level, it links up with labour value in the metaphysical sense. Many Marxists to this day maintain that it is impossible to make use of the concept of exploitation or to support the cause of revolution without believing that, in some sense, the prices of commodities are determined by their labour values. On the other level, it is merely a tool of analysis" (Joan Robinson and John Eatwell, *An Introduction to Modern Economics*, London, McGraw-Hill, 1973, p. 30).

2   "Introduction to the Critique of Political Economy," *A Contribution to the Critique of Political Economy*, Appendix 3, "The Method of Political Economy," p. 293.

3   The need for this *numeraire* has periodically impressed itself upon the economic mind since the seventeenth century. Currently, the dominant neoclassical economics of the mainstream, so called, has stumbled against the same chair in its capital theory. While she has her own difficulties with the labor theory *numeraire*, Joan Robinson is entirely correct in her criticism of conventional capital theory: "The student of economic theory is taught to write $O = f(L, C)$ where L is a quantity of labour, C a quantity of capital and O a rate of output of commodities. He is instructed to assume all workers alike, and to measure L in man hours of labour; he is told something about the index-number problem involved in choosing the unit of output; and then he is hurried on to the next question, in the hope that he will forget to ask in what units C is measured" (quoted in a volume that gives valuable guidance to the capital controversy, or the "Cambridge controversy," named after the Cambridge, England, critics of conventional theory: Hunt and Schwartz, *A Critique of Economic Theory*, op. cit., p. 22). In their own accounts of the labor theory of value, these critics of orthodox economics have, however, sought to revise rather than reconstruct Marx's work for systematic testing. (Maurice Dobb is a notable exception to this tendency.)

4   Thorstein Veblen, *The Instinct of Workmanship*, New York, Macmillan and Co., 1914, p. 188.

5   See *Capital I*, p. 41, for instance.

6   This, I take it, is one of the primary points of Piero Sraffa's analysis of *The Production of Commodities by Means of Commodities*, op. cit. Sraffa has helped greatly to make explicit, and to make economists aware of what is implicit, in the thought of Marx in this connection. His avoidance of the issues of value theory puts him in the revisionist school, however.

7   *Capital I*, p. 41.

8   Ibid., p. 38.

9   Ibid., p. 44.

10   Ibid. The student of the labor theory of value should read concurrently with *Capital I*, Pt. I, Bk. I, ch. 1 of *A Contribution to the Critique of Political Economy*, op. cit.

11   *A Contribution to the Critique of Political Economy*, op. cit., p. 25.

12   *Capital I*, p. 170. "The value of labour power is the value of the means of subsistence necessary for the maintenance of the labourer" (ibid., p. 171).

13   For examples of statistical ingenuity in processing see the works of Mage and Gillman, op. cit. Both of these theorists, in particular Gillman, perceive the important effects of unproductive consumption, but neither proceeded with a direct estimation of its value magnitude, that is, the *loss* in reproductive value that a given volume of unproductive consumption represents. That magnitude may be estimated directly in a manner similar to the estimation of the value of the surplus product. That is, the physical volume of product

directed into unproductive employment has a value, a negative value to be precise, measured by the labor time required to reproduce that volume of output, or, what is the same thing, by the labor time required to reproduce the means of subsistence of labor spent in unproductive employment.

5. VALUE ACCOUNTING, PRICES, AND SOCIALIST PLANNING

1   For some interesting work by Soviet economists bearing upon this ambition see V. Nemchinov, "Price and Value Theory," *Problems of Economics,* no. 12, 1960; S. G. Strumilin, "The Time Factor in Investment Projects," *International Economic Papers,* No. 1, 1951; L. V. Kantorovitch, "The Best Use of Economic Resources," Morton and Knightfield, eds., Harvard University Press, 1965; V. Novizhilov, "Cost Benefit Comparison in a Socialist Economy," *The Use of Mathematics in Economics,* Nemchinov, ed., M.I.T. Press, 1964. For a general and theoretically challenging discussion of the reduction of the market as a long-term objective, see C. Bettelheim, *La Transition vers l'Economie Socialiste,* op. cit., and his *Problemes Theoriques et Pratique de la Planification,* Paris, Maspero, 1970. The former is soon to be available in English translation by Harvester Press (England).

2   Compare Bettelheim, op. cit.

3   An excellent brief introduction to the subject is to be found in Oskar Lange's *An Introduction to Econometrics,* Warsaw, 1962.

4   Loc. cit.

5   Note that this is a *definition* of the coefficient by which the man-hour of skilled labor is to be multiplied in order to convert it into simple labor time units. One does *not* obtain this definition by a logical transformation of equations such as $V = V_S + V_U$ and $a = V_S/V_U$, from which it follows that $V = a V_U + V_U$. The latter suggests that the value of skilled labor is obtained by multiplying the quantity of unskilled labor extant by the coefficient a. On the contrary, the value of skilled labor is measured by multiplying the raw man-hours of skilled labor by the a coefficient whose method of estimation we are discussing.

6   *Capital I,* p. 44.

7   The impossibility of quantifying the theory has been alleged since the days of Boehm-Bawerk, who suggested, "Marx ought to have turned to experience for the proof of a proposition the correctness or incorrectness of which must be manifested in the facts of experience . . ." (*Karl Marx and the Close of His System,* Sweezy, ed., New York, Augustus Kelley, 1966, pp. 81–86 especially). Having no data-gathering agency at his disposal, Marx would have been rather hard-pressed to meet this requirement. However, all of those true scientists who might wish to confirm or refute the labor theory definitively might urge the institution of relevant data gathering as quickly as possible. For recent repetition of Boehm's charges with minor variations, see J. Schumpeter, *Capitalism, Socialism, and Democracy,* New York, Harper, 1950, Pt. I, ch. 3, "Marx the Economist." These are standard criticisms whose bases are quite insubstantial.

8 Bettelheim, op. cit.

9 *Capital III*, p. 830. See also Marx's comments in *The Critique of the Gotha Program*, pp. 27–32.

10 John Embree, *Mura, a Japanese Village*, cited in E. Mandel, *Marxist Economic Theory*, Vol. 1, New York, Modern Reader, 1972, p. 61.

11 Mandel, op. cit., ch. 2, and for other examples.

12 Pierre-Philippe Rey, *Colonialisme, Neo-colonialisme et la Transition au Capitalisme*, op. cit.

13 "If, then, first there is proportionate equality of goods, and then reciprocal action takes place, the result we mention will be effected [the rule of proportionate requital will prevail]. If not, the bargain is not equal and does not hold; for there is nothing to prevent the work of the one being better than that of the other; they must therefore be equated" (Nichomachean Ethics, Bk. V, ch. 5, *Basic Works of Aristotle*, McKeon ed., New York, Random House, p. 1010).

14 "For it is not two doctors that associate for exchange, but a doctor and a farmer, or in general people who are different and unequal; but these must be equated" (ibid., pp. 1010–1011).

15 David Ricardo's *Principles of Political Economy and Taxation* (1817) came closest in the period prior to Marx to providing a precise statement of the law of value.

16 It seems to have been his own inability to allow for differing ratios of capital to labor (as he thought of them) in relation to the functioning of competition that disturbed him.

17 Compare the famous *Capital III*, Pt. II, ch. 9, "Formation of a General Rate of Profit (Average Rate of Profit) and Transformation of the Values of Commodities into Prices of Production."

18 Op. cit., p. 1010.

19 There is the American economist Kenneth Boulding, for instance, according to whom Marx's "logical but inadequate system of economic reasoning . . . made little contribution to the broad line of development of economic thought" (*Economic Analysis*, Vol. II, 4th ed., New York, Harper & Row, 1966, p. 268).

20 Joan Robinson, "Marxism: Religion and Science." op. cit., p. 429.

21 See note 1, and for the role of labor time and labor value in fixing wages and prices in contemporary China, see Bettelheim, Charriere, Marchisio, *La Construction du Socialisme en Chine*, Paris, Maspero, 1968, especially III (Marchisio), "Les Systemes de Remuneration dans les Communes Populaires."

6. THE TRANSFORMATION OF VALUES INTO PRICES OF PRODUCTION

1 In the development of this theory, Smith's *Wealth of Nations* and the Abbe de Condillac's *Le Commerce et le Government* were early contributions. Leon Walras' *Elements of Pure Economics (The Theory of Social Wealth)* dates from 1874, and A. Marshall's *Principles of Economics appeared in 1890*. In this tradition also is the work of William Stanley Jevons (*Theory of Political*

Economy, 1871) and Carl Menger (*Grundsatze der Volkswirtshaftslehre,* 1871).

2   As the words themselves suggest, the assumption of freedom of entry and egress is mere special pleading suggesting the possibility of a frictionless movement of capitals that abstracts entirely from actuality. Again, the assumption that optimum scales of organization are small relative to total demands for products strains economic credulity beyond endurance.

3   In the struggle for shares of the aggregate profit the means utilized by the capitalists are very much a function of the level of technique. At present, with administrative technique so advanced, the devices of competition may be technically quite sophisticated. Appropriation has become highly mechanized, while often cruder forms are combined with the advanced administrative technique. Compare *The Pentagon Papers* for a revealing admixture of techniques.

4   For further discussion refer to *Science and Society,* "On the Monopoly Theory of Monopoly Capitalism," Winter 1971; " 'Terms of Exchange' and Extended Reproduction," *Science and Society,* Summer 1973.

5   Later theorists have been more careful in spelling out assumptions. Compare Walras, op. cit., Lesson I, for example.

6   *Capital III,* p. 174.

7   Ibid., p. 177.

8   Ibid.

9   This does not mean that there are no problems of formal logic involved in the Marxian explanation. For a recent discussion of the problem from this standpoint see David Laibman, "Values and Prices of Production: The Political Economy of the Transformation Problem," *Science and Society,* Winter 1973–1974, including the brief bibliography on the subject. On the transformation problem as a problem of history see the excellent and helpful essay, R. Meek, "Some Notes on the 'Transformation Problem,' " in *Economics and Ideology and Other Essays,* London, Chapman and Hall, 1967, pp. 154–157 in particular.

10 "Wherever the handicraft system reaches a fair degree of development, the daily life of the community comes to center about the market and takes on the character given by market relations. The volume of trade grows greater, and purchase and sale enter more thoroughly into the details of the work to be done and of the livelihood to be got by this work. The price system comes into the foreground" (Veblen, *The Instinct of Workmanship,* op. cit., p. 244).

11 "With the advance of technology the material equipment so requisite to the pursuit of industry in the crafts increases in volume, cost and elaboration, and the processes of industry grow extensive and complex, until it presently becomes a matter of serious difficulty for any workman single-handed to supply the complement of tools, appliances and material with which his work is to be done. It then also becomes a matter of some moment to own such wealth" (ibid., p. 277).

12 E. P. Thompson, *The Making of the English Working Class,* New York, Vintage Books, 1966, p. 67. For the stresses caused by the emergence of new price-value relations see especially pp. 63–68; for the crumbling of the traditional wage structure, ch. 8 and pp. 235–236. George Eliot remains in some

respects the most perceptive expositor of the effects of the new transformation of values upon social relations: *Adam Bede, The Mill on the Floss,* and, in a later phase, *Middlemarch.* The inability of historians and some economists to keep pace with the novelist's perception is revealed in *Capitalism and the Historian,* Hayek, ed., op. cit. For a more objective assessment of nineteenth-century developments see Eric Hobsbawm, "The British Standard of Living, 1790–1850," *Labouring Men,* London, 1971, pp. 64–104.

13 The principle of methodology utilized is no where better described than by Marx himself: "The conversion of money into capital has to be explained on the basis of laws that regulate the exchange of commodities, in such a way that the starting point is the exchange of equivalents . . . the formation of capital must be possible even though the price and value of a commodity be the same; for its formation cannot be attributed to any deviation of the one from the other. If prices actually differ from values, we must, first of all, reduce the former to the latter, in other words, treat the difference as accidental in order that the phenomena may be observed in their purity, and our observations not be interfered with by disturbing circumstances that have nothing to do with the process in question" (*Capital I,* p. 166).

14 Competition is more effective because of the improvement of circulatory mechanisms that accompanies the industrial advance. In the model we use here prices of each department's outputs are identical. This follows from the assumption that all of the constant capital turns over in a period, a greater simplification than any used by Marx in *Capital III* (compare ch. 9, "Formation of a General Rate of Profit and Transformation of the Values of Commodities into Prices of Production").

15 It should be emphasized that, since the capitalist, like his economic apologist, is incapable of perceiving the empirical reality of exchange values, surplus values, and so on, he cannot perceive either the movements of terms of exchange through which he exploits labor in other branches of production and gains a margin of surplus value in his average profit that is the result of their productivity: ". . . the mass of surplus value produced in a particular sphere of production . . . is of importance to the latter [the capitalist] only insofar as the quantity of surplus value produced in his branch helps to regulate the average profit. But this is a process which occurs behind his back, one he does not see, nor understand, and which indeed does not interest him. The actual difference of magnitude between profit and surplus value . . . now completely conceals the true nature and origin of profit not only from the capitalist, who has a special interest in deceiving himself on this score, but also from the labourer. The transformation of values into prices of production serves to obscure the basis for determining value itself' (*Capital III,* pp. 165–166).

16 There is certainly no need to credit the conventional theory in proportion to its own claims: "Orthodox economists . . . have developed a kind of price theory which is more useful in this sphere [theory of the firm, and so on] than anything to be found in Marx or his followers" (Paul Sweezy, *Theory of Capitalist Development,* op. cit., p. 129). Marx's discussion of the firm in *Capital I* is more to the point than any standard theory of my acquaintance.

17 P. Sweezy, "Some Problems in the Theory of Capital Accumulation," *Monthly Review,* op. cit., p. 40, n. 2.

APPENDIX TO CHAPTER 6

1 Paul Sweezy in his introduction to *Karl Marx and the Close of His System,* New York, Augustus Kelley, 1949, gives an excellent resumé of the development of the argument.

2 K. Winternitz, "Values and Prices: A Solution of the So-Called Transformation Problem," *Economic Journal,* 58 (June 1948), 276–280; F. Seton, "The 'Transformation Problem,' " *The Review of Economic Studies,* 24 (June 1957), 149–160; Morishima, *Marx's Economics,* op. cit., inter alia. For an interesting summary of these solutions, see Laibman, op. cit.

3 Seton, op. cit., p. 160.

4 As usual, Marx's presentation is nicely balanced between historical and logical considerations. His formulation of exchange relations perhaps begins with a consideration of industrial-agricultural exchanges (Letter to Engels, August 2, 1862, *Selected Correspondence,* op. cit.). In *Capital III* Marx refers to the interdependence of inputs and outputs through successive periods and to the need to analyze these sequences more carefully: "But for the buyer the price of production of a specific commodity is its cost price, and may thus pass as cost-price into the prices of other commodities. . . . It is necessary to remember this modified significance of the cost-price, and to bear in mind that there is always the possibility of an error if the cost-price of a commodity in any particular sphere is identified with the value of the means of production consumed by it. Our present analysis does not necessitate a closer examination of this point" (p. 162).

5 "The So-Called Transformation Problem: Marx Vindicated," unpublished manuscript, New School for Social Research.

6 Op. cit.

7 "Understanding the Marxian Notion of Exploitation: A Summary of the So-Called Transformation Problem Between Marxian Values and Competitive Prices," *Journal of Economic Literature,* 9 (June 1971), 153–308.

8 "The 'Transformation' from Marxian 'Values' to Competitive 'Prices.' A Process of Rejection and Replacement," *Proceedings of the National Academy of Sciences,* 67 (September 1970), 309–311.

9 *Marx's Economics,* op. cit.

10 W. Baumol's review of Morishima's *Marx's Economics,* in *The Monthly Review,* loc. cit.

11 *International Economic Relations,* P. A. Samuelson, ed., New York, St. Martin's Press, 1969, pp. 57–58.

7. UNEQUAL EXCHANGE

1 *Capital I,* ch. 2, "Exchange." Max Weber, *General Economic History,* New York, Greenberg, 1927, p. 195.

2 Benjamin Higgins, *Economic Development,* New York, W. W. Norton, 1968, p. 297.

3 Pierre Jalee, *Imperialism in the Seventies*, New York, Third Press, 1972.

4 Interpretations stressing a unilateral exploitation of the underdeveloped by the developed risk fomenting national animosities rather than promoting a deeper understanding of mechanisms by means of which ruling classes everywhere extort the surplus value of international labor. Compare Andre Gundar Frank, *Capitalism and Underdevelopment in Latin America*, New York, Monthly Review Press, 1969.

5 The famous scissors movement of industrial and agricultural prices in the period of Soviet reconstruction after the Revolution is of a kind by no means peculiar to that country or to that period. In Russia at the time it was an institutional hangover from the previous order, and an incomplete socialization of the productive forces still prevents its complete eradication there as elsewhere. See M. Dobb, *Soviet Economic Development Since 1917*, London, Routledge and Kegan Paul, 1972, pp. 117, 162–176, 215–216. On the matter of incomplete socialization see C. Bettelheim, *La Transition vers l'economie socialiste*, op. cit.,

6 Compare *Capital II*, ch. 20, "Simple Reproduction" ch. 3, "Exchange Between the Two Departments."

7 In his excellent study, *Productive Labour and Effective Demand*, op. cit., Coontz shows the impossibility of the balance condition being realized between the two departments when the average value composition of capital is rising with the accumulation of capital. Our own demonstration shows in a manner quite consistent with Coontz's that when value compositions in the two sectors are unequal the entire structure of price-value relations prevents equilibrium exchange. Compare Coontz, p. 81.

8 Since the nineteenth century, mercantile theorists such as the German Friedrich List, and the American Peshine Smith, have stressed the trading advantage of the more developed country without understanding the inseparability of the advantage, or, for that matter, the disadvantage, from capitalist exchange. So, too, there are some modern mercantilists in the less developed world today who argue similarly in order to gain the advantages of nationalism without acquiring the taint of socialism. The tendency to unequal exchange is seen also by many standard economists, most of whom determinedly resist any suggestion that something in the capitalist mode pushes inexorably to this effect. See, for instance, T. Morgan, "The Long Run Terms of Trade Between Agriculture and Manufacturing," in *Readings in Economic Development* by Morgan, Betz, and Choudry, Belmont, Cal., Wadsworth, 1963, pp. 274–285; League of Nations, *Industrialization and Foreign Trade*, Geneva, 1945, in *Relative Price of Exports and Imports of Underdeveloped Countries*, United Nations, New York, 1949; P. T. Ellsworth, *The Terms of Trade: A European Case Study*, New York, The Technology Press, 1956, who says, "in the European context, the terms of trade favor the developed and run against the underdeveloped countries" (p. 239); Raul Prebisch, *The Economic Development of Latin America*, United Nations, New York, 1950. Among non-Marxists concerned with the subject, Gunnar Myrdal is best known (*Rich Lands and Poor*, New York, Harper, 1958; *Asian Drama*, Twentieth Century Fund, New York, 1968), but, like other standard

economists, seems unable to devise any suitably general explanation for the phenomenon.

Among Marxists, Arghiri Emmanuel's *Unequal Exchange* (New York, MR Press, 1972) is well known. Samir Amin's *L'Exchange inegal et la loi de la valeur* (Paris, editions-anthropos-idep, 1973) gives a clean summary of the tendency to unequal exchange. While Emmanuel well describes the short-sightedness of standard economists, his own theory is inadequate, first, because he does not define terms of exchange with any suitable precision, and, second, because he is careless about distinctions between price and value and fails altogether to see that it is in discrepancies between these quantities that the root of the ailment resides; his own analysis consequently lacks an appreciation of the generality of the incidence of unequal exchange, its incidence in domestic as well as in international exchange. It is not surprising, then, that he concludes rather lamely that "mechanisms of redistribution" applied internationally will cure the difficulty.

In relation to the generality of the incidence of unequal exchange, we by no means preclude its incidence in countries where prices are politically determined and fixed over long periods. For such countries, that is, the socialist countries, unequal exchange would show itself in scissors movements in physical flows of commodities entering international trade. Since the value of an output (W) is the labor value per physical unit (W/q) multiplied by the number of units being exchanged ($W/q \times q$), indices of movements of physical flows during appropriate periods of expansion should reveal the predicted tendency where an inadequate socialization of the productive forces still obtains. An example is Soviet-Czechoslovakian trade of the late 1950s and early 1960s. See H. Starobin, "A case study in Socialist Economic Aid and Political Development," unpublished dissertation, New York University, 1969.

9　Carlos Andres Perez, "The President of Venezuela Responds to the President of the United States," *The Wall Street Journal,* September 27, 1974.

10　Final Act, Conference of Trade and Development, June 16, 1964. Cited by L. Horowitz in *Three Worlds of Development* (*The Theory and Practice of International Stratification*), New York, Oxford, 1966, p. 169. As we argue in concluding this chapter, the real issue of stratification is not between countries but between social classes. The movement of terms of exchange merely ensures that each segment of the ruling class will receive a share of profit proportioned to the amount of capital it advances. For the ruling class the particular country, nation, corporation, and so on, is no more than a vehicle for pursuing class interest.

11　Jalee, op. cit., p. 53. He declares, "Unequal exchange dominates the commercial relations of the two groups of countries. The main results of this are: the economic suffocation of the Third World countries; the camouflaging of the crucial importance of their shipments of raw materials behind a smoke-screen of figures whose value is diminished; the contracting capacity of their markets for the industrial products of imperialism, which accentuates the importance of the excess production capacity of factories in the imperialist countries" (p. 65). Abstracting from his false inference that it is a matter of countries exploiting and being exploited – rather it is a matter of class interrelations – the statement is quite correct in its reference to value effects of unequal exchange.

12 Attention must be drawn to the contribution to inflation of an extending spread of prices and wages. Given value flows, prices of labor intensive commodities will decline *relative* to those whose value composition is above the social average. As the former reach their floors (they cannot fall to zero), the rise of the latter will accelerate. This inflationary pressure may help to forestall collapse in the short run, as during the mid-sixties exchange of advanced with less developed countries. Compare Horowitz, op. cit., pp. 165–166.

13 The theory of noncompeting groups will be found in *Some Leading Principles of Political Economy*, London, 1874, pp. 66ff. The theory draws on the liberal price-equilibrating theorem discussed in the previous chapter: wage rates will be proportioned to costs of production given the mobility of labor. This mobility, Cairnes then points out, is lacking where groups fail to compete. Cairnes, in the liberal tradition, sees education as a palliative that will restore social mobility. Where the groups are social classes, as in the English case, the failure of the device is manifest.

14 Thorstein Veblen's *Theory of the Leisure Class*, New York, Macmillan, 1899, is the seminal statement of the connection between discrimination and capitalist relations of production.

15 It is social discrimination in combination with the law of unequal exchange that explains the secular tendency for labor values to gravitate from northwest to southeast along the main diagonal of the labor flow matrix. Compare Chapter 5, "Value Flows in the Matrix of Social Labor." This effect is thus brought about by the most horrendous pressures, both economic and social, upon the whole of the social labor force. The benign and insipid explanations sometimes offered of the secular movement are an offense to anyone who has thoughtfully participated as a worker within this distorted and distended system of production. See, for instance, Gary Becker, *Human Capital*, NBER, New York, 1964, in which he minimizes the cost of every man's life and death struggles to find employment on survival terms: "A simple analysis of the incentive to invest in human capital seems capable of explaining, therefore, not only why the over-all distribution of earnings is more skewed than the distribution of abilities, but also why earnings are more skewed among older and skilled persons than among younger and less skilled ones." In this work he treats social discrimination as an exogenous factor in the process of distribution to labor – a process that is altogether a process of production, as we have seen. Justification for this procedure he previously offered in his *Economics of Discrimination*, University of Chicago Press, 1957. With such Chicago school works, harmony doctrines of the nineteenth century move in the twentieth into the ranks of empirical science. A far more reasonable discussion of racism is to be found in Baran and Sweezy's *Monopoly Capital*, op. cit., pp. 249–280

16 These issues are argued by Charles Bettelheim and Arghiri Emmanuel in Appendix I to *Unequal Exchange*, op. cit. Bettelheim is entirely correct in insisting that unequal exchange follows from ruling-class activities and accrues to its benefit primarily. The argument has an important bearing on the historical development of forms of imperialism. With the consolidation of the international class and its exchange interrelations, the old rapine led by the

single nation-state becomes the exceptional form, and the appropriation of surplus value through an ever more generalized and unequal exchange becomes the modern form, particularly in evidence during expansion phases in the accumulation of capital.

17　Bettelheim in *Unequal Exchange*, op. cit., p. 295.

18　Rey, *Les Alliances de Classes*, op. cit., p. 9.

8. ACCUMULATION IN THE ADVANCED CAPITALISM

1　Discussing the transformation of the antique mode of production, Marx says: "The aim of all these communities is survival, i.e., reproduction of the individuals who compose it as proprietors, i.e., in the same objective mode of existence as forms the relation among the members and at the same time therefore the commune itself. This reproduction, however, is at the same time necessarily new production and destruction of the old form" (*Grundrisse*, op. cit., p. 493).

2　"From forms of development of the forces of production these relations turn into their fetters. Then comes the period of social revolution" (*A Contribution to the Critique of Political Economy*, op. cit., p. 12).

3　Coontz, *Productive Labour and Effective Demand*, op. cit., p. 85.

4　*Capital I*, cited by Coontz, ibid. See the famous discussion of primitive accumulation, *Capital I*, Pt. 8.

5　See Chapters 4 and 5.

6　The equations given here are modifications of those of Coontz, op. cit., with slight interpretative differences.

7　See Chapter 2. Compare Mage, op. cit. An interesting recent discussion also is that of Geoff Hodgson, "The Falling Rate of Profit," *New Left Review*, no. 84, March–April 1974.

8　*Capital I*, op. cit.

9　Cited by Coontz, op. cit., p. 150.

10　John Hobson, *Imperialism*, London, Allen and Unwin, 1902, ch. 6. At a slightly later point in the development process, Lenin generalized the theory of imperialism with his emphasis on the "export of capital," for that export provides the financial means for extending markets for both consumption and investment goods. Compare V. I. Lenin, *Imperialism: The Last Stage of Capitalism*, especially ch. 4, "The Export of Capital."

11　Beginning with the Austrian school in the past century, bourgeois theorists have treated consumption as the ultimate end of capital accumulation, the value from which the value of means of production derives through imputation. The theories that have descended from this tradition into standard economics are little more than rationalizations of capitalists' market needs, as Bukharin long ago noted in his *Theory of the Leisure Class*, op. cit. The present generation, having discovered the so-called service industries, takes their development as a sign of the perennial viability of the mode of production, not realizing the economic implications of the unproductive needs being served.

12 Lewis Corey, *The Decline of American Capitalism,* New York, Covici-Friede, 1934, p. 291. Cited by Coontz, op. cit., p. 150.

13 Coontz, op. cit., pp. 154–155.

14 The manner in which unproductive consumption leads to inflation is not easily grasped, and a further word on the subject may be helpful. Suppose that at the close of a given period, the portion of the surplus destined for unproductive use consists of means of production and means of consumption to be used in support of unproductive labor, that is, labor engaged in unproductive work, as defined. In other words, these material means of subsistence will in this case function as productive inputs in the following period. To be sure, they are inputs caught up in support of unproductive labor, but they are inputs in the next period, nevertheless. Thus in this interval from the close of the first period (t) to the close of the second period ($t + 1$), we have the equation: $M_t = O_t = I_{t+1}$, *even though* a portion of the input I_{t+1} is spent in support of unproductive labor. But we must follow this situation for at least one more period of reproduction.

At the close of period $t + 1$, the input values I_{t+1}, productive and unproductive alike, reappear as part of the value of the output, O_{t+1}. *However,* that portion of the reproduced value resulting from unproductive labor in $t + 1$ consists now of product or services useful only for unproductive work, that is, for circulatory or other unproductive work. Hence this portion of the output of $t + 1$ *cannot be used as material means of subsistence* – means of production or wage goods – in period $t + 2$, whether for productive or for unproductive labor. If the labor using these products and services is to have material support for its unproductive activities in $t + 2$, therefore, material means of support must be drawn from what is otherwise available to support productive labor. The sale of the portion of the output O_{t+1} that is usable only for unproductive purchases provides, however, the purchasing power that bids material means of subsistence away from productive employment in the required volume. Or, as we put it previously, the excess demand that appears at the close of period $t + 1$ will drive up the prices of means of production and of wage goods as these are allocated out of productive and into unproductive use.

In period $t + 2$, then, the scale of unproductive consumption – which we assume to be extending – is again maintained by bidding a portion of material means required from productive sectors together with a new increment of unproductive consumption over its level in the previous period. At the close of the period $t + 2$ the value of the output again contains a value, the value contributed by unproductive labor, in the amount of the means of consumption and of production consumed in its support. But the output materially considered will consist again of the products or services rendered by unproductive labor, and thus in the following period means of consumption and production will again have to be bid away from productive employment. Again an excess demand for productive inputs appears, and so on. In sum, the appearance of excess demand with a rise in the rate of unproductive consumption may be delayed by a period or two before its impact is felt. For Marx's analysis of the pressure of unproductive consumption on the price of necessaries, see his discussion of Malthus in *Theories of Surplus Value*, Pt. III, Moscow, 1971, "Over production, 'Unproductive Consumers,' etc." pp. 40–51.

15   See Mage, op. cit.

16   Ibid.

17   Taking the census category "Managers, Officials and Proprietors (Except Farm)" as an index of the growth of unproductive labor, we see that between 1950 and 1960 the numbers so employed increased by 10 percent, whereas between 1960 and 1970 they grew by approximately 30 percent (Census of population, U.S. summary, Table 53, P-B1, for 1950; U.S. Census of Population, Table 21, "Occupational Characteristics," PC2, for 1960).

18   *Economic Report of the President, 1974*, Table C 45, "Consumer Price Indexes," p. 301; Table C 74, "Corporate Profits After Taxes," p. 335.

19   In the estimation of real values, gnp statistics do not, of course, allow for the annual volume of unproductive consumption. Hence the standard data exaggerate growth rates, on the positive side, or understate rates of decline, on the negative.

20   *Economic Report of the President, 1974*. Table C 32, "Output per Man Hour and Related Data."

21   Particularly revealing in the *Economic Report* (op. cit.) is Table C 74, showing the rise of corporate profits after taxes plus capital consumption allowances. The rise of the capital consumption allowances reflects the growing financial distress of the managers after 1965 under pressure to maintain their liquidity. It is this pressure, tracing to the falling rate of profit, that forces financial and nonfinancial managers alike to seek to reverse the situation through the administration of inflation, the repression of wage rates, increased unemployment, and so on.

22   *Capital I.* Cited by Coontz, op. cit.

23   *Capital II*, p. 133.

9.   MARX'S FIRST AND SECOND APPROXIMATIONS

1   Usually, this interpretation is buttressed by reference to nothing more economically analytical than the *Communist Manifesto*. It is probably accurate to say that the general law of *Capital I* offers but a first test at the level of economic analysis of the general tendencies asserted in the *Manifesto*.

2   *Capital I*, p. 644.

3   Ibid.

4   Processes of interpenetrations of modes of production, or of transitions from one to another, are now receiving a good deal of attention by investigators in the wake of work by Bettelheim and Rey, already referred to.

5   *Theories of Surplus Value*, Pt. II, p. 573.

6   Ibid.

7   This is one interpretation that might be made of the phrase "stand between" in the passage just cited. In his survey of some current theories of class structure, Anthony Giddens has much to say about this thesis, and in the end

credits it with a good deal of force: ". . . the middle class rarely tends to play a direct role in manifest class struggles" (*The Class Structure of Advanced Societies*, New York, Barnes and Noble, 1973, p. 288). Giddens refers to Frank Parkin as an expositor of the buffer hypothesis (*Class Inequality and Political Order*, London, 1971). As we shall see, while Marx himself anticipates the rise of middle classes, he does not consider them a buffer. Our own appraisal of the buffer thesis is an extension of Marx's views with some modifications and will be found in the following chapter.

8   *Capital II*, p. 498.

9   The distinction is given theoretical formulation in Chapter 3.

10 *Capital II*, p. 133.

11 *Capital III*, p. 288. The importance of the administrative labor in facilitating appropriation can hardly be stressed too much. A further passage is worth citing in this connection: "In so far as it contributes to shortening the time of circulation, it [merchant's capital] may help indirectly to increase the surplus value produced by the industrial capitalists. In so far as it helps to expand the market and effects the division of labor between capitals, hence enables capital to operate on a larger scale, its function promotes the productivity of industrial capital and its accumulation. In so far as it shortens circulation time, it raises the ratio of surplus value to advanced capital, hence the rate of profit" (*Capital III*, pp. 274–275). Insofar as these advantages in the employment of administrative labor are perceived by capitalists, investment in their production and installation proceeds accordingly.

12 They have been lost except for the political economy of the Left. Even the stagnationists of the conventional economics have underrated or ignored the role of unproductive labor, and John Maynard Keynes' *General Theory of Employment, Interest and Money*, as is well known, dismisses as irrelevant to the problem of full employment the productivity of investment. A further example is Alvin Hansen's *Full Recovery or Stagnation?* New York, 1938. The Keynesians have been notoriously unable to see that their investment stimuli, stabilizers, and all the rest point toward rising rates of unproductive consumption and, therefore, toward an intensification of certain of the problems they seek to avoid. As we saw earlier, the rise in the rate of unproductive consumption is perhaps the most important factor underlying the development of rising unemployment and inflation (stagflation). As an economics of stabilization, this economics is best regarded as a scientifically defunct part of neoclassical economics.

13 *Capital III*, p. 295.

14 In the United States, for example, labor apart from manual and farm workers comprised 26.6 percent of employed labor in 1900 and 54.9 percent of employed labor in 1960. See P. A. Lester, *Economics of Labor*, 2nd ed., New York, Macmillan Co., 1964, p. 21, Table 3. For the period 1820–1940 Simon Kuznets observes: "The share of trade and other service industries, a miscellaneous group including business, personal, professional, and government services have grown steadily and continued to grow in recent decades" (*Economic Growth and Structure*, New York, W. W. Norton Co., 1965, p. 25). Like so many other economists, Kuznets is unable to resist posing the

naive question: "Why has the 'middle class' failed to disappear, and indeed flourished, particularly in countries like the United States where capitalism was most developed? These questions indicate the gap between the over-simplified terminology of the Marxian theory of class struggle and the secular transformation of capitalist society and the changes in the structure of economic organization that in fact occurred, partly in connection with the development of the nonpersonal organizational Units [corporations] in modern economic growth" (ibid., p. 103). The suggestions that Marx expected these "middle-class" layers to disappear is too absurd to take seriously.

15 *Capital III*, pp. 294–295.

16 The value of its labor power exceeds its wage cost of reproduction. Although it does not produce surplus value, its use by the capitalist enables the latter to appropriate a share of the social surplus value in the form of profit (*Capital III*, Chap. 17, "Commercial Profit").

17 "This [falling wage of the commercial laborer] is due partly to the division of labour in the office, implying a one-sided development of the labour capacity, the cost of which does not fall entirely on the capitalist, since the labourer's skill develops by itself through the exercise of its function, and all the more rapidly as division of labour makes it more one-sided" (*Capital III*, p. 295).

18 *Capital I*, p. 332.

19 Explaining why the wage of the white-collar laborer tends to fall, Marx says: "Secondly, because the necessary training, knowledge of commercial practices, languages, etc., is more and more rapidly, easily, universally, and cheaply reproduced with the progress of science and public education the more the capitalist mode of production directs teaching methods, etc., towards practical purposes." And he continues in a passage presaging the enormous enlargement in supply of this labor: "The universality of public education enables capitalists to recruit such labourers from classes that formerly had no access to such trades and were accustomed to a lower standard of living. Moreover, this increases supply, and hence competition. With few exceptions, the labour power of these people is therefore devaluated with the progress of capitalist production. Their wage falls, while their labour capacity increases" (*Capital III*, p. 295).

20 *Capital I*, p. 332.

21 Compare *Capital I*, pp. 626–628.

22 Ibid., p. 626.

23 *Capital III*, p. 379.

24 "Stock companies in general – developed with the credit system – have an increasing tendency to separate this work of management as a function from the ownership of capital, be it self-owned or borrowed. Just as the development of bourgeois society witnessed a separation of the functions of judges and administrators from landownership, whose attributes they were in feudal times. But since, on the one hand, the mere owner of capital, the money-capitalist, has to face the functioning capitalist, while money capital itself assumes a social character with the advance of credit, being concentrated in banks and loaned out by them instead of its original owners, and since, on the other hand, the mere manager who has no title whatever to the capital,

whether through borrowing it or otherwise, performs all the real functions pertaining to the functioning capitalist as such, only the functionary remains and the capitalist disappears as superfluous from the production process" (ibid., p. 380).

25 Ibid.

26 Henry Ford II, cited by Baran and Sweezy, *Monopoly Capital*, op. cit., p. 30.

27 The work of the Marxists on the question is seldom consulted by conventional scholars. The recent work of Giddens, op. cit., illustrates the point.

28 I must here point to the brilliant and pioneering work of Lewis Corey, whose *Crisis of the Middle Class*, New York, Covici-Friede, 1935, was called to my attention following recent publication of two essays of my own on the same subject ("Class Structure and Conflict in the Managerial Phase, I, II, *Science and Society*, Fall, Winter, 1973, 1974). Corey's analysis parallels my own, the substance of which is contained in the following chapters.

10. CLASS STRUCTURE AND CONFLICT IN THE MANAGERIAL PHASE I

1 Rather than provide a bibliography of agency studies, an offering of authors' names will suffice: Aronson, Kolko, D. Horowitz, Domhoff, Fitch and Oppenheimer, Galbraith, Blair, Bain, Dewey, and a long line of economists. An important current exception is S. Menshikov's *Millionaires and Managers*, Moscow, Progress Publishers, 1969, especially ch. 1, "Evolution of Capital and of the Capitalist," describing an alternative.

2 A good survey and critique of current non-Marxian theories is contained in Anthony Giddens, *The Class Structure of the Advanced Societies*, op. cit.

3 This bold statement deserves a more extended study along the lines suggested by Rey of the interpenetration of modes of production. My view at present is that the managerial capitalist is the last form in the evolution of the capitalist, although a role for him may need to be found in early phases of the transition to socialism. Compare *Class Alliances*, op. cit.

4 The same may be said of many of the works of the Marxian monopoly theorists that almost invariably focus on organizational forms and interrelations rather than on class analysis. Menshikov is again an exception to the rule.

5 The ambiguous social position of the bourgeois artisan of the seventeenth and eighteenth centuries is resolved in the twentieth century with the plunging of the bulk of administrative labor into the working class.

6 "At a certain stage of their development, the material forces of production in society come in conflict with the existing relations of production, or – what is but a legal expression for the same thing – with the property relations within which they had been at work before. From forms of development of the forces of production these relations turn into their fetters. Then comes the period of social revoltuion" (preface to *A Contribution to the Critique of Political Economy*, op. cit., p. 12).

7 In *Capital II* Marx writes: "We have already learned from the analysis of the simple circulation of commodities, that $C - M$, the sale, is the most difficult part of its metamorphosis and that, therefore, under ordinary conditions, it takes up the greater part of its time of circulation" (p. 126).

8 The computer is merely the latest, striking example of administrative technique. For previous discussion of the accumulation of administrative capital see, "Social Integration and the Power to Manage," *Quarterly Review of Economics and Business,* 5 (Spring 1965), 38–43.

9 The truth about the office boy is not at all what Horatio Alger taught. In the same issue of *The New York Times* in which republication of the Alger novel was announced (January 28, 1973), we find this item: "Charges of scandalous business conduct when he was building his fortune hang as a cloud over the reputation of Roy L. Ash as he assumes the important duties of the director of the Office of Management and Budget in the Nixon administration." Following a recitation of down-to-earth details, we find that Ash "had been in the Air Force. Although he had no college background, he went to Harvard Business School after his discharge, finished first in his class and received a master of business administration degree." The historical evolution of the new entrepreneur is relived again and again in the individual careers of the office boys.

10 *The Managerial Revolution,* New York, John Day and Co., 1941. *The Engineers and the Price System,* New York, Viking, 1921. The dates of publications of these studies, the former, apologia, and the latter, criticism, are significant in view of the impetus given by war to the ascent of the managers.

11 Burnham's total failure to understand the forces giving rise to the managers is revealed in this statement: "The position, role and function of the managers are in no way dependent upon the maintenance of capitalist property and economic relations (even if many of the managers themselves think so); they depend upon the technical nature of the process of modern production (op. cit., p. 91). Note the confusion between the origins of managerial and of administrative labor.

12 Ibid.

13 Conventional theorists are notorious in their inability to perceive differences in value compositions of capital and in assessing the economic effects of these differences. Compare Hal B. Lary, *Imports of Manufactures from Less Developed Countries,* New York, Columbia University Press, 1968. The theorist fails, for instance, to include in constant capital the circulating portion of that capital. Or, he measures capital intensity by the ratio S/V ($\Delta O/V$) rather than C/V. Or he fails to realize that it is the average value composition that governs terms of exchange, and so on.

14 This has a further practical application. The rate of interest is the price of producing financial services. The tendency for the entire structure of interest rates to rise in later phases of capitalist development reflects the necessity of covering the costs of reproduction (on an extended scale) of a growing circulatory establishment. The accumulation of circulatory relative to industrial capitals involves a change in the relative prices of these commodities. Hence the new usury.

15 On the assumption that circulatory capitals are unproductive, and are composed of $C_u + V_u$, while the productive capitals, or industrial capitals, are $C_p + V_p$, we define the value composition of the social capitals as: $C' \equiv C_u + V_u + C_p/C_p + V_p$. We are here counting those administrative capitals that are productively utilized within the p category along with the industrial labor that is productively employed. The social organic composition of capital is the traditional Marxian organic composition of capital expanded to include also capitals absorbed in circulatory work. Because this ratio comprehends all the capitals of society, we term it the social value composition to distinguish it from the industrial organic composition with which Marx was primarily concerned.

It is further assumed that the wasted and unproductive capitals of society function as constant capitals economically. The capitals C_u and V_u, along with C_p, are a part of capitalists' cost of production that yield no surplus value, according to the labor theory of value. Marx makes clear the theoretical nature of these input capitals in a letter to Engels, April 30, 1868: "According to our previous assumption the productive capital of society = 500 . . . and the formula was $400C = 100V// + 100S$. The general rate of profit, $p' = 20\%$. Now let the merchant capital = 100. The $100S$ has now to be calculated on 600 instead of 500. The general rate of profit is therefore reduced from 20% to 16 2/3%." Similar assumptions permeate discussion of merchant's capital both in the *Grundrisse* and in *Capital III*.

16 Joseph Gillman, *The Falling Rate of Profit*, op. cit.
17 The most influential work has probably been Baran and Sweezy, *Monopoly Capital*, op. cit.
18 Ibid.
19 This was explained in Chapter 8.
20 Ibid.
21 Compare the work of Mage already noted.
22 Recall Chapters 6 and 7.

11. CLASS STRUCTURE AND CONFLICT IN THE MANAGERIAL PHASE II

1 The division of the middle classes is such that the modern working class is much larger than is commonly supposed. Its true magnitude has been hidden by prattling about the great middle class, by recent puffings in regard to the growth of the service industries, and – it must be said – by the pontifications of aspirants to the managerial ranks, many of whom hold academic appointments and whose business it is to know better. Many of the bourgeois claims regarding the effectiveness of capitalism as a system of social integration hang on the claimed unity of this middle class. As the class disintegrates, so do the final claims for capitalism as an order of social integration.

2 The history of the administrative-managerial kind of differentiation that we are emphasizing no doubt extends far back. For interesting suggestions see Marc Bloch's "The Administrative Classes in France and in Germany," in

Land and Work in Medieval Europe, New York, Harper, 1969. Modern capitalism regularizes and extends the differentiation.

3   On recent trends in the recruitment of the managers see Jay Gould's *The Technical Elite,* New York, Augustus Kelley, 1966. Gould expresses the usual hope that antagonistic social relations will be mediated through the organs of education and of "rational management."

4   Gould, op. cit.

5   Menshikov, *Millionaires and Managers,* op. cit., ch. 3, "Managers at the Top." While Menshikov documents the managerial ascendancy, our concern is for its explanation. We hope to make it clear that the answer to the old question, "Why Does the Scum Rise to the Top?" (F. A. Hayek, *The Road to Serfdom*) is to be found within the history of capitalism and not, as Hayek suggests, in the deficiencies of socialist theory.

6   Gould, op. cit., offers some evidences. In general, there is less disagreement on the extent of the managers' ownership involvement than on its significance.

7   Ibid. Especially, see Gould's report on the survey of *Scientific American* magazine.

8   It should by now be evident in the wake, for example, of Watergate and other proceedings in the United States, that the rise of a client class of managers in Nazi Germany and Fascist Italy was not a special phenomenon but the result of something inherent within the mode of production. The activities of the managers in fomenting war and imperialism are well documented in *The Pentagon Papers,* although it is curious how the discussion of these documents so frequently overlooks their principal significance. The quality of managerial operations is also seen in the space race, in the petty hucksterings of the kind much publicized by J. K. Galbraith, Vance Packard, and others. On the Nazi client class see Charles Bettelheim, *L'economie allemande sous le nazisme,* Paris, Maspero, 1971.

9   *Selected Correspondence,* op. cit., letter to J. B. Schweitzer, and the summing up of Proudhon in *The Poverty of Philosophy.* The importance of the intellectual branch of the managerial assemblage should not be underrated. Recruited from vertically mobile administrative laborers, it is given over to apologetics under the cloak of science and to an unquestioning provision of tools for the managerial service. Some academic disciplines, such as economics, have become almost wholly managerial in this sense of the term.

10   The phrase "technicians and professionals," while indicating the proficiency of the administrative laborer, is unsatisfactory because it blurs a necessary distinction between the old administrative mode of capitalism with its lawyers, judges, doctors, priests, politicians, and so on, and the varieties of technically trained labor over which the former seek to maintain their dominance with the assistance of the managers. When the managers step out of line with the general capitalist interest, they must be disciplined or they will usurp (momentarily) authority from the old leaders and fascism is the result. Depending upon circumstances, a crisis of this kind can go either way, though it seldom abates in the managerial phase.

The administrative accumulation does render obsolete the older managerial divisions within the traditional superstructure of the capitalist state: Priests give way to psychiatrists, doctors to medical technicians, police to therapists and social welfare workers, judges to vendors of administrative law, and so on. As the obsolescence of the old mode proceeds, the old leaders invoke the assistance of the managers to maintain the law and order that is inexorably slipping away from them either at the hands of the managers or of the administrative laborers.

11 The worker's baptism to managerial proceedings may cause him to recoil. The case of Daniel Ellsberg and Anthony Russo and the theft of the Pentagon Papers are interesting in this connection and underscore the importance of one's drawing correct conclusions from his experience.

12 As biological producers women do not necessarily fall into the productive labor category. It is women producing productive labor who first of all fall into the working class. They are women associated with administrative and industrial work, and the activists among them derive from the former category, at the moment.

13 *Capital I*, op. cit.

14 Liberal theorists stress the individual impulse to bureaucratize, to monopolize, and so on, which avoids the proposition that general economic circumstances conduce to the phenomenon. Compare Walton Hamilton, "Institutions," *Encyclopedia of the Social Sciences*, New York, Macmillan Co., 1930–1935.

15 Menshikov, op. cit., p. 80.

16 Many will recall, however, the revolt of artists and intellectuals in the Great Depression and, perhaps more importantly, the typical role of intellectuals in revolutionary movements.

17 Veblen's *Theory of the Leisure Class*, op. cit., deals extensively with this feature of upper-upper-class existence and function.

18 Since administrative labor, and especially sections of its educating branch, is produced under above-average conditions in the value composition of capital, its wages will be above its exchange value. This, too, works to inhibit the class consciousness of this labor and caters to illusions concerning its real worth in capitalist society, for example, among college professors.

12. ROTATIONAL EMPLOYMENT AND THE TRANSITION TO SOCIALISM

1 *Grundrisse* (Nicolaus), p. 493.

2 *The Communist Manifesto*, I.

3 On the Chinese effort, see Charles Bettelheim, *Cultural Revolution and Industrial Organization in China*, New York, Monthly Review Press, 1974. In relation to the Cuban reconstruction, Che Guevara's comment indicates a focal point of socialist organization: "Youth receives treatment in consonance with our aspirations. Education is increasingly integral, and we do not neglect the incorporation of the students into work from the very beginning. Our scholarship students do physical work during vacation or together with their studies. In some cases work is a prize, while in others it is an educational tool;

it is never a punishment. A new generation is being born" ("Man and Socialism in Cuba," in *Man and Socialism in Cuba,* Bert Silverman, ed., New York, Atheneum, 1971, p. 351). The great migration of urban labor into the countryside in Cambodia has been well publicized, and viewed with considerable horror, by the Western press, but, in addition to avoiding starvation, the goal of rotational employment appears to have been involved.

4 *Grundrisse* (McLellan), no. 20, p. 144: "Capital creates a great deal of disposable time, apart from the labour time that is needed for society in general and for each sector of society (i.e., space for the development of the individual's full productive forces, and thus also for those of society). This creation of non-working time is, from the capitalist standpoint, and from that of all earlier stages of development, non-working time or free time for the few."

5 The industries of circulation dominate the functioning of the mode: "Under all forms of society there is a certain industry which predominates over all the rest and whose condition therefore determines the rank and influence of all the rest. It is the universal light with which all the other colors are tinged and are modified through its particularity. It is a special ether which determines the specific gravity of everything that appears within it" (*Contribution to the Critique of Political Economy,* op. cit., p. 302).

6 In *A Marxian Model of Growth* (master's thesis, New York University, 1975) Elsie Olsen estimates the ratio of the number of workers unproductively employed relative to the number productively employed on a decennial basis, 1900–1970. The ratio rises from .28 in the former year to .76 in the latter. As an index of the *value* of unproductive relative to the value of productive labor power, the Olsen estimate is probably a significant underestimate. The main reason this is so is that the principal categories of unproductive labor are labor powers of the more complex and expensive varieties, while productive labor tends to be simpler in form. Consequently, the numerator of the unproductive ratio needs to be multiplied by a coefficient of 2 or 3 in order to gauge the appropriate value ratio. In other words, our assumption that the unproductive ratio is 50–50 is probably a very conservative one, and the potential gain in free time may be as much as 50 percent greater than our simple calculations indicate.

As an estimate of the numbers of workers falling into the two categories of unproductive and of productive labor, however, the Olsen data are probably accurate and in full theoretical agreement with the definitions of productive and unproductive labor used in this volume. These are the operational categories used in the Olsen study to classify occupations of the U.S. Census of Occupations:

IIWm Technically unnecessary, white-collar (W) labor of management (m). Managers and executives above the ranks of functioning technicians and professionals. Juridical and traditional professionals.

IIWw Technically useful white-collar labor that is wasted (w), whether misallocated or unemployed. Consists mainly of functioning technicians and professionals employed within the circulatory system but excluding formal education and certain social service work useful to productive labor, for example, in health, communications, advisory. It is labor employed in trade, commerce, finance, the state, and the military but is potentially productive by virtue of its technique.

IIBw Technically useful blue-collar labor misspent or unemployed, for example, spent in production of military hardware or in high consumption hard- or software (capitalists' consumption). Potentially productive by virtue of its work capacities. Thus far the numerator of the unproductive ratio.

IBp Technically useful blue-collar labor producing means of production and consumption for productive labor (economic reproduction).

IBa Technically useful blue-collar labor functioning as support labor for productive administrative workers, for example, workers in education, public health, and other social service occupations.

IWa Technically useful administrative workers. Principally, this labor is employed in producing productive labor (educating labor), but in addition to teachers it includes household labor, information and communications workers, social administration and cultural producers (musicians, artists, and so on). Thus the denominator of the unproductive ratio.

7 S. B. Lindner's *The Harried Leisure Class,* New York, Columbia University Press, 1970, reveals inadvertently, in its coy tribute to what is actually unproductive labor, how much hangs on the economist's refusal or inability to distinguish between productive and unproductive labor.

8 "Capital is itself contradiction in action, since it makes an effort to reduce labour time to the minimum, while at the same time establishing labour time as the sole measurement and source of wealth. Thus it diminishes labour time in its *necessary* form, in order to increase its *superfluous* form; therefore it increasingly establishes superfluous labour time as a condition (a question of life and death) for necessary labour time" (*Grundrisse* [McLellan], p. 143). "But although its tendency is always to create disposable time, it also converts it into surplus labour" (p. 144).

9 Just as conventional economics overstates the actual level of gross national product by its failure to allow for unproductive consumption, so it understates potential production by its failure to allow for the conversion of unproductive into productive labor. For standard estimates see, for example, Arthur Okun, *The Political Economy of Prosperity,* New York, W. W. Norton and Co., 1969, "Potential GNP: Its Measurement and Significance" (appendix); Charles Schultze, *National Income Analysis,* 3rd ed., Englewood Cliffs, N.J., Prentice-Hall, pp. 130–133, "Measuring Potential GNP." More than a half-century ago Veblen estimated correctly that half the national income was appropriated by unproductive labor, and allowed for this in estimating potential income: ". . . something more than one-half of the country's industry goes to those persons in whom the existing state of law and custom vests a plenary power to limit production" (*The Vested Interests and the Common Man,* New York, Viking, 1919).

10 Conventional criticisms of growth are widely known and publicized. See E. J. Mishan, *The Costs of Economic Growth,* New York, Praeger, 1967; Donella H. Meadows, et al., *The Limits of Growth,* M.I.T. Press, Cambridge, 1972.

11 *Critique of the Gotha Program,* op. cit., p. 29.

12   Recall our discussion (Chapter 5) of the matrix of interlabor flows and the historical drift from northwest to southeast along the main diagonal of the matrix.

13   *Capital II*, p. 135.

14   "Things have now come to such a pass, that the individuals must appropriate the existing totality of productive forces, not only to achieve self-activity, but, also, merely to safeguard their very existence. . . . This appropriation of these forces is itself nothing more than the development of the individual capacities corresponding to the material instruments of production. The appropriation of a totality of instruments of production is, for this very reason, the development of a totality of capacities in the individuals themselves" (*The German Ideology*, Moscow, 1964, I Feuerbach, p. 83).

15   Emphasis is mine. "What is new in capital is that it also increases the surplus labour time of the masses by all artistic and scientific means possible, since its wealth consists directly in the appropriation of surplus labour time, since its direct aim is value not use value. Thus, despite itself, it is instrumental in creating the means of social disposable time, and so in reducing working time for the whole of society to a minimum, and thus making everyone's time free for their own development" (*Grundrisse*, p. 144).

16   *Capital III*, p. 295.

17   Aristotle, Politics, *The Basic Works of Aristotle*, McKeon ed., p. 1131.

Index

Numerals in italics indicate references to tables or figures.

315